WOMEN and the CONTESTED STATE

FROM THE JOAN B. KROC INSTITUTE
FOR INTERNATIONAL PEACE STUDIES

*Kroc Institute Series on Religion, Conflict,
and Peacebuilding*

WOMEN

and the

CONTESTED STATE

Religion, Violence, and Agency
in South and Southeast Asia

Edited by

MONIQUE SKIDMORE
and **PATRICIA LAWRENCE**

University of Notre Dame Press
Notre Dame, Indiana

Designed by Wendy McMillen
Set in 10.4/13.6 Adobe Minion by Four Star Books
Printed on 50# Williamsburg Recycled Paper by Sheridan Books, Inc.

Library of Congress Cataloging-in-Publication Data

Women and the contested state : religion, violence, and agency in South
and Southeast Asia / edited by Monique Skidmore and Patricia Lawrence.
    p. cm. — (Kroc Institute series on religion, conflict, and peacebuilding)
    Based on presentations at a conference in 2003 of the Program in
Conflict, Religion, and Peacebuilding at the Joan. B. Kroc Institute for
International Peace Studies.
    Includes bibliographical references and index.
    ISBN-13: 978-0-268-04125-0 (cloth : alk. paper)
    ISBN-10: 0-268-04125-3 (cloth : alk. paper)
    ISBN-13: 978-0-268-04126-7 (pbk. : alk. paper)
    ISBN-10: 0-268-04126-1 (pbk. : alk. paper)
    1. Women—Violence against—Political aspects—South Asia—
Congresses.   2. Women and war—Sri Lanka—Congresses.   3. Women
and religion—Burma—Congresses.   I. Skidmore, Monique.   II. Lawrence,
Patricia.   III. Program in Conflict, Religion, and Peacebuilding.
    HQ1236.5.S66W66   2007
    305.48'96920954—dc22

                                                        2007020100

Contents

Acknowledgments

We would like to thank the staff at the Joan B. Kroc Institute for International Peace Studies, especially Scott Appleby, Rashied Omar, Cynthia Mahmood, and Barbara Lockwood, for their generosity and kindness during our residence at the institute as Rockefeller Fellows. This project is funded by the Rockefeller Foundation.

Sections of two chapters in this volume are reprinted with permission and with substantial changes. Chapter 2, by Veena Das, was originally published as "Secularism and the Argument from Nature" in *Powers of the Secular Modern: Talal Asad and His Interlocutors,* edited by David Scott and Charles Hirschkind and published by Stanford University Press in 2005. Chapter 4, by Yasmin Saikia, was originally published as "Beyond the Archive of Silence: Narratives of Violence of the 1971 Liberation War of Bangladesh" in *History Workshop Journal* 58 (2004): 276–87. Figures 1, 2 and 3 are reprinted courtesy of the Liberation War Museum, Dhaka. Figures 4 and 5 are reprinted with permission from Dominic Sansoni. Figure 8 is reprinted courtesy of Dennis McGilvray. Figure 19 is reprinted with permission from Panos Pictures and Nic Dunlop. The maps were created by the Cartography Unit of the Australian National University.

Illustrations

Maps

Figures

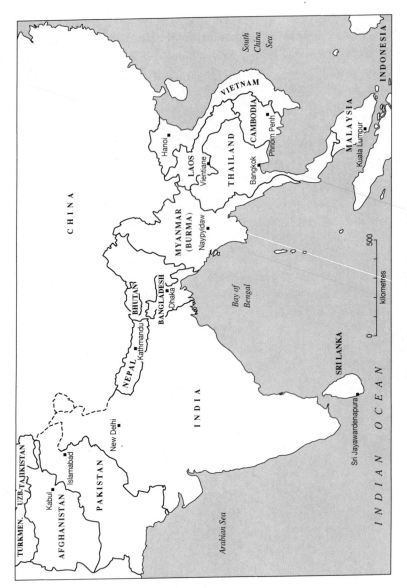

Map 1. South and Southeast Asia

Preface

This collection of essays exploring the relationship between women and the contested state through the lens of religion and conflict in South and Southeast Asia emerged from a conference on the same theme held at the University of Notre Dame in 2003. It is part of the activities resulting from the 2002–3 Rockefeller Visiting Fellowships in the Program in Conflict, Religion, and Peacebuilding at the Joan B. Kroc Institute for International Peace Studies. The present collection is one of a series of books that emerge from the theme of each year's program.

Introduction

Religion and Women in Peace and Conflict Studies

MONIQUE SKIDMORE

All the nations in which the chapters of this volume are set were part of the British Raj, and among their citizens are adherents of all the world religions. Although South Asian and Southeast Asian studies are often separated on library and commercial bookshelves, the history of these areas is interwoven through the spread of religions such as Hinduism and Buddhism from India and the similar expansion of British mercantile and political control into a "greater India" that at various times encompassed the entire region. The contested process of state making continues apace in this region of the world, but dominant ways of "seeing" this process, such as area studies or nation-state analyses, are increasingly less relevant given the historic specificities and globalized linkages among contemporary conflicts. The contributors to this volume explore the intricate, dynamic relationships that pertain between women's agency and the state-making institutions and armed forces of Kashmir, India, Sri Lanka, Bangladesh, and Burma (Myanmar) and the complex roles of Islam, Hinduism, and Theravada Buddhism in the postcolonial period.

Some of these paths are well traversed: the latter part of the twentieth century proved fertile ground for studies from a variety of academic disciplines that contextualize the effects of violence in South and Southeast Asia, its relationship to nationalism and statehood, and its diverse and historical consequences (Banerjee 2000; Basu and Kohli 1998;

1

Daniel 1994; Kapferer 1988; Kumar 1992; Ludden 1996a, 1996b; Pandey 2006; Pandey 2001; Tambiah 1991, 1992, 1997; van der Veer 1994). Studies that examine agency in this region (in particular, women's agency and agency derived from religious traditions, especially from feminist, subaltern, and ethnographic perspectives) have been equally rich, and the tradition continues in the first decade of this century (Argenti-Pillen 2003; Basu and Jeffrey 1997; Das 2000; Das et al. 2000; Lawrence 2003a; Lentin 1997; Manchanda 2001b; Meintjes, Pillay, and Thursen 2001; Moore 1998; Pettigrew 1999; Rajasingham-Senanayake 2001; Skidmore 2004, 2005). The purpose of this volume is to explore the ways in which we can move toward a productive and innovative synthesis of studies of South and Southeast Asian women's agency and social conflict in the field of peace studies. Drawing from anthropology, history, and literary studies in order to link individual voices with historical specificities, we examine the religious traditions of this turbulent region and the contested nature of nation building in the postcolonial era.

Women's Agency and the Violent Field

The theory and practice of peace and conflict studies is slowly integrating the perspectives and experiences of women, much of it informed by feminist analyses. Recent works, for example, have finally ended the simplistic and often erroneous binarisms of masculinity and war, femininity and peace (Afshar 2004: 2; Afshar and Eade 2004; Carter 1998; Lorentzen and Turpin 1998; McDonald 1987; Skielsboek and Smith 2003) and the prevalent stereotype of women as victims of war, especially with regard to sexual violence (Clark and Moser 2001; Goldstein 2001; Rostami Povey 2004; Zarkov 1997, 2001). A related strand of theoretical innovation has been research into women's role in the the perpetration of violence (African Rights 1995; Turshen and Twagiramaiya 1998) and women's roles in Hindu nationalist and armed movements (Bennet, Bexley, and Warnock 1995; Coomaraswamy 1997; Gautam, Banskota, and Manchanda 2001; McDonald, Ardener, and Holden 1987; Manchanda 2001a, 2001b; Mukta 2000; Musengezi and McCartney 2000).

Yet another series of recent studies gives voice to marginalized women and illluminates their integrity, courage, and ability to endure in the face of discrimination, forced displacement, lack of access to health and education, and other forms of social suffering and structural violence in conflict zones · (Belak 2002; Butalia 2000, 2002; Gottschang Turner 1999; Jayawardena and de Alwis 1996; Manderson and Bennett 2003; Pearlman 2003; Shehadeh 2003). These studies move between feminist analyses and gendered approaches to scholarship and into the broader arena of women's studies. They demonstrate how, in extreme situations, women are seldom able to do other than endure and foster resilience (Robben, Suarez-Orozco, and Quinn 2000), yet these are precisely the skills that allow them to move forward in peacetime (Azza 2001; Meintjes, Pillay, and Thursen 2001).

Throughout this book we refer to this broad category of women's studies concerned with describing the perspectives of women actors and their experiences. These perspectives and experiences are analyzed using theories emerging from gender studies and the various streams of feminist analyses. Perhaps the most exciting new front in the development of women's studies in the field of peace and conflict studies is the documentation of local women's organizations during times of conflict (Cockburn 1998). This research shows the importance of such organizations in war zones and under repressive regimes and the way in which these groups become integral to peacemaking in the postconflict period. Elaheh Rostami Povey (2004), for example, has written of middle-class and professional women of Afghanistan who did not flee the country during the Taliban period but instead created networks with poor women. She writes, "For over 20 years, and especially under Taliban rule, these networks and forms of solidarity became mechanisms for women's empowerment" (176). In the post-Taliban period in which the state is both weak and contested, women's nongovernmental organizations (NGOs) are vital in the reconstruction process, "particularly in relation to education, training, and skills to create opportunities for women to have access to income-generating activities" (184).

Palestinian women have formed equally vital networks and organizations, but the political situation has moved in reverse. In Lebanon, Palestinian women found a means to "activate" the domestic sphere to which they were relegated from the 1920s onward. They "incorporated political actions into their domestic routine and interpreted domesticity as a form of political activism" (Peteet 2001: 137). After the siege of Beirut in 1982 and the shifting focus of Palestinian resistance to the Occupied Territories, women's grassroots organizations needed to concentrate on legal and human rights issues. Most recently, these organizations have been forced to concentrate on the basics of survival, forming old-style village associations rather than the more liberal women's groups of the pre-1982 era (Peteet 2001: 146–47). The ability of such networks not only to continue but also to adapt dramatically to worsening political situations represents a formidable and potentially rich basis for communal peacemaking and the endurance of such efforts in post-conflict societies.

In South and Southeast Asia, grassroots activism and the creation and maintenance of women's networks often emerges from a particular religious framework. In this volume we begin precisely at this frontier of gender and peace studies theorizing and examine religion as a fruitful site for under-standing further how women's agency is constituted, created, and constrained in the region during times of conflict with the state and other armed actors such as guerrilla groups, paramilitaries, and parastatal organizations. Con-flict can be both empowering and disempowering for women (Eade 2004: 2; Kumar 2001; Lorentzen and Turpin 1998; Manchanda 2001a), and focusing on women's agency enables us to illustrate how local community organiza-tions run and managed by women play a key role throughout conflict situ-ations, not only for meeting basic needs, but also as advocates fostering the trust and collaboration—the social capital—that are so critical to reconcili-ation and to the postconflict and postaccord phases of societal rebuilding (Clark and Moser 2001).

Religion and Agency

Like other studies of the role of religion in everyday life (Kendall 1985; Mahmood 1999; Mahmood and Brady 1999; Mulder 2001; Ram 1992; Tay-lor 2004), we recognize religion as a conceptual and moral framework for understanding and ordering lives and communities. As a unifying element in quotidian life, it can transcend gender, ethnicity, and class divisions but can equally be used as a justification for shoring up these same social and geo-graphic divisions (Kelly and Messina 2002: 167). As the September 2001 at-tacks on the World Trade Center and other contemporary terrorist warfare tragedies demonstrate, aspects of religious doctrines can be used to justify even the gravest acts of murder and the infliction of suffering. A focus on the importance and contested nature of religious doctrines and practice in times of conflict and the growth of religious fundamentalism is critical for even a basic understanding of so many contemporary conflicts, from Northern Ire-land to Afghanistan and central Africa.

In South and Southeast Asia, religious traditions are inseparable from the social and cultural fabric of family, community, and national life (Kakar 1996;

Kapferer 1991; McKenna 1999; Mahmood 1999; van der Veer 1994). Rita Manchanda (2001: 11) writes that South Asian women's visions of peace "tend to privilege the notion of a 'just' peace, as defined from the perspective of the discriminated and disempowered." To understand the relationship between women and the contested states of South and Southeast Asia, therefore, the first chapter in this volume is a historical overview of the claims to a "just peace" in the religious traditions of India. In "Contesting Traditions: Religion and Violence in South Asia," Peter van der Veer examines the historical recourse, among Muslims and Hindus, to religious frameworks for agency, suffering, the infliction of violence, and the pragmatics of peace building.

Van der Veer's chapter provides the conceptual basis for the examination of the relationships between women's engagement with religion, the state, and violence. Accordingly, the book is divided into three parts. Part I deals with Hindu-Muslim dynamics in India and Bangladesh. Part II is concerned with Theravada Buddhist and Tamil conflict in Sri Lanka. Part III explores the relationship among Theravada Buddhism, Nat spiritism, and the military dictatorship of central Burma (Myanmar). One of the most interesting aspects of compiling this volume has been to see how the epistemological approach and tone adopted in the three parts differs according to the nature of the conflict with the states in question and is consistent within each of the parts. These similarities are explained in the introductions to the three parts of the book. In moving away from a traditional area studies perspective, *Women and the Contested State* demonstrates how geographic regions of study stimulate their own well-developed sophistication of knowledge and analysis. In integrating these different approaches, we hope to open a pathway for broader academic and "on the ground" analyses, that is, analyses more conscious of the conditions of epistemic knowledge generated in this part of the world.

Throughout the chapters, women and religion intersect in contemporary arenas of conflict in South and Southeast Asia in complex ways. Together gender and religious stereotypes perpetuate violence and inequality as women are represented by Islamic clergy, Hindu nationalists, Buddhist generals, and armed groups such as the Tamil Eelam as belonging to the private or the domestic sphere. They are charged with acting in ways appropriate to their religious traditions and transmitting the fidelity and integrity of the family and community as well as the nation-state during times of conflict. Other case studies presented here show small spaces for community networking and the fostering of solidarity in conflict zones by women using particular religious traditions and forums. Women's agency is made manifest in the creation of these networks during crisis periods and their continuation in the aftermath. In addition to forming networks and NGOs, individually and in groups some women adopt religious roles under repressive state apparatuses and in violent situations that allow them a measure of freedom or personal and psychological respite from which resilience, creativity, and peacemaking may emerge (Kumar 2001; McKay 1998; Manchanda 2001a). A contextualized understanding of these complex relationships among women, agency, religion, and the contested states of South and Southeast Asia show where women and women's organizations emerge from and how they can be supported when the violence ends and building a sustainable peace begins.

1

Contesting Traditions

Religion and Violence in South Asia

PETER VAN DER VEER

According to Annie Besant, India is the spiritual leader of the world and even Nehru believed what she said (van der Veer 2001). One could say that Robert Oppenheimer followed an established tradition when he quoted the Bhagavad Gita at the first test of the atomic bomb. Perhaps that was a warning for believers in India's spiritualism, since today politicians in India and Pakistan have raised the possibility of using nuclear weapons in their current standoff over Kashmir. The current conflict between Pakistan and India is one in a succession of violent conflicts since Partition, always related in some way to communal antagonisms between Hindus and Muslims in India. Since 1980 communal violence in India has been on the increase (van der Veer 1994). Much of this violence originated in the campaign to replace the sixteenth-century Babar Mosque in Ayodhya with a temple to the Hindu god Ram. In 1992 activists of the Hindu nationalist organization Vishva Hindu Parishad (VHP) and its political partner, the Bharatiya Janata Party (BJP), both allied to the Hindu nationalist group Rashtriya Swayamseval Sangh (RSS), destroyed the mosque. Widespread violence followed, especially in Mumbai and cities in Gujarat. In subsequent years these activists have continued to demand that a temple be built. In the early morning of February 27, 2002, *karsewaks* (volunteer builders) on their way back from Ayodhya provoked Muslims in Godhra in Gujarat to attack their train. According to reports, some of the Muslim attackers had contacts with the Pakistani secret service. Although the details are disputed, it is clear that some fifty-eight people, mostly women and children, died in the clash. In the following months more than one thousand Muslims in nearby Ahmedabad were killed and more than one hundred thousand people (mostly Muslims) made refugees in makeshift camps. The killings have followed a pattern of ethnic cleansing that has completely transformed the nature of this Muslim-named city, in which about six hundred thousand Muslims live among about three million Hindus. The kind of violence as well as the nature of the responses by the authorities show a pattern chillingly similar to that of 1992. This replay of events seems to make even critical reporting by the media and human rights organizations part of an already existing script.

All this is well known by those who follow current events in India, but how should we interpret the violence between Hindus and Muslims today? Violence is a social fact that has many sides: social, economic, political, religious. Violence is also an intrinsic part of human relations and thus can be found everywhere. Causal explanations are often not easy to give. For every instance of large-scale violence in which two communities (ethnic, religious, racial) are involved, one has to come up with a detailed analysis in which all these elements are taken into account. In such a way one finds out what triggered the violence, who participated, the economic circumstances of competition and conflict, what happened in the political arena, and the role of the police. In cases such as Ahmedabad, one finds an institutionalized system in which specialists turn small-scale violence into large-scale mob violence (Brass 1996). These specialists build on experiences in earlier riots and may be organized by political parties (such as the Shiv Sena, or Army of Shiva political party, in Mumbai), trade unions, or criminal gangs. Communication plays a significant role in the spread of violence, and it is the media in particular that narrate the story of violence. As has also been shown in the case of Gujarat, English-language newspapers tend to be more evenhanded in their reporting and are branded as pseudosecular by their opponents, whereas Gujarati-language newspapers are seen as taking sides with the Hindu majority for a number of reasons, including circulation. There is clearly a split public; neither side trusts the other (Rajagopal 2000).

The difficulty, as always, is also one of representation (van der Veer 1997). After a riot occurs, a struggle emerges over how to represent it—in terms of number of casualties, who started it, and the role of the police. That struggle makes use of certain master narratives and tropes that one finds at random in Indian newspapers, such as "communalism or the ingrained antagonism of Hindus and Muslims" or "the machinations of dirty politics behind the scenes" or "the foreign hand." Hindu-Muslim violence since the 1980s can be explained in a variety of ways, but at least at some level it is connected to the rise of Hindu nationalism and the success of the VHP and the BJP in the social and political arenas. These organizations have an ideology claiming that the Hindu majority has the right to balance wrongs from the past and that Hindu religious traditions should be the core of national identity (Pandey 1990). Minorities, in this view, have to submit themselves to the majority perspective. In that master narrative the secular state is seen as pseudosecular because it pampers minorities and demands that Hindus should be proud of their traditions and not marginalized in their own country.

In this chapter I examine references to religious traditions in the antagonistic and continually contested relations between Hindus and Muslims (Ali 1999; van der Veer 2002). The past is sometimes invoked in connection to utopian views on the "just state." It is also sometimes invoked in relation to traditions of conversion (religious expansion) and conflict as well as to traditions of harmony and tolerance. But first it is useful to discuss what can be meant by the concept of tradition.

Tradition, Invention, Modernity

References to tradition are mystifying. As a textual scholar, one can adopt a superior position (such as that of Max Muller [1876]) from which one adjudicates what is invented and what is authentic, but such ex cathedra judgments are often unacceptable to the players in the field and also from a scholarly point of view, as authenticity is an intractable concept. The predicament of anthropologists is not much better than that of the textual scholar. Today anthropologists often forget about the text and focus on practice, the cultural performance of a tradition (e.g., a ritual) in a certain context. Cultural meaning is produced in symbolic action, and it has both subjective (intentional) and objective components. In the view of many anthropologists, ritual enactments of tradition are demarcated from the practices of everyday life (Bloch 1977; Tambiah 1985). Again, anthropologists put themselves in a position to adjudicate this demarcation and what to make of it. The native's point of view may be authentic (in Clifford Geertz's terms [1973]), but the anthropologist's superior interpretation of that view may be *authoritative.* References to cultural praxis and to everyday life are thus not a solution for the problem of the interpretation of tradition. This is even clearer when the anthropological understanding of a community's culture provides a key to understanding violence as resulting from some deeper cultural logic. It is then the interpretation of a particular cosmology that makes violence culturally interpretable. For example, in Bruce Kapferer's (1983) work on Sri Lanka there is a hierarchical cosmology in Sinhalese society that sees demonic possession and violence as a sign of an inverted hierarchy and exorcism and counterviolence as a means to return from chaos to order. Similarly, Tamil violence against the Sinhalese is interpreted as demonic. This kind of argument in which violence is an enactment of culture is often counterbalanced by an argument that shows tolerance and syncretism to be culturally embedded. In such instances an anthropological notion of "culture" is akin to the textual scholar's notion of "tradition," and these notions can be referred to for all kinds of purposes.

Following the philosopher Alasdair MacIntyre, Talal Asad (1986: 14) has given the following definition of tradition that is relevant for both historians and ethnographers: "A tradition consists essentially of discourses that seek to instruct practitioners regarding the correct form and purpose of a given practice that, precisely because it is established, has a history. These discourses relate conceptually to a past (when the practice was instituted, and from which the knowledge of its point and proper performance has been transmitted) and a future (how the point of that practice can best be secured in the short or long term, or why it should be modified or abandoned), through a present (how it is linked to other practices, institutions, and social conditions)." Central to this, then, is a community's debate about boundaries and transgressions, about orthodoxy and orthopraxis. This understanding of tradition stresses its reflexivity and is contrary to Anthony Giddens's (1991) view that tradition is static and not reflexive and that late modernity is posttraditional in the sense that it is reflexive. Nevertheless, traditions often project themselves as timeless, transcending history and politics, and part of their discursive power lies in that claim, so that historicizing them is often felt by practitioners as "debunking" and showing a lack of respect. This is even worse in situations in which Western modernity is perceived as the enemy of tradition. Those who use modern scholarly methods and observations are then declared to be with the enemy, as Nasr Abu Zaid, the Egyptian scholar of the Qur'an who is currently exiled at Leiden, experienced. Again, the outsider's point of view is also problematic given the fact that orientalist scholarship is so much a part of authorizing discourses.

Traditions are crucially concerned with correct practice and opinion. Therefore, it is in the field of boundaries and transgressions, of syncretism and conversion that some of the most contested issues lie. These issues are not only strenuously debated; they also often lead to violent conflict. That conflict is perhaps even more intracommunal than intercommunal. The most heated debates are between competing groups, and these tend to be close together. A good example is the Khalistani movement of Sant Bhindranwale, who rose to power because of his claim to defend orthodoxy against heterodox Sikhs and who played a role in the murder of the Nirankaris, Gurbachan Singh, in 1980 (Kapur 1984). In addition, there is considerable intercommunal violence. This is true of both the colonial and precolonial periods. Criticism of Sufi saint worship predates Shah Waliullah of Delhi and Muhammad bin Abd-al Wahhab of Arabia both of whom are eighteenth-century thinkers who predate colonialism proper. We know also of a lot of conflict between Shaivas and Vaishnavas, partly doctrinal, partly about control over resources. Of course, there has been precolonial intercommunal violence also, as Chris Bayly (1985) has argued, but what is interesting is how the arena, the participants, and the political context all change in the colonial period and thus give old issues of syncretism, conversion, and conflict a new salience. To some extent it is attractive to posit a traditional opposition between the defenders of orthodoxy, the Brahman or Sayyid jurists and the bringers of poetic syncretism and transgression, the leaders of the Bhakti and Sufi movements. The recurring problem with posing this kind of structural opposition, however, is that it fails to do justice to the historical salience of recurrent traditional arguments in changing contexts. Traditions do have continuity, but their transmission is historically and contextually specific.

The colonial state and the practices of modern governmentality have had a huge impact on the conditions of transmission of tradition, on the questions asked and the answers given by practitioners. This is immediately clear in the field of education where modern education and new fields of knowledge compete with traditional education. It is not only that other languages and other forms of knowledge push existing ones aside but also that modern and traditional forms of knowledge penetrate each other. This was obviously not a level playing field, since knowledge of languages, such as Persian, Urdu, Hindi, and English, gave access to some opportunities for jobs and money. This is a complex field of interaction that can only be touched in passing, but for our purposes it is important to note that Christian missionaries were active in the field of education and that this forced Hindus, Muslims, and others to respond. This response was very much in terms and organizational forms adopted from the missionaries. The Arya Samaj, for example, a Hindu reformist society founded in 1875 to preserve Vedic heritage, wants a rational religion with one god and one central text. It organizes schools with a mixture of traditional and modern subjects. Swami Dayanand Saraswati was a great debater and staunch critic of Christianity and Islam, and a public sphere of debate on religious and social issues emerged through his teachings. The importance of modern forms of knowledge and especially the authority of science is immediately clear from these debates. This produces a creative mixture of argumentative styles, sources of authority, and so on. The Arya Samaj is at the same time at the forefront of a movement to create a national state on the basis of "tradition."

Let me now turn to the discussion of traditions of the "just state," traditions of conversion, and traditions of syncretism.

The Just State

BJP politicians make increasing use of references to Hindu traditions. They do not have to be very learned in these references, as they can choose what they need for a particular purpose. This is the feeling one gets when political leaders all over the world use traditional references in order to place their political programs in a moral framework. A well-known example is American presidents' references to the biblical tradition in their inaugural or State of the Union addresses. In Robert Bellah's (1970) much-cited view, these references constitute a civil religion, a religion of the modern nation-state. Many of the references made by political leaders in India seem to be of the same category. However, whereas in the United States such references are more or less interpreted as metaphors with an emotional appeal to what constitutes the Moral Majority, in the case of Islam and Hinduism, there is a tendency to take them much more literally. This is especially true for Islamic and Hindu references to a "just" state; it is sometimes suggested that those who make these references desire a return to ancient political practices.

The state can be seen as a nexus of institutional arrangements in which power and violence are crucial. According to Max Weber, the state has a monopoly on legitimate force in society. Similarly, Norbert Elias's (1994) story of Western civilization connects the civilizing process with the growing monopolization of violence by the state. It is odd that Elias wrote his book during the formation of the Nazi totalitarian state and ignores Weber's dark misgivings about the dangers of state bureaucracies. There is enough reason to be less optimistic than Elias about the modern state. Moral arguments against the actual practices of the modern state often take the shape of utopias referring to an idealized past. Colonized people who object to a "foreign," colonial (and "Christian") state in particular sometimes couch their criticism in terms of a religious past. This is in principle not so different from, say, the neo-Gothic fantasies that characterized nineteenth-century nationalism in Europe, but the reference to the past by the colonized is primarily in opposition to a colonial state that itself has a nationalist project "at home" but not in the colony. While the romantic impulse is strong in all nationalisms, it refers in colonial nationalism to a past that is seen as essentially the opposite of the present form of the state and thus a source of resistance. This continues after independence, when the postcolonial state is seen as the instrument of a deracinated, Westernized elite.

This is the background to references to the Islamic state *(dawla)* or to Ram's Rule (Ramrajya).[1] The first thing that has to be observed here is that references to earlier political forms show a deliberate misunderstanding of the radically different nature of the modern, developmental state. Those who call for the foundation of an Islamic state often use the Arabic term *dawla,* which refers to "dynasty," and indeed the premodern societies are governed by sultans, nawabs, rajas, and the like. The modern state, conversely, is ideally an instrument of the will of the people and penetrates deep into people's lives with a number of development projects, such as education and health care. Even when it is a weak state in Gunnar Myrdal's (1968, 1970) sense, the modern state is still a beast of a completely different nature from the premodern state.

The second observation to be made is that references to a religiously based "just state" are relatively recent in modern Indian history and are actually quite marginal in Indian political thought and practice. The call for a return to the time of the Prophet or the time of Ram and the establishment of a so-called theocratic state is a very recent demand that has to be understood in the framework of modern political ideas of true Islamic democracy. Contrary to what is often thought, there is no clear definition of the Islamic state in Pakistan (Zaman 2002). What should one think of the tradition of Dar-al-Islam (Abode of Islam) to which Muslims should migrate *(hijrat)* if they are in a minority position, or that of the jihad (holy war) against the *dar-al-harb* (house of war, a term used to refer to countries administered by non-Muslim governments or thought to persecute Muslims)?

None of this makes much sense in India, where Muslims were always a minority and there were no Islamic states but merely Muslim dynasties with

Islamic legitimation. It also ignores the fact of current large-scale migration to the *dar-al-harb* (the West) rather than away from it. Similarly, the reference to the rule of Rama, the virtuous king *(dharmaraja)* and the Lord of Propriety *(maryada purushottam),* has very little specific content, even less than in the Islamic context, where the establishment of the Law *(shariat)* can at least be part of a political program, as it was in Pakistan under Zia-ul-Haq (1977–88) and Nawaz Sharif (1990–93, 1997–99). Certainly in Hindu kingdoms the Ramayana may have given some guidance to the behavior of rulers, but there is little in it that specifies the nature of the caste order and the rules of politics. Where authors such as Sheldon Pollock (1993: 288) see continuity between the politics of the Ramayana and the politics of the BJP, I see a significant rupture. One should understand references to such traditions in the modern period primarily as a utopian rejection of current political formations rather than a theological interpretation of the tradition. This is not to say that there are no theological interpretations of the tradition that have political implications. They certainly exist and are important, because they show that the tradition is alive. The violent political projects of activists such as Osama bin Laden, however, do not engage the tradition in such a fundamental manner. It is, in fact, striking how little theological training leaders of the major religious nationalist movements have had. They tend to be journalists, engineers, or graduates in the humanities, educated in modern topics rather than in the tradition.

The same is true for leaders of Hindu and Muslim movements who desire a just rule. Gandhi was absolutely not a theologian, and when he came up with the notion of Ramrajya he used a cultural repertoire in which he had been socialized from his early youth but not a political theology. In the case of Gandhi and many other great populist leaders one sees the function of a traditional religious repertoire for bridging the gap between elite politics and mass politics. However, it is also clear that this kind of reference to tradition for purposes of mass mobilization needs to allow for a wide range of interpretations, as Shahid Amin (1988) has beautifully demonstrated in his piece on Gandhi as Mahatma. Similarly, Gananath Obeyesekere and Richard Gombrich (1988) have mapped what they consider the major departures from Buddhist tradition in Sri Lanka and the invention of new traditions, such as the Sarvodaya movement,[2] which purports to give a Buddhist model of development. Here we get to the heart of the matter: Eric Hobsbawm and Terence Ranger's (1983) "invention of tradition" or what recent scholarship has called "the manufacturing of religion" or "the invention of religion." I would suggest that while the universal category of religion is a European invention that affects the development of religious traditions (of a Hindu, Buddhist, Christian, Muslim nature), these traditions exist and have a history of change, polemics, and so on, that cannot be reduced to the encounter with European thought. I do think that modern references to Ramrajya and Dar-al-Islam are inventions of tradition, but at the same time there are a number of living traditions in which there are discourses and practices relating to state and violence. However, we are not speaking about separate universes (one of tradition, one of invented tradition) here but about interaction, conflict, polemics. Some people are willing to use a great deal of violence to establish their idea of traditional justice in the form of an Islamic state or a Hindu state, and others who think they are living in harmony with tradition are completely mystified by what the first are doing.

What about women and the "just state," the main subject of this volume? It has often been observed that gender is a way of signifying relationships of power. An important transformation in these relationships in the nineteenth century is the rise of the gendered distinction between public and private. This distinction is crucial to the development of a modern ideology of the family, domesticity, and the moral order of the nation. The bourgeois ideal of the domesticated housewife had strong religious overtones in many European nations but also in many nations outside Europe. Religious traditions (Christianity, Islam, Hinduism) provided a gendered language to deal with the new realities of the imperial nation-state and of the colony in the nineteenth century. Symbols of masculinity and femininity were crucial in the development of imperial attitudes both in the metropolis and in the colony, and they were embedded in new conceptions of religiosity and secularity. A dominant line of interpretation in the study of nationalism is to argue that the nation is often imagined in terms of a brotherhood of men protecting their womenfolk. Men are portrayed as strong and powerful; women, as weak and powerless. Protection implies the exertion of male authority, to which women have to submit. The state represents male authority as if it were the father of the nation. While this pattern can be found everywhere, religious traditions shape this configuration in different ways in different cultures. While, for instance, Victorian ideas about "domesticity," "companiate marriage," and female education were influential all over the empire, in Hindu India, according to Dipesh Chakrabarty (1993: 7), "the ideal of the 'modern' educated housewife was almost always tied to that of Lakshmi." The problematic we need to address therefore is how such traditions are transformed under the pressure of modernity. Let me briefly examine the transformation of some Hindu traditions in nationalist discourse.

In a well-known argument Partha Chatterjee (1993: 8) has suggested that under colonial conditions Indian nationalists divided the social world into two domains: spiritual and material. In the material, outer domain the Western colonialists are superior; in the inner spiritual domain Hindu values are superior. This division is gendered. On the one hand, the inner spiritual domain is feminine and Lakshmi reigns supreme; on the other, there is the misogynist notion that the female body is a prison of wordly interests, in which the family man is trapped (Chatterjee 1993: 63). I have argued elsewhere that nationalists actually appropriate a contemporary Western discourse on spirituality and use that to translate Hindu discursive traditions. In the Hindu monk Vivekananda's discourse,[3] spirituality stands both for the outer world of material science and rationality and for the inner world of ascetic discipline. Vivekananda creates a sanitized translation of the religious ideas and practices of Ramakrishna for a modernizing middle class in Calcutta.[4] In Ramakrishna we find the ascetic discursive tradition of the necessity of detachment for men. While this tradition in many ways is misogynous, Ramakrishna actually propagates an androgynous state, in which the male ascetic realizes the feminine within himself in a way that is reminiscent of the Ramanandi ascetics I have studied.[5] Ramakrishna's discourse stresses the dialectic of femininity and masculinity in the detachment of men. This detachment is necessary not only for spiritual perfection but also for recovering masculinity that has been sapped by colonial domination. The British colonial stereotype of the effeminate nature of Hindus is thus countered and transformed in the Hindu theme of the dialectics of femininity and masculinity. Gandhi's ideas and practices can be interpreted in this light and have been countered by a very different tradition of warrior-masculinity that has been espoused by Maratha nationalists. Gandhi's assassin, Nathuram Godse, a Maharashtrian Brahman, declared in his trial, "I firmly believe that the teachings of absolute ahimsa as advocated by Gandhiji would ultimately result in the emasculation of the Hindu community and thus make the community incapable of resisting the aggression or inroads of other communities, especially the Muslims" (Godse, quoted in Mehta 1993: 175–76). What we have here is the contestation of the concept of the just state—Gandhi's Ramraj or Godse's Hindu Sangathan and Hindutva. There is not a simple, straightforward patriarchy promoted in these forms of nationalism but a contestation of the dialectic of femininity and masculinity that is central to Hinduism.

Conversion

Conversion from one tradition to another is probably the most contentious issue in India today (Viswanathan 1998). This perception clearly has to do with the rise of communal politics of numbers after the first colonial census of 1872. Political mobilization and strengthening of Hindus and Muslims as antagonistic religious and political communities made the issue of conversion, of moving from one community to the other, into a crucial one. It also created an anachronistic history of Islam in India as one of violence, of invasions, of destruction of Hindu shrines, of mass conversions by the sword. Conversion to Islam is often read by Hindus today as the result of coercion—either by violence or by economic and political means—while "being a Hindu" is seen as a fact of nature, a natural identity. Muslims, obviously, regard conversion to Islam very positively, as a moral and religious change. Hindu leaders often see conversion to Christianity in the light of their view on conversion to Islam as a sign of coercion but now with an emphasis on mental coercion of the disenfranchised poor by way of education and spreading literacy. While Islam spreads through oil money, Christianity spreads through literacy programs paid for by Western philanthropy. When Amartya Sen received the Noble Prize in economics, Ashok Singhal, president of the VHP, argued that Sen's plea for spreading literacy was part of a plan to spread global Christianity and wipe out Hinduism (Viswanathan 2002). In recent years there have been a number of attacks on Christian missionaries by the VHP in the context of their own expansion in tribal areas.

The upsurge of Hindu nationalism and the successes of the VHP/BJP began with the highly publicized conversions to Islam of untouchable communities in and around Meenakshipuram in South India in 1981. The press interpreted these conversions as "induced by oil money" and "a threat to Indian unity." Indira Gandhi and her Congress Government warned against the Muslim conspiracy, in line with a long-standing secular apprehension about conversion, expressed in recurring debates about the constitutional right to proselytize. A fear of "the foreign hand," of global developments such as migration to the Gulf, and of a severe weakening of national unity when untouchables and tribal peoples would leave the Hindu fold all come together in a fierce rejection of Muslim and Christian religious activities. The slippage from "Hindu" to "national" in the secular Congress response to Meenakshipuram is interesting, and this aspect has, unsurprisingly, been brought to the forefront by the VHP. It plays on a notion that was prevalent in premodern

Europe, *cuius regio eius religio* (whose rule, whose religion), that relates political loyalty to religious allegiance. In the modern European nation-state this has been disentangled in a long history of creating national identities, but this process cannot be taken as a model for India, where in modern history communal identities have been politicized in opposition to the (colonial) state.

It is important to point out that the "naturalness" or "givenness" of Hinduism is a myth. Saints, traders, and soldiers were agents of Muslim and Christian expansion but also of Hindu expansion. Often Sufis were all in one. Sufi shrines were spiritual and material centers, just as *baraqa,* the concept of spiritual power derived from the grace of God, had political and economic aspects associated with it. Like their counterparts, Brahman priests and ascetics were the vanguard of the expansion of agrarianism and civilization and played a significant role in the settlement and very slow conversion of nomadic and tribal peoples to Hindu traditions. Hindu *sadhus* (ascetics) have always been soldiers as well as traders and fighting ascetics during the larger part of their history. Militancy, not pacifism, is the core of their traditions, whatever nineteenth-century views on Hindu spiritualism may have posited. The current activities of the VHP among tribal peoples[6] are therefore to be regarded as part of a longue durée expansion of Hindu traditions. It is one of the saddest aspects of the recent conflagration in Gujarat that Muslims have been widely attacked by tribal peoples, showing the success of the VHP strategy.

Hindu revivalist movements and certainly the contemporary BJP argue that Hindus have been too tolerant, that they have been taken advantage of for too long, and that in independent India they have to take what is theirs. This is the rhetoric behind the Ramjanmabhumi-muktiyajna that led in 1992 to the destruction of the Babar Mosque in Ayodhya.[7] It is in fact also something all Indian schoolchildren learn about in their history lessons, even long before the "textbook controversies" of the late 1990s. Mahmud of Ghazni is the well-known villain of that story while similar raids by Shaiva rulers on Vaishnava temples, or vice versa, are hardly mentioned. At the same time, it is clear that this story of "foreign invasions" into pristine India is now so well entrenched that it is almost unassailable. It is hard to see what the role of modern history writing is in the face of popular history. One wants to talk truth to power, but when there is a discursive framework that one is challenging, courage is not enough. The flat denial of violence and destruction by Muslim conquerors is in any case too ideological to be either true or powerful. It is the nature of violence and the conceptualization of it in history that is important.

The story of conversion is decisively reshaped under the conditions of modernity (van der Veer 1996). In North India the reformist Hindu movement, the Arya Samaj, despite the hybridity of its Hindu ideology, wishes to strengthen the ranks of the Hindu community. A series of successful but aggressive campaigns, such as the very violent Cow Protection Movements and the equally important reconversion or *shuddhi* (purification) movements are initiated. The latter movements to reconvert Muslims, Sikhs, tribal peoples, and low castes created an immensely contentious atmosphere in North India and were in some important respects forerunners of the ethnic cleansing *(safaya)* that took place during Partition. *Shuddhi* built on accepted elements of Hindu tradition, such as *prayascitta* (expiation) rituals, but these had never been used in collective action for reconversion of the lapsed *(patita)* before. Conversion and violence were very close together and experienced as the same: an attack on the boundaries of the community. *Tabligh* (internal mission) was the answer given by Muslims to the *shuddhi* activities of the Arya Samaj. To prevent the Arya Samaj from making inroads in the Muslim Meo community in Mewat near Jaipur,[8] small groups *(jamat)* of dedicated Muslims (mostly Deobandis from Nizamuddin in Delhi) tried from 1925 onward to educate the Meo in proper, orthodox Islam (Mayaram 1997). The Meo, like so many other groups, had a wide range of traditions in common with their Hindu neighbors, and these traditions were taken by both the Arya Samaj and the Tablighi Jam'at as a sign that they were not really converted to Islam. The Meo are Muslim, but the boundaries between them and their environment had to be redrawn in the arena of communal politics in the 1920s and 1930s. The practices of groups such as the Meo can be called syncretistic, and this brings us to the other side of religious expansion: syncretism.

Syncretism

"Syncretism" is historically a term that refers to attempts in the seventeenth century to promote tolerance among Protestant sects in the context of religious war and violent conflict in Europe. The term is therefore less a descriptive than a prescriptive one. It shows an acceptance of a multiplicity of truth-claims and of fundamental difference within a polity. This use of the term is also found in writings on Indian traditions. Ashis Nandy (1990), for instance, has a strong belief in the syncretic traditions of ordinary Indians and blames the modern, secularizing state for the communalism that rips apart the social fabric. In Nandy's view it is in particular the modernizing, Western-izing middle class that has lost touch with India's syncretism and thus with tolerance. Nandy (1990: 91) refers to Gandhi as the apostle of this culture of tolerance: "Gandhi used to say that he was a sanatani, an orthodox Hindu. It was as a sanatani Hindu that he claimed to be simultaneously a Muslim, a Sikh, and a Christian and he granted the same plural identity to those belong-ing to other faiths. Traditional Hinduism, or rather Sanatan dharma, was the source of his religious tolerance." Nandy does articulate here something that is found in Gandhi and perhaps in Hindu traditions more generally. I inter-pret this tradition of tolerance as a tradition of inclusivism, a form of hierar-chical relativism: there are many paths leading to God and there are many Gods, but that does not do away with the fact that there is a hierarchy of these paths. People follow paths that belong to their "being"; there is a cosubstan-tiality between believer and his dharma. That includes Muslims and Chris-tians but in an inferior position. When Nandy therefore argues that "it is as religion-as-faith which prompted Indians to declare themselves as Moham-medan Hindus in Gujarat in the census of 1911" (70), he forgets that the VHP does not demand that Muslims give up their religion but rather that they rec-ognize themselves as Hindus first. Islam becomes, then, a *sampradaya* within Hinduism.[9] It should be clear that Muslims do not want to be syncretized in such a manner. Nandy's argument ignores completely the internal debate among Muslims about orthodoxy.

The most important example given of Hindu-Muslim syncretism in India is always the Sufi shrine (Werbner and Basu 1998). Observers report that both Hindus and Muslims frequent this kind of shrine and that members of both communities worship the saint for all kinds of purposes. Such observations lead to the notion that popular (or "folk") Islam is as tolerant as Hinduism and that it is only modern fanatics who want to destroy this and replace it with intolerant purism. Unfortunately, one has to reject such easy views. First of all, there is a long tradition of Islamic criticism of Sufi saint worship as *bida* (innovation) or as *shirk* (polytheism), even by some Sufis themselves. The issue is as usual the definition of orthodoxy. This debate about the orthodoxy of some Sufi practices is an internal Islamic one of which Hindus mostly have no clue. Moreover, historically, Sufi saint worship has been in decline since the late nineteenth century, not only in India, but in the entire Muslim world as well. Mass education and direct lay access to sacred scripture and the debate about it, as well as the waning of the economic and political power of shrines, seem to be factors in that decline.

Hindus often have their own motivations and stories that led them to seek the blessing of the Muslim saint. In some cases this is precisely because the saint—as a Muslim—is seen as having power over a world of demons and dangerous ghosts. From a sociological point of view, it is important not only to observe that Hindus and Muslims participate in the same Sufi rituals but also to consider the why and how. In my own ethnographic experience, traditions on which participation was based were often understood and recited in very different ways. Moreover, the shrine is often part of a larger complex of Islamic institutions of prayer and education such as mosques and madrasas, in which Hindus do not participate, as long as they are not converted. It is perhaps better to see the Sufi shrine as an arena of contestation and conversion than as a site of interfaith dialogue.

This is also clear from recent work by Shahid Amin (1988) on the famous Sufi shrine of Ghazi Miyan or Salaar Masud, in Bahraich. Over the past century or so this has been an arena of contestation in which the Arya Samaj attacks some popular versions of the founding myth of this shrine. But not only modern nationalism and reformism has brought contestation and violence. These are elements at the heart of the shrine itself. Like many other Sufi shrines this is a shrine for a warrior-saint *(ghazi)* who was martyred on that spot. The founding myth of the shrine deals directly with violence and conversion. It is the constant reworking of this myth in history that gives us a perspective not only on the changing relations between Hindus and Muslims but also on Hindu and Muslim understandings of violence itself. In the Ghazi Miyan story one element is striking: the killing of the virginal saint at the time of his wedding. It is this story of mystical power that emerges from an act of violence against it that is such a powerful metaphor we live by. It can be found in the story of Jesus Christ, of African earth cults, of Mahatma Gandhi. Such root metaphors can trigger collective memory and bring Hindus and Muslims together with interpretations embedded in their own traditions. The story of violence is thus multifaceted and religiously potent.

Gendered Markers of Communal Identity

Reference to traditions is made in debates about correct beliefs and practices, about orthodoxy and orthopraxis. Such debates may not only be verbal. Liberal government allows for debates in the public sphere and for the expression of the will of the people in elections, but, according to its own theory, it has to monopolize violence by suppressing it between individuals and groups in society. The theory presupposes, therefore, a distinction between the free expression of opinion and the use of violence, between speech acts and other acts. However, words can hurt, and the role of insults, slander, rumors, and propaganda is important in the dynamics of civil violence. When slogans such as "Babar ki santan: jao Pakistan ya kabristan" (Descendants of Babar—Pakistan or the grave, take your choice) are uttered freely in the streets and in writing, there is reference to tradition and to certain understandings of history. Physical violence is an extension of verbal engagement.

Debates about tradition define the boundaries of a community. They define the "other" of the community, and this is done in different contexts. In some contexts Shi'a-Sunni or Sanatana-Arya antagonisms are relevant; in others they are replaced by Hindu-Muslim or Hindu-Christian antagonisms. In some cities in India one finds elaborate riot systems with collective memories of previous violence, with rituals of provocation that feed on religious traditions of purity and impurity. One would expect to also find systems of pacification with rituals of tolerance that feed on traditions of syncretism and nonviolence. A sad story about the Ahmedabad riots of the recent past was that Gandhi's Sabarmati ashram in the city closed its gates for refugees at the moment of the riots. In such circumstances one might expect the state to be proactive in controlling communal violence, but this expectation is based on another tradition, the liberal tradition of the state as arbiter between interests. In the instance of Gujarat and in other cases such as the destruction of the Babar Mosque, it is clear that the institutions of the state are involved in civil society to the extent that political leaders are the main instigators and organizers of communal violence. Democratization in India implies a growing participation of larger sections of the population both in the political process and in communal violence (Hansen 2001). To expect that the liberal tradition will give answers that religious traditions will not provide seems to be a fallacy of the secular mind.

The traditions dealt with in this chapter crucially engage the contested terrain of gender politics. Devotionalism that is foundational for many Hindu and Muslim traditions in South Asia is often seen as feminine, but at the same time there is a narrative of female subjugation under the legitimate rule of patriarchy. The rhetoric of communal violence is often couched in terms of the emasculation of the Hindu majority by secularism or by the greater prowess of Muslim men. One of the greatest markers of communal identity is Woman as a symbol of the integrity of the community, which is one of the reasons rape is such an important element of communal violence. In our discussion of religion and violence the problematic of gender is central.

NOTES

1. Gandhi argued that Ramrajya was the rule of dharma and that it was primarily about a "desire for the welfare of others" (Parkel 1997: xvii).

2. Sarvodaya is a large Sri Lankan charity whose mission is the sustainable alleviation of rural poverty across all ethnic groups and empowerment of individuals through self-help and collective support. It was founded by a Sri Lankan schoolteacher in 1958 and is based on a Buddhist-Gandhian philosophy.

3. Swami Vivekananda (1863–1902) was a Hindu monk and thinker who is considered one of the major spiritual leaders of the Vedanta philosophy. He was a disciple of Ramakrishna and founder of the Ramakrishna Mission.

4. Ramakrishna Paramahamsa (1836–86) was an influential Bengali Hindu sage.

5. Ramanandis are a sectarian group dedicated to the worship of Vishnu, a high Hindu god.

6. Whom they call *vanavasis* instead of *adivasis* in line with their theory of the original Aryan inhabitants of India.

7. Ramjanmabhumi-muktiyajna is the movement to free Rama's birthplace from remnants of Islamic rule. See Ludden 1996, especially the introduction.

8. The Meo are a tribe from the Punjab and Sindh provinces of Pakistan and Haryana and Indian states of Punjab, Rajasthan, and Delhi. Many Meo migrated to Pakistan after 1947, and the group is known for their mixing of Hindu and Islamic customs, practices, and beliefs.

9. In Hinduism a *sampradaya* is a tradition encompassing a common philosophy but embracing many different schools, groups, or guru lineages.

Part I

Between Subjects and Citizens

Women, the "Modern" State, and Violence in South Asia

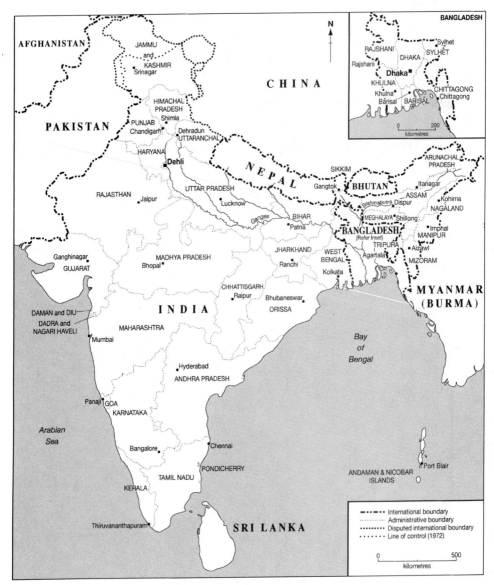

Map 2. India and Bangladesh

Part I is concerned with how the processes of nationalism, development, modernization, and nation building intersect with ethnic and religious identities in South Asia and the abuses and negotiations accompanying these processes. It brings together critical perspectives on these issues from anthropology and literary studies and focuses on Hindu-Muslim conflict in India and Bangladesh. In South Asia national sentiments and religious identities have often become densely and inextricably entwined, and they are wielded strategically by the state and by various political groups as instruments of political power over targeted populations. Each chapter explores the various ways in which "woman" becomes the site of multiple contestations—political, legal, and religious—in order for the postcolonial state to reinvent itself.

In "The Citizen as Sexed: Women, Violence, and Reproduction," Veena Das delves into Indian colonial courts of law to show how the founding narratives of sovereignty draw from the life of the family. She rethinks the relationship among reproduction, death, and sovereignty during the colonial encounter to show how "bare life" is already socially constituted as gendered and as embodying Hindu, Muslim, or Christian passions. In this dual marking of its citizens, the Indian postcolonial state rationalizes violence against the bodies of women, and Das demonstrates this theory through an analysis of the plight of abducted women during the Partition riots of 1947.

In "The Nuclear Fetish: Violence, Affect, and the Postcolonial State," Betty Joseph examines a second manifestation of the gendering of "nature" in contemporary India. She questions the ordinary basis of "fundamentalist" movements in South Asia through an examination of contemporary postcolonial texts and shows how the rise of religious militancy in South Asia, which takes gender and ethnicity as its defining tropes, is commensurate with the rise of the technological violence of the state. Joseph analyzes *Wings of Fire,* the 1993 autobiography of the Indian president, A. P. J. Abdul Kalam, arguing that "all talk of nuclear violence is inevitably a gendered discourse." Joseph draws our attention to the link between the representation of female figures as organic unity and real violence against women, specifically the consequences for future generations of nuclear war between India and Pakistan. She argues that in many developing nations women represent and must shore up cultural autonomy, purity, and nationality through attention to such values in the private sphere, whereas in state discourses technological violence is represented using male metaphors. Joseph contends that the gendered nature of such discourses is outmoded when applied to the scientific abilities of the modern nation-state and its desire for new defense technologies and that religious and gender stereotypes together "perpetuate forms of violent sublimity in the modern [Indian] state."

Yasmin Saikia, in "Overcoming the Silent Archive in Bangladesh: Women Bearing Witness to Violence in the 1971 'Liberation' War," examines the roles of silence and memory in the creation of a national history that erases the trauma of Bengali and Benhari women raped by the Pakistan military and Bangladeshi men in 1971. Saikia notes the way in which nationalist and Islamic discourse reconfigured the liberation war's effects on women as matters of private or domestic concern except where all pregnant women were required by the first prime minister after liberation to undergo abortions. Saikia draws on Renan to suggest that in this active national process of silencing memory and the pain of women, sorrow and suffering are powerful resources for women's collective agency to emerge in postliberation Bangladesh. Empathy, dignity, and survivorhood form a possible basis for victims, perpetrators, and survivors to recast the suffering of the past in such a way as to make the future more palatable and less riven for the ethnically and religiously diverse peoples of South Asia.

These chapters do not claim to be representative of the huge body of scholarship and diverse conflicts and histories of the subcontinent. But together they offer nuanced and rigorous examinations of how nationalism, religion, and politics intersect to operate as instruments of power in these emergent and contested locations and where and how women locate themselves, and are located, within these sites.

2

The Citizen as Sexed

Women, Violence, and Reproduction

VEENA DAS

What are the practices of the self by which the subject comes to be attached to the nation-state and its law, and how are forms of transgression themselves premised on this form of attachment? Paradoxically, the claims of modern states that they are dedicated to the rule of law and to the building of enduring social peace and toleration are coupled with atrocities committed in the name of the nation-state against populations that threaten existing perceptions of national unity and security. Two of the most powerful thinkers on the biopolitical state, Giorgio Agamben and Michel Foucault, have shown how calculations about life and its management are the defining feature of the modern state. However, the very project of enhancement of life determines, as a corollary, that either certain forms of life are not worth preserving, as Foucault's formula of "letting die" as a form of biopower makes clear, or selective populations are targeted for active destruction, as Agamben's location of the camp as the paradigm of the biopolitical state and its manipulation of "bare life" demonstrates. Modern ideologies of progress, then, are not so much about *ending* violence as distributing and rearranging forms of suffering so that the violence of religious wars is shifted into another terrain — that of the violence of national and colonial wars (Asad 2003). Feminist philosophers, such as Rada Ivekovic who has studied comparative partitions in India and the former Yugoslavia, argue that it is the ideology of the *masculine* state that accounts for the gendered violence of the modern state. Whatever adjectives we attach to the idea of the state under modernity—biopolitical, progressive, secular—the route by which violence becomes part of the subject's attachment to the modern state remains a pressing question. My aim here is to examine the foundational stories that make clear why the nation-state comes to have an interest in issues relating to the biological life of the individual and to ask if there are specific questions regarding sexuality and reproduction that might illuminate questions of violence against women.

One of the places to begin an examination of these foundational myths is to consider the place of nature in thinking about the creation of the political. The problem, as I see it, is that once the idea of God as the author of nature and time is displaced and the political body is seen as subject to death and decay, secular means have to be crafted to ensure that the sovereign receives life beyond the lifetime of its individual members. Thus the state has to reimagine its relation to the family, particularly to women's sexuality and reproduction, in denser ways than simply assigning it to the realm of the private. Since the state of nature is seen as the point of mythic origin of the state (as in Hobbes), it seems appropriate to begin this analysis with the way in which bodies are imagined in the state of nature.

One of the frequently cited quotes in Hobbes refers to the mushroom analogy, in which we are asked to consider men as sprung out of the earth and suddenly "like mushrooms, come to full maturity, without all kind of engagement to each other" (Hobbes [1651] 1991: 205). Many feminist scholars have noted the exclusion of the woman, especially the mother, from this originary imagination of social order. Thus Carol Pateman (1988) notes that the invitation to think of men as springing up like mushrooms is designed to obscure the fact that contractual individualism is grounded in the husband's subjugation of the wife. Similarly, Seyla Benhabib (1992) cites this analogy as evidence that the denial of being born of a woman frees the male ego from the natural bonds of dependence on the mother. While this line of argumentation is powerful in showing how the profoundly masculine Leviathan is formulated on the explicit exclusion of women, there is some scope for thinking about this issue beyond questions of exclusion.

One point of entry into these questions is to track the way the so-called natural life enters into the mechanisms and calculations of power—in short, the domain of biopolitics. In his recent writings Agamben (1998) offers us the concept of bare life to suggest a constitutive principle of modernity, namely, that of the coinciding of biological life itself with the life of the citizen. In Agamben's words, "European democracy placed at the center of its battle against absolutism not *bios,* the qualified life of the citizen but *zoe,* the bare, anonymous life that is as such taken into the sovereign ban" (124–25). He locates the first rendering of bare life as the new political subject in the 1679 writ of habeas corpus for here he tracks the idea that what has to be produced before the law is literally the body: "It is not the free man with his statutes and the prerogatives, nor even simply *homo,* but rather *corpus*—that is the new subject of politics" (125). This bears some affinity to the idea of the individual sprung from the earth, as it were, although its location is shifted from the origin of social contract to that of anonymous life as the subject of the law. I propose a different trajectory and argue that even when the law is demanding a body to be produced before it, this body is already constituted as a sociolegal subject rather than a natural body. In the Indian context this turns out to be based on two interrelated conceptions about the "state of nature" and its relation to the political community. The first assumption is that the individual who comes to be the "subject" whose attachment the state seeks to secure is a sexed individual; the second, that the natural "savage" is in fact a communally constructed subject whose passions as "Hindu," "Muslim," or "Christian" come to the fore when the social order is threatened. Both conceptions bear the mark of colonial history in subject formation that always assumes that but for the constraining hand of colonial governance there would be no politics in India except in the form of a succession of communal riots.

Law, Paternity, and the Facts of Nature

Let me first ask the question, how is nature constituted in the legal imagination in the colonial archive? The colonial archive is particularly instructive in this regard since taken-for-granted notions of nature and culture had to be explicitly articulated in the context of subjects whose integration into the law was mediated by the notion of custom; or else for citizens who were domiciled away from the metropolitan centers. In this section I draw from judgments of the Supreme Court in Bombay in the mid-nineteenth century regarding questions such as the "natural" rights of the father over his child after the father had converted to Christianity or the validity of marriages when all legal provisions could not be fulfilled. As the British view of their role in India was not that of aggressive proselytizers, such cases raise important issues regarding what is seen as natural and universal and what belongs to the domain of custom and religion. Beyond the obvious questions about how colonialism had to adjust to local conditions, these cases are important, in my view, for addressing the place of nature in a colonial, secular modernity through pathways of birth and reproduction. I hope to show that there are subtle connections between the regulation of birth and the figuration of death in thinking about sovereignty and citizenship—a theme I take up later for more sustained discussion.

I start the consideration of these matters with a particular problem that colonial law faced in India: did conversion to Christianity alter the rights of the father over the custody of his child? The first case I present, *The Queen v. Shapurji Vezonzi and Bezanzi Edalji,* came before Justices C. J. Roper and J. Perry on February 28, 1843.[1] It concerned a Parsi man named Hormazji Pestonji who had converted to Christianity and consequently was denied access to his wife and female child by his father-in-law. The petition by the father-in-law submitted that the Parsi Panchayat had already given judgment on the matter, dissolving the marriage of Pestonji, whose wife had now married another Parsi man. Further, the petition stated that the child over whom he sought custody was already betrothed and that her grandfather had settled an amount of Rs. 3,000 on her. The petitioner submitted that these were sufficient grounds (the dissolution of the marriage and the betrothal of the child) for denying Pestonji any claims over his wife and child. I will not go into all the questions raised by the case but concentrate instead on the observations of the court regarding the natural rights of the father over his child. The case summary provided by the judges is as follows.

It appeared from the affidavit on which the ruling of habeas corpus was sought on behalf of Hormazji Pestonji, the father of the child, that he converted to Christianity in 1839. Before this conversion he lived with his father-in-law, the defendant. After his conversion, however, he resided at the house of the mission of the Church of Scotland, leaving his wife and child at his father-in-law's house; and he swore that he abstained from going there because he feared of ill treatment on account of his conversion. Hormazji said that he had frequently asked the defendant, Shapurji, to return his wife and child to him, but the defendant refused, on the ground that Hormazji's conversion to Christianity constituted dissolution of the marriage. In January the defendant and his family married off his wife to another Parsi man. It was also sworn before the court that the defendant was about to betroth Hormazji's daughter, according to the custom of the Parsis; that he had refused to give her up to him; and that they believed the child would be removed from the jurisdiction if the writ of habeas corpus was not issued.

The question before the court, then, was whether Hormazji Pestonji's actions amounted to a desertion of his wife and child and whether the custom of the Parsi community, as the court put it, was to be ascendant over the natural rights of the father to have custody of his child. The petition from the child's grandfather and the new husband of the woman stated that the man had deserted his wife and child and went on to claim that he had consented to the child's betrothal so that effectively he had agreed to forgo custody. The observations of the court on this matter are worth producing in detail.

Justice Perry stated that none of the affidavits submitted to the court supported the claim of the father's acquiescence and assent to the child's betrothal:

> If Hormazji is sincere in his embracing of Christianity, it is impossible that he could ever consent to his child being educated in a faith that he believes to be false. . . . The cases in which a father has been held to have waived his right to custody of his children, all shew either gross immorality on the part of the father or a distinct assent on his part to a separate custody in which case the arrangements having been made on the strength of such assent, court would not allow the father capriciously to interfere; . . . but here the whole conduct of the father shews that he has always been desirous to have his wife and child restored to him. *Rex v Green* . . . is a clear decision that the proper custody of an infant child is with the father.

The judgment continues:

> There is a statement in this return that bears improbability on the face of it. The child was betrothed, it is said, a month after the baptism of the father. She must then have been betrothed at the age of one year. Is it in accordance with the custom of the Parsis to betroth so early? I believe it is not; let me be corrected if I am mistaken. Say, it was betrothed; it was plainly done to annoy the father. Done by whom? By the grandfather; but the grandfather had not the slightest right to do so. If he betrothed the child, the father not consenting, then the betrothment was decidedly an illegal act. The man had embraced Christianity and therefore he is to be deprived of his natural right as a father? I can only say that if the Parsis set up such a claim as that, they will find they are grossly mistaken.

There were similar cases in which the issue of conversion and custody of children came up before the court (e.g., *The Queen v. Rev. Robert Nesbitt* [1843]). The application of the writ of habeas corpus was always alluded to not as producing a body that was under illegal detention but as determining what constituted illegal detention; it was the socially constituted person that was at stake rather than a biological body. Thus, for instance, the failure to produce the child in court had to be interpreted juridically. Was it illegal for the grandfather to refuse to give custody of the child to its father? Did it violate the natural rights of the father? But in interpreting what were the conditions under which such *natural rights* could be asserted, the court had to give due consideration to Parsi custom. It had to determine further whether conversion to Christianity constituted an act of desertion. Thus the centrality accorded to the "natural rights" of the father arose not from the mere fact of the birth but from the acknowledgment of the father as one who transforms birth from a natural event to a social one.

I suggest the body of the child over which the writ of habeas corpus was applied in courts of law was not a simple body unattached to the social, as Agamben's argument would have us assume, but the body of a socially and legally constituted person already located in a system of relationships. It is the symbolic weight of the father that makes the court read the biological function of fathering in this way, for no corresponding discussion occurs about the natural rights of the mother over the child. It was paternity that was seen to transform sexuality from private pleasure to an obligation that the citizen had toward reproducing the political community. Thus the right of the father over that of the child that seems to stem from the natural fact of birth and thus to cut across race and religion, in effect, carried already constituted ideas of paternity that allowed family and the state to be linked together. Below I provide the intellectual and moral context that makes the father such a pivotal figure in the imagining of the political community. But first I want to consider one more case, *Maclean v. Cristall,* that came before Justices Perry and Yardley in September 1849 in the same court. I give the case summary from the court records and then quote from the judgments that link issues of reproduction with the issue of citizenship. The essential question here was whether the common law of England regarding marriage, as it applied to British citizens living in India, imported with it the provisions that made the presence of a minister in holy orders essential as it was in England. The details of the case are as follows.

On November 6, 1834, a marriage was performed between the plaintiff and Miss Mary Lewis Pelly, a resident of Surat. Both parties to the marriage were members of the Church of England. Mr. William Fyre, a missionary who was then residing at Surat, performed the ceremony. The court noted that Mr. Fyre had not been episcopally ordained; he belonged to the Congregationalist sect and had signed the register in which the marriage was entered as "Minister of the Gospel and Missionary." The court further noted that no person of holy orders was present at the time of the marriage and that although there were several civil functionaries who lived in Surat, a person of the holy order was not easy to find. In their summary of the case, the justices put the question before the court as follows: "The question for the opinion of the Court, is, whether the preceding facts constitute a valid marriage, as stated in the plaint."

The counsel for the plaintiff brought a passage from an earlier judgment *(Reading v. Smith)* before the court: "What is the law of marriage in all foreign establishments, settled in counties professing a religion essentially different? . . . An English resident at St. Petersburgh does not look to the ritual of the Greek Church, but to the rubric of the Church of England, when he contracts a marriage with an English woman. Nobody can suppose that while the Mogul empire existed, an Englishman was bound to consult the Koran for the celebration of his marriage." Another counsel suggested that only parts of English law were suitable to the conditions in India so that it was open for the court to consider whether this portion of the common law was indeed appropriate to the circumstances of the country.

The judges themselves were quite clear that the "common law of England is the law of this country [i.e., India] so far as respects Europeans." This would imply that the marriage would have to be declared void. But as Justice Perry noted, "The effect of such a conclusion would be to pronounce a vast number of marriages that have taken place in India during the last 250 years, invalid,—to extend the stain of illegitimacy to many a pedigree hitherto deemed spotless,—and, above all, to carry error and dismay into numerous innocent and unsuspecting households." Accordingly, Justice Perry concluded that "the fund of good sense which is contained in the most valuable collection of jurisprudence in the world—I mean the English Law Reports— furnishes forth ample authority for denying a rule so inconvenient to mankind as has been alleged at our Bar to exist."

The historical and anthropological literature on colonialism recognizes that the entire process of applying legal rules to new circumstances arising from the expansion of empire led to adaptations of the law to local conditions. The very question of where authority of law is to be located came to be debated. Thus, for instance, Justice Perry talked about the *unstable* foundations of law in such a case as the present one. Reflecting on the conflict of opinions in the judicial archive on this question, he referred to the great masters in law, the classical Roman jurists, who, when they found that propositions and dicta, laid down in early times, led to a conclusion "opposed to the best interest of the Common wealth vigorously appealed to the foundation of all human law." He saw these foundations to lie in common sense and the principle of *utilitas causa* and *jus sigulare ad consequential non productur.* Thus if the consequences were against the welfare of mankind, then the law was to be rejected.

We now have the building blocks necessary for my argument on the links between an appeal to common sense about the "natural rights" of the father and the welfare of mankind as opening a way to consider how reproduction linked the citizen to the secular state. After all, certainty about paternity is not necessary to reproduce the population conceived as a numerical entity, but the reproduction of the social body seems to call for reiterating the role of the father. To anticipate my later argument, I claim that regulating birth and reproduction was the other side of the concern with the sovereign's rights over life and death and that life for the political body required not only that "correct" children be born but also that they should as *citizens* be ready to die for continuity of the political body.[2] Thus while the father's right over the life and the death of the son was reconfigured so that even the natural right of the father seems to stem now from some notion of consent and capacity to provide care for the child, the sovereign now demands that citizens be ready to give life to the sovereign *voluntarily.* However, as we saw in the judgments of the Supreme Court, such citizens are not seen as springing from the earth but rather from the normatively configured order of the family.

Revisiting an Old Debate

This scene of colonialism obliged administrators and judges to refer to a world populated with other religions and customs: their notions of natural rights were pitted against other people's ideas of what constituted nature. Thus a form of secular reasoning had to be applied to cases in which the private domains of marriage and reproduction met the public domain of making loyal subjects and citizens for the nation. As we saw in the *Maclean v. Cristall* case, this was not a matter of religious rites becoming redundant as marriage became a secular affair. We witness instead the state's concern to produce legitimate members of the political body when this body was dispersed in sites away from home. The judges seem to have rearranged the relative importance of legal rules concerning what constituted legitimate marriage and used the welfare of mankind argument for suspending the application of the rules in these cases. This is not, then, a simple story of the secular emerging out of the religious and leaving it behind, nor is it one in which religious life is now consigned to the sphere of the private: what is at stake is precisely that marriage and reproduction cannot be relegated to a private arrangement. Instead these cases provide a different line in support of Asad's sense that secular concerns of the state stand ascendant over other concerns as far as the production of legitimate subjects or citizens is concerned. Thus the founding moment of the social order that conceives of a state of nature as consisting of autonomous individuals must meet its limits in the sexed individual whose reproductive functions place the individual as born within a family rather than produced from the earth.

The line of argument proposed here does not see family simply as the institution from which civil society arises and separates itself but proposes that sovereignty continues to draw life from the family. An important debate that has bearing on this question relates to the nature of patriarchal authority in seventeenth- and eighteenth-century England when the framework for a liberal polity based on consent was in the process of formation. Was patriarchal authority derived from God so that the father was the head of the family according to the divine law of nature; or was secular or civil power to be seen as instituted by men? Another way of putting this question is to ask whether the power of the king was an extension of the power of the father or whether that power was given to the multitude by the king, who ruled by their consent. Whichever events we emphasize in determining what constituted the historical context—the execution of King Charles in January 1649, the problems of succession, reformation, or the discovery of Aristotle via Arabic—there is little doubt that theological considerations were intertwined with political philosophy.[3]

My interest in revisiting the debate about the relationship between family and the state is for the limited purpose of thinking the relationship among reproduction, death, and sovereignty. Was the place of the father under what has been called the new framework for liberal thought a complete break from the earlier patriarchal doctrine, a transformation, or a transfiguration? If we look at the relationship between reproduction and death in relation to continuities of the political body, then the symbolic weight of the father is transfigured (in the way in which, say, a walk may be transfigured into a dance or speaking may be transfigured into singing), but he neither disappears from the political scene nor does his authority become redundant in the efforts to reimagine the place of family within political community. In emphasizing the continuing importance of "reproduction" as that which links the state with the family, I am suggesting that though notions of fraternity are important for some purposes, as emphasized by Pateman (1988),[4] the life that sovereignty draws from the family is that which can ultimately be "sacrificed" for the maintenance of the nation-state as in war.

If we take Filmer's text *Patriarcha* ([1652] 1991), then, fatherly or patriarchal authority was derived from God, and the authority of the father over his children was similar to the authority of the king over his subjects; in fact, the latter was a direct extension of the former. Filmer states that the father was head of the family according to the divine law of nature: his wife, children, and servants owed obedience by the will of God himself. According to Filmer, "Fatherly power over the family was natural and God was the author of nature" (31). Thus fatherly power was not something that law authored. Rather the social order was itself founded on the fact that this power embodied the law. The father of the family governs by no other law than by his own will, not by the laws or wills of his sons or servants. Filmer's insistence on grounding kingly power in the natural and originary authority of fatherly power escaped the impasse that Hobbes faced in somehow deriving the social from the fully formed autonomous individual arising from nature and contracting to make up the political.

In her acute analysis of the relationship between fatherly authority and the possibility of a woman citizen, Mary Laura Severance (2000) argues that in Hobbes we have fatherly authority predicated on consent rather than on something that is natural or originary. But, as she notes, the consent of the family to be ruled by the father is, in effect, to neutralize his power to kill. For Filmer, the family is insulated against the power of the father to kill because the laws of nature would ensure that the father does not use this power but instead does his best for the preservation of the family: "There is no nation that allows children any action or remedy for being unjustly governed and yet for all this every father is bound by the law of nature to do the best for the preservation of his family. By the same move is the king tied by the same laws of nature to keep his general ground that the safety of his kingdom be his general law" ([1652] 1991: 42). Analogically, the king also would not use his power to kill under normal circumstances. Since the father (and by extension the monarch) *embodies* rather than *represents* law, it is up to him to decide what constitutes the state of exception, and there can be no remedy in law against this.

By grounding the power of the father in the consent of the family, Hobbes is able to draw a distinction between fatherly and sovereign authority as two distinct but artificial spheres. However, this is done within the framework of the seventeenth-century doctrine that women are unfit for civil business and must be represented (or concluded) by their husbands. The sexual contract and the social contract, then, are two separate realms, but the relationship between them is much more vexed than Asad is granting. Certainly, as Severance (2000: 464) notes, the idea of the state of nature as that in which every man is in a state of war with every other man should be modified to read as that in which every father as the head of the family is at war against every other father: "The members of each individual family 'consent' not to the sovereign's but to the father's absolute rule; they are not parties to the 'contract' that brings the commonwealth into existence." Unlike the consent to be ruled by the father, which protects the family against him such that political society stops at the doorstep of the family, the consent to the social contract protects individuals against each other by vesting power in the sovereign.

Paternity, Secular Time, and the Life of the Sovereign

One might expect that once biblical notions of time were displaced in the nineteenth century in favor of the secular notions of time, derived from evolutionary theory, one would find the symbolic weight of the father in determining the nature of political community lifted. Turning to the studies of kinship as instituted by legal scholars such as Johann Jakob Bachofen, John Ferguson McLennan, and Lewis Henry Morgan,[5] we find that though family now acquires a history, this history is staged around the curious question of the conditions under which it became possible to ascertain paternity. Thus, for instance, Bachofen characterized primitive promiscuity as problematic because it made it impossible to determine paternity with certainty. McLennan, similarly, thought that the problem with polyandry was that while the mother was known under this system of marriage, it was impossible to determine who the father was. Morgan and later Engels asserted that the beginning of civilization can be traced to the decisive victory of the monogamous family "the express purpose being to produce children of undisputed paternity" (Engels 1942: 125). Though Engels saw in this rise of monogamy the establishment of the power of men and the world historic defeat of women, one can read passages in both authors that are based on the premise that the desire to pass on property to sons was a *natural* desire. Bachofen famously talked about the "spurious" children brought about by women among the Cecrops, since the woman was not bound to any one man exclusively.

Although Filmer's claim that the father had absolute right over the life and death of his son was refuted by Locke on the ground that the facts of begetting would give joint dominion over the child to both parents, he too thought that women were by nature weak and hence needed to be represented by their husbands. Moreover, Locke claimed that the father's authority over the child, necessary in childhood, has a natural limit when the child becomes older. It is interesting that in introducing a temporal element in the relationship, Locke shifts the emphasis to the anatomical child, whereas for Filmer, the status of the son was relational (i.e., even adult sons were children of their respective fathers). Severance points out that the performative nature of the father's authority is overlooked in discussions of Locke, especially by those who feel that he did not go far enough in refuting the patriarchal grounds of political authority.

Does the father then act in the Lockean view only as the symbolic place holder for the political order? For Severance (2000: 491), the father functions not as an individual but as a symbolic principle: "He is a necessary presupposition in Locke's attempt to maintain a distinction not between the natural and the political but the political and the social." Yet, as the legal scholarship at the moment of the institution of kinship studies attests, the concern with certainty of paternity as a necessary condition for the establishment of the political in the context of the state cannot get rid of the "natural" so easily. The symbolic weight of patriarchy, it seems, can only be borne by biological fathers, and the evolution of the monogamous family is the best guarantee within evolutionary time for political authority to be securely grounded in fatherly authority. So how is the sexed individual to be placed in the imagination of the secular? If individuals are sexed, then they are also mortal. Both are facts that the mushroom analogy manages to obscure. The final text I want to consult for the place of men and women in the creation of political community is

Rousseau's *Emile,* specifically the figure of Sophie, for some guidance on this issue (Rousseau 1911; hereafter cited as *Emile*).

On Sexed and Mortal Individual or Rousseau's Woman

Many scholars of Rousseau have held the view that book 5, "Sophie or The Woman," is a minor text marked among other things by a break in genre from the earlier sections of the book. Ronald Grimsley (1982), for instance, argued that not only are Rousseau's ideas on men and women conservative and reactionary, but in this section Rousseau is unable to detach himself from his personal fantasies. Others have abstracted the observations on the masculine and the political from this section but held that the figure of Sophie does not offer any philosophical challenge. I want to make a limited point here. I ask, what promise does the figure of the woman hold for introducing the themes of love and citizenship, and how are these themes conjoined?[6]

Earlier, at the conclusion of book 4, the tutor announced that Emile was not made to live alone; he is a member of society and must fulfill his duties as such. Thus the appearance of the woman, first crafted in imagination and then given a name and thus made concrete, is to teach Emile the meaning of sociality. Sophie, as the tutor says, is the name of a good omen. If Emile is a man of nature not spoiled by artifice, then Sophie is not so much the symmetrical opposition but the obligatory passage through whom the man will move along the road of marriage, paternity, and citizenship. While the scene of seduction is necessary for the pupil to be inserted into the social, his capability to be a citizen is proved by learning how to renounce the very lure of the woman that was his passage into sociality. In an intriguing episode in which Emile and Sophie are betrothed, the tutor tells Emile that he must leave Sophie. The argument presented to Emile is that he must wait until Sophie is older and able to bear healthy children. But an earlier episode in which the tutor tells Emile that Sophie is dead, in order to test his reaction, shows that there is a close relationship between learning how to inhabit society through the engagement with sex and learning how to become a good citizen by overcoming the fear of separation and death. It is worth pausing here to reflect on this.

In educating Emile in a manner that his natural inclinations are not shrouded by the artifice of society, the tutor had taken care to see that he overcomes the fear of death that Rousseau sees as a sign of this artifice. "Death is the cure for the evils you bring upon yourself," he exhorts, "nature would not have you suffer perpetually" (*Emile* 146). So when the announcement of Sophie's death happens, Emile has already learned not to fear death in general. But what of the death of the other? By fearing that Sophie might be dead, Emile has learned that the fear of death can be expanded to include those one loves: "You know how to suffer and die; you know how to bear the heavy yoke of necessary ills of today; but you have not yet learnt to give a law to the desires of your heart; and the difficulties of life that arise rather from our affections than from our needs" (146).

It is then from Emile's journey into citizenship that we learn the multiple chains of signification in which the figure of Sophie is inserted. She is the chimera who is inserted into the text—figure of seduction, future mother of a family, and one through whom Emile learns that to be a good citizen is to overcome his fear of death by giving a law to the desires of his heart. Hence she is seductress in the present, the maternal in the future, and the teacher of duty and code of conduct. Without her he can overcome physical ills, but with her and then despite her he will become a virtuous citizen: "When you become the head of a family, you are going to become a member of the state, and do you know what it is to be a member of the state? Do you know what government, laws, and father land are? *Do you know what the price is of your being permitted to live and for whom you ought to die?*" (*Emile* 448; emphasis added).

There are two thoughts here. First, in order to be a citizen of the state, you must be the head of a household; and second, you must know for whom you ought to die. It is important not to confuse this virtue of the readiness to die with a simple picture of the heroic. In earlier sections, while learning about the arts, Emile had expressed derision at the idea of the heroic, and in considering the careers that do not obstruct the naturalness of Emile, the tutor says with irony, "You may hire yourself out at very high wages to go to kill men who never did you any harm" (*Emile* 420). Then what does the readiness to die signify?

For the woman, the duty as a citizen is confounded with duty to husband. A woman's comportment must be such that not only her husband but also his neighbors and friends must believe in her fidelity. When she gives her husband children who are not his own, we are told, she is false both to him and to them, and her crime is *"not infidelity but treason"* (*Emile* 325; emphasis added). Thus woman as seductress holds danger for the man, because she may use her powers of seduction to make the man too attached to life and thus unable to decipher who and what is worth dying for. In her role as mother, she may deprive him of being a proper head of the household by giving him counterfeit children. That this is treason and not infidelity shows how the mother, who was completely excluded as a figure of thought in Filmer and Hobbes, comes to be incorporated into the duties of citizenship. For Rousseau, the individual on whose consent political community is built is no doubt a sexed individual, but the woman has the special role of not only introducing the man to forms of sociality but also teaching him how to renounce his attachment to her in order to give life to the political community.

The fear of death in Rousseau is aligned with the fear of extinction. "My personal identity," as he tells Emile, "depends upon my memory. In order to be the same self, I must remember that I have existed" (*Emile* 246). But then existence is not only a matter of bodily continuity, for "the life of the soul only begins with the death of the body." Thus self-preservation for Rousseau demands that the person be initiated into citizenship by overcoming the fear of bodily death. What, then, is the life of the soul that he talks about? In book 5 where the figure of Sophie appears, the child is being taught that the beginning of the human race is the father and mother who did not have a father and mother and the end of the human race would be when there are children who did not have children. There are no references to creation and apocalypse, which is why one can see the complex relation established among the obligation to reproduce, the idea of individual mortality, and the fear of extinction. I submit that the relation between the state as a passive entity whose active face is sovereignty allows a slippage between the idea of the human race and the idea of the life invested in the sovereign. This is evident when Rousseau expounds on the idea of good government and says that increase in population provides a kind of moral compass through which we can judge the goodness of a government. Thus good governance is indexed in the fact that citizens would want to reproduce and the population would be augmented not by "artificial" means such as colonization but by natural means of reproduction.[7]

Within this scheme women's allegiance to the state is proved by their role of bearing legitimate children (recall the remark about the crime of bringing illegitimate children in the world being not about infidelity but about treason); and men learn to be good citizens by being prepared to die in order to give life to the sovereign. To be sure, there is a shift in the conception of paternity, for if the father's authority provides the foundation for the authority of the sovereign it is not because the father has a right over the life and death of his son but because the natural right of the father stems from his natural tenderness toward his son.[8] There is a natural joining of the will of the father and son that provides the model for the joining of the will of sovereign and citizen in Rousseau, but as I have indicated, the symbolic weight of paternity continues. For the individual to be located in the state as citizen (and not merely a subject who obeys laws), he must first pass through the detour of sexuality and seduction. This is a more complex picture than the simple opposition of active and passive rights would suggest and gives at least a clue as to why paternity remains at the center of debates about citizenship and sovereignty. I prefer to think of this as a transfiguration rather than a transformation in the figure of the paternal and the sovereign.

An Interlude

I give a somewhat over schematized account of my arguments regarding the complex nature of the transfiguration of the figure of the father and what that has to say about the way nature functions as a trope within the overall arguments examined here. I try to give an imaginary matrix in which the figure of the father provides a kind of keyhole through which we can see the complex relations between ideas of god and nature, family and political community and what constitutes sovereignty. Instead of starting with Justice Perry as I did above, I want to place his arguments as an end point of my argument.[9]

In Filmer God is the author of nature and Adam as his direct creation is the figure of the father who combines different kinds of power. Thus for Filmer, political power is fatherly power and earthly fathers as direct descendants of Adam have absolute power of life and death over their sons. Inasmuch as fathers embody law rather than simply represent it and kingly power is simply an extension of fatherly power, it is laws of nature that instill in both fathers and kings the desire to preserve their children and their subjects respectively. This is the only protection that sons and subjects have against the sovereign's right to kill. Hobbes, on the other hand, would place God and family completely offstage for his imagination of political community. In his rendering there are two kinds of contracts: the family consents to be ruled by the father, and this is their protection against the father's power to kill. The men who arise like mushrooms from the earth are, nevertheless, heads of households. In the war of men against men (read Fathers) in the state of nature, the capability to enter into a social contract produces the sovereign who now gives men protection against each other. The sexed individual is recognized but placed just at the threshold of political community.

In disputing Filmer's patriarchal absolutism, Locke famously argued that God is the maker of mankind, and thus even if his power is to be read as fatherly power, it excludes all pretense of earthly fathers that they are the makers of their children. In the earthly register begetting would give joint dominion to men and women over their children, but since it is God who is the maker, the dominion over children does not give rights over life and death to either parent. One could argue that the father is merely the place holder—a name in Locke, as argued by Severance[10]—but the slippage between the father as the biological begetter and the father as the symbolic place holder for the Law does not vanish.

Once the individual is recognized as social because he is sexed, he is also recognized as mortal. In Rousseau man is said to receive life from the sovereign. Political community as population is dependent on reproduction, but the citizen's investment of affect in the political community is attested by his desire to reproduce and to give the political community legitimate "natural" children. A corollary is that immigration is not an authentic way to augment population—and further that a woman's infidelity is not only an offense against the family but against the sovereignty of the state as well. Once biblical time is replaced by secular time, the entire course of the history of the family is arranged around the question of certainty of paternity on which institutions of private property and state are made to rest.

Within this particular field of forces, we can see now that colonial encounters would pose significant questions about the relation between family and state. Since the political community becomes dispersed and pluralized under colonialism, the person has to be seen as situated in a socially and legally constituted community, with further possibilities of changing his or her own religion. Conversion, then, opens up the space for imagining bodies even at the moment when bare life is being asserted, as in the cases in which writs of habeas corpus are brought before courts, as socially and legally constituted. Family cannot be left offstage in imaginings of the political, but fathers now cannot be seen as either embodying or representing law. As either husbands or fathers their rights over children or wives have to be ascertained in the face of the astounding possibility that religion cuts through and divides family instead of uniting it. This development is addressed in the law courts and already complicates the relations between sovereignty and family and also between the founding stories of the origin of sovereignty in the West and the applications of these notions in a dispersed political community. In the next and final section, I argue that the issue of Hindu-Muslim conflict and forcible conversions exploded at the time of the Partition violence in 1947 in India precisely around the question of the sexual and reproductive violence and the rights of the state over "its" women.

Women, Reproduction, and the Founding of the Nation

I hope that the way in which founding narratives of sovereignty is troubled in colonial courts of law with regard to the place of the father as converting the natural event of birth into a social recognizable event is sufficiently clear. The colonial context makes it obvious that something like "bare life" is seen as already socially constituted in that the person in nature in fact embodies passions as a Hindu or a Muslim or a Christian and the colonial administration sees it as part of the exercise of sovereignty to regulate these "natural" passions. In his stunning work on the colonial censor, Deepak Mehta (forthcoming) shows how colonial governance in India was tied up with questions of regulating hate between Hindus and Muslims, which the colonial state saw as primordial. What interests me in Mehta's acute analysis is the way in which questions of reproduction appear as either giving or depriving life to the "other" community. Quoting from various Urdu and Marathi newspapers and other popular tracts that came under censorship, Mehta argues that the theme of fecundating the women of the other community is a frequent source of insult in the triad of Hindu-Muslim-Christian relations of hate. As an example, Mehta cites passages such as the following:

> What a change has been brought about by this story of Niyoga: Do you desire any son by our semen? If you have got any barren sweetheart in your mind, then send her to the stud of the Musalmans. By our Islamism we shall certainly produce a son: and we shall show that even dried up branches can fructify.[11] (From the tract *Mazhab ka Danka*)

On the other side, Hindus also imagine that the Muslim woman needs to be rescued from Islam just as they also imagine that the Christians and the Muslims use all kinds of deceptions to lure away innocent Hindu women.

Charu Gupta (2001) has similarly marshaled important evidence from vernacular tracts published in Urdu in the late nineteenth and early twentieth century to show how Hindu reform movements presented the image of the lustful Muslim as a direct threat to Hindu domesticity. The tracts attack forms of popular religiosity in which Hindu women worshiped Muslim *pirs* (saints), especially making votive offerings for the birth of sons. All this is interpreted as an affront to Hindu domesticity and Hindu community. I have argued elsewhere that the anxiety over the reproductive powers of women and the fear that these could be stolen by the enemy community set the stage for the salience that the figure of the abducted woman acquires during the Partition riots in 1947. I summarized the argument as follows:

> The story of abduction has implications for the very staging of sovereignty, such that when this story appears magnified at the time of the Partition, it becomes the foundational story of how the state is instituted and its relation to patriarchy. It invites us to think the story of the imaginary institution of the state in Western theory from this perspective rather than the other way around. (Das 2006: 33)

The perspective that I was referring to came from my analysis of the manner in which the state staked its claim in the recovery of women who had been abducted and forcibly converted. The figure of the abducted woman became important because it posited the inauguration of the Indian state not in a mythic state of nature but in the "correct" relations between communities that it had to establish. The mise-en-scène of the state of nature was not that of men in their individuality, appearing like mushrooms, but rather men as heads of households who were at war with heads of other households over the abduction and forcible conversions of "their" women. The large-scale abduction and rapes of women, as well as questions of what was to be done with children born of "wrong" sexual unions, had to be settled by the state before it could claim sovereignty and thus the right to draw life from its citizens.

I hope that revisiting some of the foundational stories of the inauguration of the nation-state in Western theory and analyzing the way in which thinking of citizens as both sexed and mortal allows us to think of gender as essential to this story rather than something that could be added or subtracted at will. These stories acquire different lives in the colonial and postcolonial contexts and compel us to think that the notion of bare life itself needs rethinking as the bodies of the citizens come marked as Hindu or Muslim as well as sexed and mortal. In some ways the postcolonial scene punctures the notion of bare life. In other ways it tells us that the intimate relation between the life of the sovereign and the life of the family determines both forms of disorder.

NOTES

1. The cases reported here can be found in Sir Eskine Perry, *Cases Illustrative of Oriental Life, and the Application of English Law to India, Decided in H.M. Supreme Court at Bombay* (London: S. Sweet, 1853).

2. Charles Taylor (1998: 44) asserts that the modern democratic state needs a healthy degree of patriotism—"a strong sense of identification with the polity and a willingness to give of oneself for its sake." Asad (2003) provides a stringent critique of the simplistic notion of belonging in this text. I simply want to add to Asad's points that the entire question of what it is to give oneself—to be ready to die for one's country—requires a complete description of who is called to die, whose death counts, and who determines what constitutes the state of exception in which one can be asked to die for one's country. One aspect of this call to patriotism is that a myth of voluntary sacrifice has to be carefully maintained and stories of suffering of soldiers, especially their dissent, carefully suppressed in myths of patriotism. In any case, with the new doctrines and technologies of high-tech wars, the risks of death are disproportionately distributed and major casualties are inflicted on civilians as collateral damage. See Humphrey 2002.

3. The precise nature and direction of the influence of religious thought on political philosophy is the subject of much debate but see the classic contributions of John Dunn (1969); John Marshall (1994); J.G.A. Pocock (1971); Joshua Mitchell (1993).

4. See esp. chap. 4.

5. See Bachofen [1897] 1967; McLennan 1970; Morgan 1877.

6. The theme of incorrect children being born of sexual violence that could jeopardize the honor of the nation is pursued in Das 1995.

7. Mario Feit (2003) has examined the implications of Rousseau's theory of the relation between sexuality and mortality for same-sex marriage in an innovative and interesting way. While I see that there are important implications of Rousseau's thesis of citizenship for non-normative forms of sexuality, I am much more interested here in the way in which the figure of the father places Rousseau in the debate on fatherhood in Filmer, Hobbes, and Locke. I have learned much from Feit's discussion on population.

8. One can see the slippage between reproduction as an act of biological begetting and as an act of socially creating the child in such statements of the tutor as "It is I who am the true father of Emile, it is I who made him into a man." The dispersal of the "I" in the text often allows a slippage between the tutor and the author: here the functioning of the father as a Name is very evident.

9. In assembling the authors in the manner that I have done, my intention is not to give a comprehensive account or even to consider the chronological developments of

ideas discussed here but to see how, specifically, the mutual determination of theological and political informs the way the father is positioned.

10. Severance gives this marvelous quote from Locke: "the Husband and Wife, though they have but one common Concern, yet having different understandings, will unavoidably sometimes have different wills too; it therefore being necessary that the last Determination, *i.e.*, the Rule, should be placed somewhere, it naturally falls to the Man's share, as the abler and stronger" (*T*, 321, quoted in Severance 2000: 491).

11. Niyoga refers to the provision in some of the Dharmashastras such as the Laws of Manu by which a woman can contract sexual relations with a man (not her husband) for the purpose of raising children. Clearly the insult here is to refer to Hindus as incapable of producing offspring and hence needing Muslims to do that for them. Mehta interprets this rightly as emasculating the enemy, but the underlying structure of claiming that Hindu men cannot get their women to produce offspring for them seems to allude to the question of where the community is to draw life from.

3

The Nuclear Fetish

Violence, Affect, and the Postcolonial State

BETTY JOSEPH

Postcolonial politics in India is being violently inscribed today as a politics of time. In this disturbing scene when historians are receiving death threats for representing the national pasts in a manner that refuses to privilege any single "origin," or community,[1] the seemingly benign conjurings of the future by technocrats may pass unnoticed. This chapter is an attempt to read between the lines of A. P. J. Abdul Kalam's 1999 best-selling autobiography, *Wings of Fire*. Before he became president of India in 2002, Kalam was better known as the architect of its missile systems and the chief scientist behind the nuclear test blasts of May 1998. The autobiography caught my attention when a review by R. Ramachandran appeared in the *Frontline* news magazine. The reviewer can barely contain his disappointment as he writes:

> Published in the wake of the nuclear tests conducted by India in May 1998, of which Avul Pakir Janulabdeen *[sic]* Kalam was one of the key architects, one expected this autobiography to provide personal insights into the scientific, technological and politico-strategic compulsions that led to India's nuclearization. Sadly, the book falls well short of that. Indeed, but for a passing mention in the epilogue, the nuclear tests do not figure in the book at all. (Ramachandran 1999)

The reviewer, like many others, believes that a group of scientists, including Kalam, garnered support from the new breed of technocrat-politicians in the 1980s and pressured successive governments to go ahead with the tests. The tests announced that the Indian state was officially a nuclear weapons power in contrast to the 1974 test, which has always been characterized by the Indian government as a peaceful nuclear explosion. Ramachandran asks in his review, "Why did Kalam think that the nuclear tests were a necessity?" He then goes on to give his readers the last word on *Wings of Fire*: "Unfortunately, the book provides no answers. One gets the impression that it is precisely to avoid the predicament of answering this question that the book has been published now—before the consequences of the nuclear tests begin to overshadow all the other events in Kalam's life."

Ramachandran's phrasing is tantalizing because it signals a set of relationships between the acts of writing and violence.[2] When we talk of representations of violence we usually imply two things. First, there are symbolic forms and practices through which one group achieves domination and another resists it. Thus forms of violence are represented in cultural texts, whether calendars, posters, paintings, films, novels, or autobiographies. This is to say that there is a social reality that is processed whether in writing, orally, or visually. Second, violence is often committed through representation. In other words, writing in a general sense or inscription of meaning not only re-presents violence but also can be a form of violence itself.

How is writing a form of violence in its own right? When Ramchandran asserts that Kalam's autobiography is trying to displace the silence left by the overwhelming question—Why were the nuclear tests necessary?—he is reading the autobiography as a discursive act, a sleight-of-hand that deflects and thereby refuses to answer a question that the public has a right to ask of the bomb's architects. Ramachandran also adds a provocative temporal twist to the autobiographical act. The autobiography appropriates, he argues, a present that is seemingly innocent or oblivious to any possibility of disaster in the future or the future violence that could result as a consequence of these nuclear tests. In characterizing Kalam's autobiography as evasive and holding back on important issues, Ramachandran is posing questions that the postcolonial state, let alone Kalam, has refused to answer for decades: Why have we gone nuclear? When and why did public discussions about the peaceful uses of nuclear energy in the 1950s go underground? And why, shrouded in secrecy, did the nuclear program gradually emerge in the 1990s as the full-blown, violent fetish of the postcolonial state?[3]

Just as the Indian public lost an opportunity to debate the need to hand over the most powerful weapon of sanctioned violence to the Indian state, the readers of Kalam's autobiography cannot miss a similar irony operating at the textual level. India went from "peaceful" user of nuclear energy to nuclear weapons power in four decades. In the very same period, Kalam went from being a rocket engineer to a weapons scientist. Given that Kalam's life story has become a kind of metonymic representation of nuclear thinking in the postcolonial state, the text's silence on what had been the core event in his life—the 1998 nuclear blasts—begs a closer reading.

Silence is never absolute in texts, for it always leaves the tracks of various decisions: to speak, not to speak, or to replace one form of speech with another. Thus it is possible to "read" silence, trace its edges in Kalam's text, and by doing so, ask how state-sanctioned violence is mediated and represented in the language of bureaucrats and scientists. What words replace others? What metaphors do the work of deflecting and obscuring? And if the nuclear bomb is the ultimate sublime object of destructive power, and a nationalistically inflected one at that, then somewhere in Kalam's text must be the signs of that affect. And if the question of nationalist violence is intimately linked (as it has been for some time in India) with the discourses of religion, gender, and cosmology, then what occupies the power of the "other" in such forms of speech? What, in the midst of the violence of representation, and the representation of violence, carries the burden of the subdued but inescapable moral and ethical questions about the future of the social—of human society in general?

The entry of ethical and moral questions into official discourse is not surprising. I use the term "official discourse" here in the sense in which the cultural critics Frank Burton and Pat Carlen (1979: 48) have used it: "the systematization of modes of argument that proclaim the state's legal and administrative rationality." This discourse also often needs a discursive "other" to legitimize its claims; an "other" that appears in governmental publications as a "guarantor of the discourse" and is therefore characterized by a "constant appeal to, and commentary of, a third party (constructed by the discourse) as a guarantor of the truth of the discursive fiats, claims and silences" (Burton and Carlen 1979: 23). This "other" in official discourse is especially effective when it appears in a domain often seen as antithetical to the political desiderata of the modern state: religion, affect, family, women, and the private sphere. These domains, by their seeming disinterestedness in the workings of governmentality, dissimulate state power by presenting "uncontaminated" and "sincere" takes on politics. Thus one of the key effects of such harnessing of ethical and moral questions in these domains of discourse, especially insofar as these questions appear in the work of intellectuals whose confidence the state must retain—parties, elite groups, bureaucrats—is that these affective tropes lend a unity and coherence to the state's rationality and hegemonic functions. I spell this out in some detail in the following section.

State violence is sanctioned violence. But if Ashis Nandy (2002) is right, and even that has its limits, we may encounter within the text of rationalization of official violence a deflection or a "defense" or "denial" of rationalization. Nandy's example will suffice here: a scientist such as Norbert Wiener might refuse to join his fellow scientists to compute the number of possible deaths at Hiroshima, but others (nonscientists) who manifest more "moderate" versions of such rationalizations may only display ambivalence at the linguistic level. "What looks like the stylized pastoralism" [of Tolstoy, Thoreau, Gandhi, and Tagore]," Nandy tells us, may be "an attempt to break out of the violence of rigid intellectual frames" (215–16).

What Burton and Carlen and Nandy are suggesting, albeit in different historical and geographic contexts, is that no clear-cut boundaries exist for the operation of power within the modern state. Writing and aesthetics are signifying practices that materialize discourses of state power. In a variety of cultural texts (autobiography, literature), the psychic division between art and science break down and reveal their potential for cross-hatching. Similarly, the confidence and assurance of official discourse may inscribe through another register the ambivalence, guilt, and contradictions of its rationalization—the destruction of the social. This is especially so, it seems to me, because violence and destruction exist in a kind of temporal relation: it is a giving up of the future, as well as a giving up *on* the future. When state violence is multiplied into the possibility of mass destruction such as a nuclear weapon, there is an unavoidable fracture in the present and thoughts of future destruction/destruction of the future are haunted by their opposite—the anticipation of the future as one occupied by continuing generations. The future, needless to say, then inescapably has a gendered structure; it is most often *intimately* understood through figures of reproduction—children, infants, nature, and so on.

I approach Kalam's autobiography with this prestructured frame of reading driven by the hunch that in the end all talk of nuclear violence is inevitably a gendered discourse. And even if one refuses to talk directly about the destruction of the future, the shadowy presence of the woman emerges within the text as its unconscious; as a partially developed position pointing to what has to be negated so that the text can validate the possibility of using awesome forms of state power. While it is often difficult to see the connections between a personal text like Kalam's and the larger plane of politics, it is not difficult to acknowledge that the object of both—psychobiography and human subjectivity on the one hand and political society and political action on the other—often run close together. Nowhere is this more evident than in the powerful rhetorics of nationalism and affect, where the line between rational and irrational, between power and repression, between love and hate become dangerously unclear and yet significant motors of action that cannot be ignored in social analysis.

Understanding how women are figured in these discussions is crucial for understanding how representations of women may result in real violence against women. When the figure of woman is used as a symbolic resolution of social fractures (of class, caste, religion, etc.), she provides the means by which ideologues can preserve social totality as an organic whole. However, this use of female figures as symbols of organic totality does not advance feminism. In his work on colonial science, Gyan Prakash (1997: 537) shows that in the late nineteenth century the condition of women was one factor summoned by Hindu intellectuals to speak of the progressive and scientific nature of the "true religion of ancient Hindus." They contrasted it with "the irrationality and corruption of contemporary Hinduism," arguing indeed that the degradation was a result of the loss of Hindu science (537). It is important to note that the condition of women (like the caste system or priestly superstition) operated both as a point of resistance to cultural change (one must resist modernity) and as an impetus for a reactionary change ("progress" lay in reclaiming a past image and regaining the vigor of an archaic Hinduism).

In such a scenario the gendered positioning of the female subject reveals an already existing fundamental contradiction in modern national temporal imaginings. Anne McClintock (1995: 395) has called this the "temporal anomaly within nationalism," where the "veering between nostalgia for the past and the impatient sloughing off of the past . . . is typically resolved by figuring the contradiction in the representation of time as a natural division of gender." Women stand in for the "atavistic and authentic body of national tradition (inert, backward-looking, and natural) embodying nationalism's conservative principle of continuity," whereas men represent the "progressive agent of national modernity (forward thrusting, potent, and historic) embodying nationalism's progressive or revolutionary principle of discontinuity" (McClintock 1995: 358–59).

In the context of a third world nation such as India trying to "catch up" with the West, the temporal contradiction plays out thus: Indian men represent the progressive elements of the nation as it tries to catch up with the developed world; women represent the anxieties and fears about its cultural consequences—the loss of cultural autonomy, purity, and markers of national identity. The former play their part in the world system while the latter stave off its effects in the private sphere and in private values by becoming the symbol of its organic unity and purity.[4]

In Kalam's autobiography the veering between state violence and affect demonstrates how these realms of human subjectivity rather than being incommensurable actually consolidate each other's power and relationship to each other. The female and the feminine become powerful motors here. The autobiography begins with a poem titled "My Mother," which recounts the memories of a ten-year-old Kalam sleeping on his mother's lap. He remembers her touch as she removes his pain, her tears falling on his knee, and describes the moonlit setting for this perfect mother-son moment of communion. This affective thread runs throughout the autobiography, as Kalam quite unselfconsciously inserts his own poetry whenever confronted with moments that seem to require a more heightened and emotional response. Tears are not held back when Kalam expresses grief about the deaths of parents and family members, and this sensibility is also mirrored in his sorrow at the loss of misfired rockets and surrogate scientist fathers—Vikram Sarabhai, Homi Bhabha, and Brahm Prakash. In extending this affective, aesthetic, and feminine mode of subjectivity, the scientific community is unhinged from its political and statist role and cast into that of a surrogate family. Other examples from the autobiography make the work of this narrative structure clearer.

By any count Abdul Kalam's story is a remarkable one: the meteoric rise of a young Muslim boy, the son of unschooled parents from Rameswaram, an isolated island-town in Tamil Nadu. The autobiography records how Kalam made his way from the simple surroundings of a local village school with meager resources to the Indian Institute of Technology in Madras and later into the inner ranks of scientists, who, in postindependence India, worked closely with the Indian government to produce space launch vehicles, nuclear bombs, and finally missile delivery systems. In 2002, two years after the publication of the book, Kalam was sworn in as the eleventh president of India.

On a first reading the book reveals a noticeable refusal to talk about politics. References to political debates are couched in terms of commonsensical patriotism: the need for national self-reliance in defense technology or the need to assert national sovereignty and strengthen Indian security. But the irony cannot escape the reader who is aware of the resurgence of right-wing politics in India since the 1980s, that, at the very time that Kalam, a Muslim, was awarded the highest civilian award for his services to the nation, the technological capability he engineered, as well as its potential for mass violence, were being appropriated by the Bharatiya Janata Party (BJP) and elements of the Hindu religious right.[5] What does it mean to be a Muslim scientist and participate in a discourse of national protection in India when Muslims are increasingly being stereotyped as "foreign"? Or when the BJP government's constant rhetoric of the fanatical and traitorous Muslim continues to "denationalize" the Muslim as Indian citizen (Prakash 1997: 556)?

As expected, Kalam never discusses these fractures in the national imaginary in an overt way. But there is something that clearly marks the autobiography as a 1990s, post-BJP text, and that is Kalam's constant attempt to represent his religious values as that of an enlightened scientist. Science, for Kalam, invokes the image of a universal and singular religion. In the autobiography he quotes liberally from various religious texts, the Upanishads, the Qur'an, and the Bible alike, and validates these religious references by making them all sources of inspiration for his scientific pursuits. Kalam resolves the expected religion/science schism by weaving the destructive power of modern defense technology with the sublimity of divine creationist power and thus poses an undivided origin for science, nation, and religion. This move also authorizes potential state violence as the recovery of an awesome power that is greater than any narrow interest group, whether nations, political parties, or communal groups. Indeed, it is not impossible that the infamous Oppenheimer moment is part and parcel of a nuclear sublime and that such discrepant power lines connect the nuclear scientist to the religious fundamentalist. Arundhati Roy (1999: 120) puts it best, "Yes, I've heard—the bomb is in the Vedas." She also describes one Indian scientist who, while witnessing the blasts of May 1998, said, "I can now believe stories of Lord Krishna lifting a hill."[6]

Before I chart the arrival of the figure of woman in Kalam's text as a palliative as well as a counterpoint to the question of the nation-state's sanctioned mass violence, I want to trace the subtler ways in which the book attempts to respond to the violence within the nation against the Muslim. The point is this: the autobiography presents three distinct genealogies, each of which places Kalam's narrative in a different order from that of the externalized, denationalized Indian. These genealogies may be read as responding in an indirect way (what I have termed affective) to the violence directed against the minority Muslim community in India. But in an almost similar way, though in a much more coded medium, the "response" to the other level of violence—nuclear violence—is also present in the text. This surfaces when responsibility or ethics-talk is managed in the text by various structures of feeling such as love, kinship, and the feminine.

What are these three genealogies? First, there is the one I have already mentioned—a kind of secular religious tradition forged not as might be expected by Nehruvian or Western principles of secularism but through a Gandhian ethic: Rameswaram as an exemplar of South Indian small-town values, where communities lived in peace without politicizing religion. In a narrative demonstration of this ethos, sections in the book are introduced by quotations from the Qur'an and the Vedas. Kalam's earliest memories of life in Rameswaram are also carefully chosen: his best friend is the son of the high priest of the Rameswaram Hindu temple. The priest himself is cast in the role of an organic intellectual whose principles reflect the town's peaceful community life. Kalam recounts an incident from his schooldays when Lakshmana Shastry, a high priest, publicly berates a caste-conscious schoolmaster for trying to place his son and Kalam on different benches in the schoolroom.

Then there is the description of the deep friendship between the boys' fathers, the high priest and the Muslim boat owner, who would spend evenings on each other's porches discussing theological questions. And finally there is the shared religious everyday: daily trips for young Kalam to the temple and the mosque; bedtime stories told by the Muslim grandmothers about events from the Hindu epics. Through these memories Kalam constructs his childhood in Rameswaram as an idyllic intersubjective one. It is of course quite possible that this intersubjective Muslim is a guarded construction—the only acceptable one perhaps for a prominent, highly placed Muslim in post-BJP India. However, the power of this construction is not diminished when we realize that this sort of nostalgia has its own politics. For one, it contests the constant revisiting of the trauma of the 1947 Partition as the originary moment for Muslim-Hindu identity and violence. Kalam charts an alternative genealogy for the South Indian Muslim, one whose cultural memory is not directly inscribed by the violent history of the partition.

The second genealogy constructs a family of scientists comprising many institutional fathers: teachers and mentors; Muslims, Hindus, and Christians who encouraged Kalam and shepherded him to the top. The third genealogy, one that is especially important because of its contested place in the BJP's rhetoric, is described through a painting in Kalam's story. The painting displayed at the Wallops Flight Facility at Wallops Island, Virginia, drew Kalam's attention when he visited there during a trip to the United States in 1963. He credits it with providing him with inspiration for the nascent Indian missile development program:

> It depicted a battle scene with a few rockets flying in the background. . . . The painting caught my eye because the soldiers on the side launching the rockets were not white but dark-skinned, with the racial features of people found in South Asia. One day my curiosity got the better of me, drawing me towards the painting. It turned out to be Tipu Sultan's army fighting the British. The painting depicted a fact forgotten in Tipu's own country but commemorated here on the other side of the planet. I was happy to see an Indian glorified by NASA as a hero of warfare rocketry. (Kalam 1999: 38)

In his assertion that Tipu Sultan is forgotten in his own country, Kalam makes an obvious dig at Hindu nationalist, revisionist historians who have been trying to rewrite Tipu Sultan's reputation as a resister of British colonialism. Although celebrated in Indian schoolbooks for almost half a century as a military genius who, while ruler of the South Indian kingdom of Mysore from 1782 to 1799, fought fiercely against British incursions on the subcontinent, his reputation has taken a beating from the Hindutva revisionists. By their calculations, when Indian Muslim rulers were not destroyers of Hindu temples or violent proselytizers, they were collaborators enabling foreign invaders such as the British. Kalam's attempt to restore a genealogy of a Muslim national hero (as "Indian") is one part of the counternarrative here. The other inserts Muslim science as a foil for the recent attempts to resuscitate the notion of a Hindu science. By referring to the recognition given by a painter to Tipu Sultan's rocketry, Kalam suggests that India finds its national achievements reflected abroad through the very figure targeted by Hindu nationalists as anti-Indian.

In a reflective moment in the autobiography, Kalam brings these various genealogies into narrative unity but does so through the figure of the woman. Kalam is describing the day in 1990 when the Indian government celebrated the success of its missile program by conferring a national award on him. As

Kalam sits in silent contemplation of the long road to this eventful day, his mind flashes back over his life:

> The sand and shells of Rameswaram, the care of Iyadurai Solomon in Ramanathapuram, the guidance of Rev. Father Sequiera in Trichi and Prof. Pandalai in Madras, the encouragement of Dr. Mediratta in Bangalore, the hovercraft ride with Prof. Menon, the pre-dawn visit to the Tilpat range with Prof. Sarabhai, the healing touch of Dr. Brahm Prakash on the day of the SLV-3 failure, the national jubilation on the SLV-3 launch, Madam Gandhi's appreciative smile[,] . . . Dr. Ramanna's faith in inviting me to DRDO[,] . . . a flood of memories swept over me. Where were all these men now? My father, Prof. Sarabhai, Dr. Brahm Prakash? I wished I could meet them and share my joy with them. I felt the paternal forces of heaven and the maternal cosmic forces of nature embrace me as parents would hug their long-lost child. (1999: 160)

This list mimics through its geographic unity in diversity theme the common format of a national anthem—the piling up of series of places and things that connote continuity. It is ironic that Indira Gandhi is evoked but erased at the same time so that Kalam can insert himself into a male genealogy: "Where were all these men now?" he asks. In such an erasure we see the very power of masculine tropes within images of state power and science. But I want to draw attention to the last line, because that is going to be the point of departure for the final part of this chapter: the gendering of the nuclear sublime. Here we come back to questions of literature, of futurity, and of the repression of violence. But first, a small excursus to get started.

Violence, the feminist critic Teresa De Lauretis (1989) tells us, is often gendered even if never admitted. As she explains it, "When one surveys the representations of violence in general terms, there seem to be two kinds of violence with respect to its object: male and female. I do not mean by this that the 'victims' of such kinds of violence are men and women, but rather that the object on which or to which the violence is done is what establishes the meaning of the represented act; and that object is perceived or apprehended as either feminine or masculine" (249). De Lauretis cites the obvious examples: nature in the expression "rape of nature," for instance. Here nature is feminine and the violence done to it is shown to be a gendered one: done to an object whether animate or inanimate. Similarly, nature appears in scientific discourse as a feminine position while masculinity and phallic power, the surmounting of a problem mastery over a set of conditions, create in turn an adversarial relationship to the object of study (De Lauretis 1989: 249). This spills over into the prowess that comes with the technological power. "We have proved that we are not eunuchs anymore," said Bal Thackeray, leader of the ultra-rightist Shiv Sena party in the days following the tests. Roy, in her eloquent response to Thackeray, says, "(Whoever said we were? True, a good number of us are women, but that, as far as I know, isn't the same thing.) Reading the papers it was often hard to tell when people were referring to Viagra (which was competing for second place on the front pages) and when they were talking about the bomb—'we have superior strength and potency' (this was our Minister for Defence after Pakistan completed its tests)."[7]

Is it possible that one is overreaching here? How did we get from the benign picture of the paternal forces of heaven and the maternal cosmic forces of nature that embrace Kalam as "parents would hug their long-lost child" to Viagra? When Kalam invokes "the paternal forces of heaven," these forces represent a masculine force of creation and destruction, whereas nature represents nurture, mothering, or reproduction (but not creation). Indeed, in this twin parenting scenario, the masculine metaphor reveals its limits, because no continuity of human society, and its endless reproduction into the future, can be imagined only cosmically. At some point it all comes down to the vulgar images of reproduction—bodies of women and children. To provide an example from fiction we can say that the scientist is caught up in the fantasy of autocreation (without either parent) or Frankenstein's monster. In the famous nineteenth-century Gothic tale, the fantasy of the male scientist creating life by himself, without female reproduction, turns into a nightmare that ultimately destroys both creator and creation.

In a similar way the arrival of nurturing nature as woman is to be expected in Kalam's text because the unspoken core of his autobiography, as Ramachandran's review suggests, is the justification of a creation, one that ultimately intends or considers the possibility of mass destruction of others. Kalam, his sensibility neatly divided into the aesthetic and the scientific realms, manages to hold the two together through a feminized vision of nature—as woman. In a brilliant essay on the nuclear sublime written more than twenty years ago, Frances Ferguson (1984: 7) makes the point that the threat of complete annihilation can have at least two effects: it can sharpen our sense of self-preservation or make us, in a reverse gesture, love even more the conditions of our existence. It is easy to see how this recommitment to the world often manifests as an ideological shoring up of the world of society and the gendered space of "domestic life." For this reason, Ferguson goes on to say, community-organized nuclear protests in the seventies and eighties often staged the moral authority of pregnant women as well as infants and children—thus conjuring up the destruction of the generations of the unborn. In this appeal to the world of "generation" and the unborn (shorthand for "consciousness of the future") a problematic contradiction also opens up (Ferguson 1984: 8). The world of generation (embodying the future of the social) offers itself as that which is being erased by the spiritual and technological sublimity of nuclear power. To be antinuclear may cross paths, then, with a natalist or pro-life position in the narrow sense.

Thus while Kalam celebrates the male genealogical power of the Indian male scientists' community at one moment, he also celebrates a sort of womanless, Gandhian asceticism as part of his scientific prowess at another. There is both self-negation and pride when he talks about his series of one-room apartments, the years of meals in cafeterias and canteens, and the solitary, workaholic existence of the man without a family. Yet the autobiography ends on the curious note of reproduction; a reaching out toward a sociality imagined as the continuity of sexual reproduction. In the final chapter titled "Contemplation," introduced by the Qur'anic epigraph "We create and destroy and again recreate in forms of which no one knows," the text reveals its uncanny Frankensteinian desire when, in a concluding gesture, after recounting the most significant events of his life in the final pages of the book, Kalam adds this paragraph: "This story will end with me, for I have no inheritance in the worldly sense. I have acquired nothing, built nothing, possess nothing—no family, sons, daughters" (1999: 177). But confronted by this infertility and the dead end of the masculine legacy—a tradition that establishes the continuity of fathers and sons—Kalam introduces a poem in which the feminine metaphor of the breast is reworked as a well, a nurturing well from which Indian children will draw sustenance. For those brought up on a dose of nationalist symbols galvanized through popular culture media in the subcontinent, "Mother India" will come to mind when reading Kalam's verse:

I am a well in this great land
Looking at its millions of boys and girls
To draw from me
The inexhaustible divinity
And spread his Grace everywhere
As does water drawn from a well. (177)

And then in the final words of the book, the self-consolation for Kalam, faced with the impossibility of male lineage, comes from the endless continuity of divine power: "God's providence is your inheritance. The bloodline of my great-grandfather Avul, my grandfather Pakir, and my father Jainulabdeen may end with Abdul Kalam, but his Grace will never end, for it is Eternal" (178). Though the book's last dominant image is of the nurturer and provider of succor, the world of female reproduction momentarily alluded to in the poem above is at once subsumed by the eternal but undeniable masculine power of the Divine.

While there is no doubt that the personal narrative format of the auto-biography in the end gives us only one version of the world—one person's way of seeing—the autobiography is always a way of writing oneself into the world and thus gives us an important way of seeing how individuals, especially individuals with some proximity to policy making, imagine their relations in the various levels of the social in which they participate and how they make the decisions they do. In that sense a reading against the grain of Kalam's autobiography allows us to answer the question that the reviewer asked.[8] Rephrased at this point, the question would be, What impulses drive state-identified individuals and members of the intelligentsia to make certain claims and perform certain services for institutions such as the state? What operations of subjectivity may be rightly termed symptomatic of certain contradictions of modernity? Here, the overriding anxiety of the third world intellectual who takes pride in being Indian, indigenous, and native, but constantly stages the need to catch up with the advanced industrialized nations, is one indication of such a subjective fracture. We see that modernity fractured further by globalization ensures the survival of "outmoded" ideologies, whether Gandhian forms of self-discipline, Nehruvian secularism, religious chauvinism, or gender nostalgia. None of these ideologemes are incommensurable with the scientific prowess of the modern state or the desire for new defense technologies. Indeed, the place of gendered and religious affects as they further and perpetuate forms of violent sublimity in the modern state will need careful analysis rather than dismissal. And just when we think that the battle between messianic and national time (or secular homogeneous time) has ended in favor of the latter, we are actually witnessing forms of messianic time enshrined in cosmologies of the nuclear sublime, the woman, and religious nationalism—not only in places like India or the third world, but also in the very slips of the tongue of first world leaders who speak of a "crusade" against terror.

NOTES

1. The recent effort to discredit the historian Romila Thapar, whose work has been paradigmatic in studies of early India, is part of this agenda. See "Romila Thapar's Appointment to the Library of Congress Opposed," www.rediff.com/us/2003/apr/25us1.html. For a text of the petition by diasporic Hindu nationalists protesting Thapar's ap- · pointment as Kluge Chair in Countries and Cultures of the South at the Library of Congress, see www.petitiononline.com/108india/petition.html.

2. Given the mutually reinforcing rhetoric of war and masculinity, feminized language in a male defense intellectual's text signals a change. This reading is related to feminist critiques of nationalism: when "woman" becomes metaphor for "nation," the ideas of mothering and of a common origin and "birth" promote a new idea of community. When mutually assured destruction or the end of society is imagined, violence is often gendered through a paradoxical use of birthing metaphors—birth is attached to male creation of destructive force. In India such language is already visible both in nationalist ideologies and in women's responses to state violence.

3. For a detailed discussion of this history, see Abraham 1999.

4. See my discussion of this phenomenon in Joseph 2002.

5. See Chatterjee 1993: 8–9 for a genealogy of this contradiction.

6. The BJP won successive elections in the center and the states from the 1990s onward by propagating the antisecularist principle of an India where Hindu culture (Hindutva) would become the official state ideology. The naming of missiles is usually a ritual to invoke cosmic, mythological, or national signifiers, but it takes on more insidious overtones as the gradual entry of religious symbolism into the following list proves: *agni* (fire), *prithvi* (earth), *akash* (sky), *trishul* (trident), *nag* (snake, cobra). The last two signal the shift from cosmic to Hindu religious symbols—both the *trishul* and the *nag* are associated with Shiva, the god of destruction. The politics of the *trishul* has come to the forefront recently as right-wing associations such as the Bajrang Dal and the Vishwa Hindu Parishad have begun distributing tridents all over India in an attempt to mobilize people and consolidate the Hindutva political base in untapped areas. See Shrimali 2003.

7. Thackeray, quoted in Roy 1999: 93.

8. We cannot use conventional political labels for Kalam (i.e., nationalist or patriarchal) because his self-representations are also Gandhian, secular, religious, poetic, humanitarian, cosmopolitan, pacifist, and feminine. The autobiography exposes elements that are excluded from scientific discourse but serve to constitute it—the female, the subjective, the emotional and religious. These "non-rational" elements ground and permeate the nuclear past and present. And just as bomb projects are rife with images of male birth, autobiography ensures a kind of immortality. Freedom to narrate the story of the bomb is only possible for those like Kalam with established scientific reputations and bureaucratic positions of authority, for whom autobiography serves as a tool to consolidate the hierarchy in nuclear research. However, by introducing a plurality of voices, autobiography also undermines claims to rationality. These unguarded voices interrupt scientific language and its power to define the world. Such "misreadings" of his work can help delegitimate powerful state languages that seek transparency.

4

Overcoming the Silent Archive in Bangladesh

Women Bearing Witness to Violence in the 1971 "Liberation" War

YASMIN SAIKIA

This chapter is part of a larger project that I have undertaken to reconstruct through oral history, fieldwork, and archival research the history of survivors—men and women in Bangladesh, Pakistan, and India who participated in, experienced, and suffered but lived to tell about the violence in the war of 1971. I intend to write a "public biography" (Bar-On 2002) of survivors in order to rethink issues of religious communalism, nationalism, and violence in postcolonial South Asia as well as engage the ambiguity of history evident in event and narrative. By "public biography" I mean a text that incorporates the investigation of violence at a theoretical level as well as through autobiographical testimonials of survivors. By "survivors" I mean both victims and perpetrators, because in a strange, problematic way they were bound together; and it is by framing them together in the context of violence that we can begin to understand what happened in the war of 1971 fought by Pakistan, India, and the Mukti Bahini (Bengali militia founded and supported by the Indian government) that led to the creation of Bangladesh.

Here I focus on a small segment of my larger project—the historiographical silence concerning gendered violence in the war and the mechanisms used by both state and society in Bangladesh to keep the experiences of the victims secret. Specifically, I am interested in the

Figure 1. Bewildered woman and child. Liberation War Museum, Dhaka.

politics of active national forgetting of the violence committed against women. I ask the following questions: Should we not interrogate the patriarchal society that has colluded with the government to marginalize women's voices? Can we move beyond the official silence and create a new space of understanding the meaning of violence and the human cost of war? I conclude by looking at the pain of women to highlight it as a possible site for generating a new regional history of postcolonial South Asia.

Background of the War

In 1947, at the end of British colonial rule, the Indian subcontinent was partitioned and two nation-states, India and Pakistan, were created. Whereas India claimed to be a secular republic, Pakistan declared itself a "Muslim homeland." Multiple ethnic and linguistic communities—Punjabi, Bengali, and Bihari (who migrated from India), along with Sindhi, Pathan and Baluchi—made up the new state of Pakistan, which was divided into two wings, east and west. In West Pakistan, Punjabis dominated; in the East, Bengalis constituted 90 percent of the population. Bihari immigrants claimed a special place in the nation-state for being actively involved in the making of Pakistan.

The Bengalis launched a separatist movement in the 1950s that culminated in 1970 in a freedom struggle. The major grievances that motivated this movement were the inequitable distribution of resources, economic exploitation, restrictions on Bengali speech in the public sphere, and lack of political representation in Pakistan's national parliament. The military dictators who ruled Pakistan from 1958 to 1971, however, were unwilling to accommodate the demands. After the first general election was held and Sheikh Mujibur Rahman, a Bengali, won the position of prime minister, the military junta reacted by deploying the national army against the Bengalis. From March 25 until December 16, 1971, a reign of terror and violence took over East Pakistan.

During the period of nine months, two wars, civil and international, were fought in the east. In the civil war, West Pakistani troops along with local "Bihari" supporters terrorized, raped, looted, and killed nationalist Bengalis, who were deemed "Hindu turncoats," thereby justifying Muslim (Pakistani) violence against them (Mascarenes 1971; Sisson and Rose 1990). In turn, the Bengalis formed a guerrilla army, the Mukti Bahini, which wreaked havoc in Bihari communities. State violence combined with ethnic struggle led to the victimization of women and children, who became the main casualty of "male warriors."

The international war between India and Pakistan, with the support of the Soviet Union and the United States, was part of a long-drawn-out series of cold war battles in the Indian Ocean region. Further, fueled by the memories of hate lingering from the Partition of 1947, India found the opportunity in the Bengali demand for freedom to fight against its enemy, Pakistan, and break it up.[1] At the end of the war Pakistan was dismembered, and in the east the new nation-state of Bangladesh was created. The war of 1971 was the first successful overthrow of a military dictatorship by common people in twentieth-century Asia, but alongside this heraldic feat was a terribly dark human story of loss and destruction. Ten million people became refugees, two hundred thousand women were raped, and several hundred thousand Biharis became "stateless" in Bangladesh and Pakistan.

The existing historical literature on 1971, written primarily by former army men, journalists, and civil administrators, projects formulaic representations emphasizing battle plans, conflicts, strategies and tactics of armed combat, and failure of diplomacy, within which only the activities of national actors and international players are highlighted. In other words, the existing histories of 1971 are framed within the established and standard genre of war literature and national histories of male heroes but are terribly incomplete and parochial. The lived histories of victims, the women of East Pakistan who experienced the direct impact of the war on their bodies, is carefully suppressed and cautiously silenced. As such, although the rape of women in 1971 is considered one of the most intense cases of brutalization of women in twentieth-century wars, there is no history of this. Scholars of postcolonial South Asia as well as gender studies internationally have overlooked and forgotten 1971; the rare exception is Susan Brownmiller's pioneering book *Against Our Will: Men, Women, and Rape* (1975). Was gender violence a random outcome of the breakdown of civil society, or was it part of a carefully planned strategy to terrorize and force enemy communities into submission? What happened to gender relations when neighbors turned into enemies? Did violence against women reinforce maleness and masculinity? Is there a memory of 1971 in South Asia that can be retrieved?

Theoretical Framework

Understandably, interrogation will reveal disturbing remains of history that the nations of Pakistan, India, and Bangladesh prefer to forget. But we cannot continue a limited narrative and present it as the "true" history of 1971. The traumatic experiences of people in the subcontinent should not be reduced to fit into categories that serve as tools for nation-state politics.

The unthinkable violence can be made somewhat thinkable and speakable if we approach 1971 as a manifestation of the violent ethos of the state, which sanctions killing and excluding "bare life" to establish its power of sovereignty (Agamben 1998). Drawing on this premise that the states in postcolonial South Asia are machines of terror and killing, I offer the testimonies of victims to bear witness to state violence, and by speaking about them, I transform the unspeakable in order to historicize the suppressed memory of a horrific war.

The question that one may ask is, what good will it do? The sheer brutality of the kind and intensity of violence that women endured in 1971 may seem to defy analysis, and the effort to find a language to communicate the traumatic memories is daunting. Recounting violence is not enough; the pain of survivors can never be fully communicated (Das 2001). Nonetheless, a space must be created for a new vocabulary to emerge, for it is only in language that communication becomes possible and the search for the meaning of violence and what it breached can continue (Arendt [1953] 1994). The distance between victim and listener hence cannot become an obstacle, nor can we continue to treat violence "like someone else's history—or even, not history at all" (Pandey 2001: 6).

Reflecting on Veena Das's (1995) seminal research on critical events in South Asia that challenged the limits of narrativizing violence, I argue that the experience of violence is shareable and the act of telling makes history both immediate and communicable. Using the feminist approach of first-person narratives as the beginning location to tell history, I intend to overcome the silent archive of national history that has privatized and abandoned the investigation of women's experiences and give "retrospective significance" to women's memories (Trouillot 1995). I am instructed by feminist scholars and activists such as Gerda Lerner (2002), Susan Brison (2002), Urvashi Butalia (2002), Kamla Bhasin and Ritu Menon (1998), and Virginia Held (1993) to refuse to accept that there is a gap between the personal and the political, the self and the other, the individual and the community. Like them, I acknowledge the possibility of understanding what it is like to be a survivor and claim "imaginative access" to history (Brison 2002). The goal of this epistemological quest is to emplace the experiences of violence and trauma as a historical subject so as to deepen our understanding of political and cultural issues in South Asia and insert into the narratives of the state people's memories and lived experiences that have been suppressed and forgotten.

Listening to women's narratives, I would argue, is crucial. Listening, like telling, as Cynthia Enloe (1990) reminds us, is a political act. In her eloquent narrative of rape and recovery, Brison (2002) convincingly argues that sympathetic listening reexternalized the event for her and allowed recovery. These feminist theorists emphasize that self and community are in a symbiotic relationship and that the act of telling and listening reconstitutes relational understanding in which language becomes the location to create identity and fight silence in both the political and cultural arenas. Assuming this premise of women's agency, I ask, can women in Bangladesh begin to claim a space within the nation and practice resistance against the silencing of women's traumatic memories to create a site for feminist nationalism and shape the narratives of 1971 in Bangladesh in the future (West 1997)?

By "feminist nationalism," I mean reconstituting the national in terms of the constituent factor, that is, people, men and women, citizens and subjects, so as to emphasize characteristics such as family, community, health, welfare, pain, and emotions that are considered feminine traits (Scott 1988; West 1997). The goal of this feminism is to create societies that do not automatically divide men and women into a fixed hierarchy of superior and inferior, "us" and "them," but open a variety of spaces to encounter nation and nation building beyond and outside gendered experiences of inequality, aggressiveness, leadership, patriarchy, kinship, and so on. I had found in the course of my research in South Asia that survivors of 1971, although various, have a common feature: they suffer from a deep sense of shame and anguish, considered feminine traits. Neither the victims nor the perpetrators can "understand" the purpose of the violence in the war. The perpetrators, however, understand that the nation called on them to take up arms as soldiers, gave them a purpose to kill the "enemy," and in the process transformed them into tools to fulfill the ambition of nationalism and state power. Although they are celebrated as heroes by their nations, the men, like their victims, the women, live their lives in silence, repulsed, puzzled, and tormented by the past. The shame and the anguish of survivors, I suggest, are powerful tools to reveal the violent masculinity of state ambition that created policies and actions in 1971 and produced traumatic outcomes for people in the subcontinent today.

I am aware that men and women—Pakistani, Bangladeshi, Indian, and Bihari—experienced 1971 differently. Heterogeneous pasts and pain cannot be submerged into a homogenized discourse of victimhood. I do not want to gloss over these different encounters and the memories they produced. Multiple narratives of 1971 are possible. But they have not yet been produced. I am making a pioneering effort and thus do not have pathways to follow. I am breaking new ground when I ask, can we begin with a human (feminist) understanding for telling 1971? Can we recover and piece together the fragmented women's bodies—Bengali, Bihari, tribal, Hindu, and Muslim—and make them a human subject for reintegration and understanding through remembrance and speech?

The Intimate War

The backdrop of the 1971 war, as I stated earlier, was both political and cultural. On March 25, 1971, Operation Searchlight was launched by the West Pakistan Army to establish military control of the capital city of Dhaka and force the nationalist Bengalis to give up their struggle for independence. As a result of the military campaign, a vast majority of the civilian population fled from the city to outlying villages and provincial towns. The news of the crackdown on Dhaka was received with anger and violence in the towns and villages, and local Bengalis went on a rampage against the non-Bengalis living in their midst (there are various reports that violence started even earlier). The Bengali population terrorized and killed non-Bengali and Urdu speakers—Biharis—who were symbolized as supporters of their enemy, the West Pakistani administration. To quell the spiraling ethnic violence the army was deployed to the provinces, but the presence of the West Pakistani military made matters worse. The opportunities for looting, killing, raping, and torturing increased, as did the number of perpetrators. The Bengalis, Biharis, and West Pakistanis became embroiled in fighting against each other and targeted the most vulnerable among them, the women, in order to claim a position within the hierarchy of masculine power.

The army, which stood in for the state, was most visible in terrorizing women in East Pakistan. Pakistani men, representatives of the army, established sex camps where they held women captive to serve the soldiers and officers. These women were abducted and kidnapped from their homes or arrested during ambush, and some were handed over by their neighbors to "teach women a lesson" about male power.[2] Sexual violence against women was not confined to the Pakistani army. The soldiers and supporters of the Mukti Bahini also raped, tortured, and brutalized Bengali and Bihari women.[3] Being a clandestine, underground organization, however, the Mukti Bahini could not set up camps and keep women in captivity. Most of their actions were carried out surreptitiously for fear of exposure and apprehension by the Pakistani forces. The third group of perpetrators, the Bihari men, indulged in sexual violence in a devious, underhanded manner. They kidnapped and raped individual Bengali and tribal women, mostly neighbors, and often killed them afterward to hide their violence.[4] Sometimes they handed their victims to Pakistani soldiers who took them to their camps and kept them confined for sex work.

Rape was not all men did to terrorize women. Often they tortured them for secret information, beat, and otherwise abused them to make them willing, bit and marked their bodies, sheared their hair, and even dismembered them after killing. "I have seen with my own eyes men throwing away bags containing parts of women's bodies into the river," a Bengali woman told me (Mirpur, June 26, 1999). A seventy-six-year-old Bihari eyewitness and survivor of 1971, who today lives in a camp in northern Bangladesh (one of sixty-three camps) told me, "Don't ask me who killed whom, who raped whom, what was the religion, ethnic, or linguistic background of the people who died in the war. The victims in the war were the women of this country—mothers who lost children, sisters who lost their brothers, wives who lost their husbands, women who lost everything—their honor and dignity. In the war men victimized women. It was a year of anarchy and the end of humanity. Is this something to talk about?" (Rangpur, February 20, 2001).

A profound understanding of the rampant violence in 1971 that included within its grip all kinds of women is generally expressed by most victims. In addition, most survivors engaged in active disassociation, trying to make the degraded body invisible by not talking about what they suffered. After three decades of silence women have almost forgotten how to relate their experiences. The lives of these women are fractured, and the moment of shattering is marked as "life before the war" and "life after the war." The hidden archive of women's memories is a challenging excavation. Occasionally, when women did speak, they could not create a narrative for there is no seamless way to tell their experiences in war and the impact on their lives. The only way they could begin to tell about the violence is to describe their condition as "like being dead" since the war.

The deadness of female victims is actively supported by the state to make the past incomprehensible and to obliterate women's voices. National history in Bangladesh today, like most nations' histories, is an instrument of the state, not a site for memories and experiences. Added to this, the patriarchal Islamic society of Bangladesh has supported the state's program to keep women silent. Society has deemed women's experiences private matters to be dealt with by the family and has done all it can to remove the embarrassing traces of women's experiences from public and social memory.

Soon after the liberation of Bangladesh, women's bodies were, once again, made into a site for Bengali men to write and exercise their language of power by establishing a gender hierarchy of experiences during the war. In public space men's experiences were eulogized; the print media gave front-page coverage to the sacrifices men made during the war. Women's experiences were hardly mentioned, except for occasional news reports on the rehabilitation programs organized by the government. The media and the state sought to "domesticate" the "fallen" women, often manifested in reports on women's programs in sewing and weaving, midwifery, caregiving, and so on. In turn, the silencing of women's bodily experiences in the war into a matter of private concern immediately made atrocities committed against women an unthinkable subject in the public arena of postindependence Bangladesh. To a large extent it has been made unspeakable among the victims themselves because no support groups, counseling services, or rape crisis centers were established after the war.

Added to the social and collective silence, the postliberation Bangladeshi government created and added a new problem. The chilling mandate of the government headed by Mujibur Rahman, the hero of 1971 who became the first prime minister after liberation, was to implement abortion for all pregnant women. The idea was to rid the nation of the "bastard Pakistani." The government's mandate reduced women to objects, took away their agency, and labeled them as things on which both men and government could inscribe their language of violence all over again. The intrusion into women's private space became so normalized that, like cattle, women were strapped to makeshift boards and operated on in emergency mobile clinics, even during late-term pregnancy.[5] So many abortions were performed that the nation became hardened to the plight of women and unmoved by the condition of the victims. The survivors did not have the control to tell who had raped them. Many women I spoke to in Bangladesh assured me that if they were called on to identify their rapists they could do so. These women were raped in sex camps or in their neighborhoods. Rape was not happenstance but a carefully plotted strategy executed by all groups of perpetrators who were known to the women.

Women's enemies were all around and within. The postliberation Bangladesh government, however, refused to admit women's testimonies for fear of exposing that Bengali men, alongside the Pakistani soldiers, had been the perpetrators. One can argue that the national story is an epistemological effort to find a way of thinking about the violence and what it breached for admission of violence, as part of the national self, would be self-condemnation. Hence blame is shifted to the other, represented as "evil" outsiders who transgressed the sacred unity of the national body. Three decades later, however, the lies of national histories have become embedded and people easily believe the official history of 1971 without question and without demanding evidence. In turn, the national policy of silence and the retraining of people to believe the official narrative have forced women to erase the details of their victimizers; it is a survival strategy. The long silence and the active national forgetting have blurred the memories of women's experiences in the war. The distance between experience and testimony today is clear.

Immediately after the "liberation" of Bangladesh the view that it was only Pakistanis who inflicted violence on Bengali women was officially enshrined in the term *birangana*, meaning "female hero," and it became the category within which survivors were classified. That description, with no explanation of the history of the event, allowed society to immediately rethink and reframe the violence in ways that suited the newfound pride in Bengali masculinity, and the term *birangana* was folded into another level of men's speech. *Birangana* was transformed into *barangana*, meaning "promiscuous women" or "prostitutes." Women's corporeal experiences thus came to be viewed as a site of national shame that allowed for interpreting rape during the war as sex, not violence. As a result, although people were willing to hear the stories of heroes so as to laud them for their glorious feats of victory in war and commiserate with them for their suffering and losses on behalf of the nation, they did not wish to hear about the suffering of rape survivors. Reduced to the level of prostitutes, women were made guilty of the crime of rape. The denial of voice was thus justified. National history became an extension of men's history. Military and civilian men who participated in the war were rewarded with high-sounding titles, their actions were memorialized in public ceremonies, and their deeds were enshrined in public, collective memory. The memory of the "liberation war" became the story of the *mukti-judha,* the male hero, who symbolically and literally vindicated the colonial effeminization of the Bengalis in order to create a discourse of remasculinization of Bengali men and the nation-state.[6]

Shaming women into silence was not enough in postliberation Bangladesh. The strategic claim by the state that the enemy Pakistani had raped two hundred thousand Bengali women transformed real women into an abstract number of bodies. The claim became a handy tool for expressing anger and taking a moral position by condemning the enemy's barbarity. Bengali men and society also made up new rules to condition women's speech. By and large, women, deemed men's property, were denied the right to speak.

Within the strictly limited scope of memory building that is slowly emerging after three decades of silence, there are many terms and conditions whose

trauma can be recalled, remembered, and heard in Bangladesh. Pain is culturally and ethnically divided, and only Bengali women's experiences are given
limited voice. Even today minority women, such as the Bihari women, are
not included in women's efforts to memorialize their experiences in 1971.
Viewed as subhuman (other), the Bihari women are deemed objects that are
undeserving of a human language of understanding, according to Bengali
society.[7]

Women's trauma has survived and grown in the lives of the children born
out of the violence of rape. During my stay in Bangladesh in 2001, I met
two so-called war babies, now adult women. Beauty is one of them. Having
grown up in an orphanage, Beauty did not know her birth mother until the
age of thirteen. The meeting between mother and daughter proved disas-
trous. Her mother was divorced by her husband when he learned of Beauty's
existence, although he had received state benefits for marrying a *birangana*.
Beauty's husband, too, divorced her when he found out that her mother was
a *birangana;* he obtained court orders forbidding Beauty to meet her two
children and tried to sell her into prostitution. Beauty's mission now is to
find the truth about her mother's pregnancy in 1971, which, she believes, will
help her to reconstruct a self in order to make sense of herself as a human
being and find meaning in her life. To this end she has identified and spoken
to many survivors of the sex camp in which her mother was held captive
in 1971.

From the disjointed narratives she has pieced together, Beauty knows that
her mother was a beautiful woman who was held in sexual slavery for many
months, but she does not know, nor can her mother tell her, who impreg-
nated her. The confusion of birth, rejection, and despair has made Beauty into
what she herself calls a "cadaver." She told me, "I look like a human being because I have a human body, but my life is not human." The annihilation of self
in victims and war children by family, community, and nation violates them in
the deepest sense and makes them into "nomadic subjects" without the choice
to claim the disjunctures that make their lives (Braidotti 1994). The nomadic
self of women, survivors of 1971 like Beauty and her mother, is not a politically conscious self but a person reduced to living like a shadow because both
community and culture refuse her admission and accommodation in their
ranks.

How does one retrieve and recover the nomadic subject without agency?
Feminist theorists have privileged first-person narratives for telling history

to recover the traumatized self. This is a way to control, subvert, and develop a new discourse, which Jonathan Dollimore (1991) identifies as the stages in the process of resistance. For its success, this process requires an ongoing conversation with people and events beyond the personal and investigation of different voices from the past (Waller and Rycenga 2000). The words of female survivors of 1971 have not come to us through the national will to remember them in sites where history is created. There are no archives, no written documents to corroborate and contextualize self-constructed narratives. Silence enters at the source of making history in postliberation Bangladesh and makes us aware of how power works even before a narrative is made. Silence is not simply cultural and political in this case; it is epistemic. Documents of survivors, case histories of *biranganas,* photographs, police reports, medical records, family documents, letters—all have been destroyed, erased, lost, and removed.

The Ministry of Women's Affairs at Dhaka told me its records had been lost in the process of three moves to different buildings. In Dinajpur, a border town in northern Bangladesh that is infamous for intense ethnic and communal violence during the war, officials declined to dig out the files because they "were too dusty and messy." Often in the regional offices I was told that the documents had been sent to Dhaka. In Dhaka I was told I was misinformed. When I tried to meet the chairperson of the Women's Rehabilitation Commission, Justice Sobhan, who spearheaded the commission in 1972, I could not get a date for an interview. However, important sources close to him and the rehabilitation process confided that the documents and case histories of women, victims of 1971, were destroyed to maintain their confidentiality. The ludicrous rhetoric of protecting women's honor by making them invisible in the government's reports and documents exposed a deep social and cultural misogyny, evidence that the male-controlled state could not interact with the survivors of rape as human selves but had to hide, disperse, and dismember their memory and speech to regain manly honor. The national archive at Dhaka does not have a single record on women's experiences during the war, nor does the national museum want to make available any documents on women's experiences.[8] Mishandling, willful neglect, and loss and theft of files are ways to discourage research on the subject—as I found out when I tried to access the museum archive. In the audio archive at the national radio station, likewise, there is no information on the corporeal experiences of women.

In the rare cases when documents are available they are suppressed, neglected, and glossed over. In a regional office in the town of Sylhet, in northeastern Bangladesh, I found a moth-eaten list containing the names of more than five hundred Hindu and Muslim women, ranging between the ages of twelve and fifty-seven, all of whom were victims of men's violence in the war. Some were single, some married, and some widowed in 1971. When I asked why they had not taken good care of such an important historical document, the director apologetically told me that "probably no one thought it would be useful." Even more telling was another document I found by chance. It was a First Investigation Report (FIR) on rape filed by twelve survivors from Mymensingh, in central Bangladesh. Today this priceless document is hidden from public view in the storeroom of a private library. Taken as a whole, silence is a state policy, and the relational nature between masculinity and Bengali identity obscures and makes women's silence an instrument of the state; survivors are reduced to objects without agency, and, worse still, made into an instrument of others' agency.

The way other people's agency is exercised on the survivors of 1971 became explicit during a mock trial organized in 1996 in Dhaka. A group of privileged urban female political activists encouraged four survivors, very poor women, to give testimony about their experiences in the war. The survivors were assured state protection and assistance as a reward for testifying. Immediately after they went public, the village community shunned the four women, branded them prostitutes, and denied them access to the commons. Threatened by further backlash, their children disowned them. In the end, the women were duped to participate in the trial, but they did not get what they were promised—houses, jobs, and social dignity. The fiasco of the public encounter with the traumatic past discouraged other women from disclosing their memories of violence. So far, only one woman, Firdousi Priyabhasani, has publicly acknowledged her corporeal experiences. Though denied a voice and compelled by circumstances and society to silently bear their trauma, the women cannot forget what they endured. Their bodies that were attacked, assaulted, and marked by male aggressive power and sexual violence have become sites for remembering personal and traumatic memories (Reilly 1996). The cuts, gashes, scratches, and toothmarks, though faded, are reminders of the physical violence; but they are more than that. The violence that women endured has created fear and uneasiness with the physical body and destabilized them. The "body memory" (Brison 2002) that is inscribed in their minds as well as on their physical being continues to remind the victims of the past and disrupts any sense of a possible wholeness, for "to know oneself as not only rapable, but as raped, is to become a different self" (Cahill 2001: 133).

Women Speak

Let me recount a few stories to create an outline of women's experiences and memories as they were revealed to me. None of these women had previously spoken about their experiences in 1971. The three decades of silence made the initial recollection of the violent memory extremely difficult and heartwrenching for both the speaker and me, the listener. I try to convey the stories as the women told them to me. They are graphic recollections centering on the body. For almost all survivors, the body is the location of the violence and the site of the silenced memory.

Halima Parveen of Jessore (in central Bangladesh) was fifteen years old, a student in the eighth grade, in 1971.[9] She is a member of the majority Bengali Muslim community. During the war, she received guerrilla warfare training and participated in two ambushes. In the second ambush she was apprehended and arrested by Bengali men from her adjoining village. They took her to the local police station where they brutally and repeatedly raped her, before handing her over, the next morning, to Pakistani soldiers. Held in captivity for five months thereafter, Halima was regularly raped, brutalized, and humiliated. At the end of the war, when she emerged from sexual slavery, Halima found her body branded and marked with violent sexual acts by her rapists, Bengali and Pakistani men. Today when she thinks and talks about herself she no longer refers to herself as a whole person but as body parts that highlight some extreme violence done to them and still bear the wounds of that memory. After the independence of Bangladesh, neither Halima nor her two friends, Rukiya and Fatima, who were also used as sex slaves during the war, were acknowledged for "fighting with their bodies," a term they used for remembering their struggle in 1971. Rather, they were stigmatized, driven out of their villages, and deleted from the collective memory of friends, neighbors, and community. Halima admitted that the betrayal of community is something she cannot come to terms with. It is not the Pakistani soldiers whom she sees as her enemy but her neighbors, the men who inflicted such intense bodily and emotional pain and who dehumanized her into a sexual object. "How can my body forget?" she asked. Every day she has to deal with the men who raped her; every day she is reminded of the fear and pain of the merciless violence they inflicted on her virginal body.

In Khulna, in southeastern Bangladesh, a Bihari woman, Nurjahan, narrated a horrific story of the dismemberment of her daughter's body. Her married daughter, Fatima, was pregnant during the war. Since they could not escape, Nurjahan and her family moved in with other Bihari families hoping they would be safe together. On March 28, 1972, several months after the war had officially ended, a group of Bengali men stormed into their compound. After killing Nurjahan's son-in-law, they dragged her daughter, Fatima, out of her room and into the courtyard, where they disrobed her and then slit her throat like "a chicken, to bleed her to death." As Fatima lay dying, her attackers ripped open her stomach, pulled out the fetus, and tore it into two.

Mansura Khatun (a pseudonym), a poor Bengali woman from Rangpur in northern Bangladesh, did not join the guerrillas to fight against the Pakistanis; her husband did. For this, the village decided to punish her. They invited a group of Pakistani soldiers to take her to a camp and teach her a lesson. Mansura was a mother of seven children and seven months pregnant at that time. For twelve days in the camp she was repeatedly raped. Even today, thirty-four years later, she struggles for words to articulate what she endured during her captivity. Pain is the only retrievable memory. As she said, "I was in so much pain, my body gave up after some time. They did whatever they wanted. I do not remember what it was like, who those people were, what they did to me, and how many times." When I asked her if there were other women in the camp who were also tortured, she said, "I did not see other women, but every now and then, when I was conscious, I would hear blood-chilling cries, like a dying puppy's yelp, but I did not see the women." Although Mansura forces her mind to forget the horrible days and she blots out the faces of other women so that recognition of self and others is totally obliterated and she cannot stop thinking about the violence they suffered, her body does not let her. During the twelve days she was held in captivity, her perpetrators raped her so many times that her vagina was torn. She did not receive medical treatment, and to this day, she said, she "continues to suffer intense bodily pain." Her pain is not merely physical; it is also ontological and spiritual. When she returned to her home, the village ostracized her as a "fallen woman" and forced her out. Since then, Mansura and her husband have been landless, laborers on other people's land. Neither her village nor the government of Bangladesh has acknowledged her sacrifices in 1971. In fact, no one had ever approached Mansura and her husband to listen to their

Figure 2. Salinda Parveen, journalist, abducted and killed in 1971. Liberation War Museum, Dhaka.

experiences in the war. This, they said, hurts them (although they are very proud to have contributed to the freedom struggle), for no one sees them—poor, ordinary people—as actors in history.

The point of these stories of extreme violence is not to shock or sensationalize. I am, however, compelled to voice women's words and bear witness. The violence committed against women were not accidents of a private history but carefully planned by state and community to victimize, terrorize, and dehumanize them into fear and submission. How can we continue to narrativize war as an act of glory for the cause of nation and make men heroes while simultaneously neglecting the pain and undying trauma that war unleashes on vulnerable groups of women? How can women be asked to uphold the cause of nation and nationalism when their basic right to dignity is under siege in times of war? How can women be asked to claim a nation as theirs when they do not have the right to speak as citizens? Can women in Bangladesh, despite state silence and the social and cultural denial of their experiences, transcend and make the unspeakable speak in Bangladesh today?

Conclusion

To answer some of these questions, I conclude by drawing on Renan's lecture of 1882 in which he made an evocative appeal to rethink a new location for making community and nation. In his public lecture Renan pondered the question, what makes a nation? "National unity is realized by brute force," he answered ([1882] 1999: 145). History, he reminded his audience, however, is charged with the responsibility to bear witness and reveal the episodes of violence that accompany the making of a nation. The motivations for the use of "brute force" may often remain unclear, and a different and more acceptable version of commonality based on language, geography, culture, race, and so on, could be developed and circulated to create cohesion. In such deliberations there is a strategic formulation "to forget and to get one's history wrong . . . for making a nation; and thus the advance of historical studies is often a danger to nationality" (145). In other words, Renan makes us aware that silencing, erasing, and forgetting a violent past and in its place creating a seamless story of contiguous region, language, religion is an intentional political strategy of the state. To overcome the lies of national history, another site, a more potent and powerful one, can be cultivated for telling a story of the national community (in this case, the regional history of the subcontinent) without silencing the violent past. This, according to Renan, is the site of suffering: "To have suffered together is of greater value than identity of custom houses and frontiers . . . for indeed common suffering unites more strongly than rejoicing. Among national memories, sorrows have greater value than victories, for they impose duties and demand common effort" (153). Renan's argument for the value of suffering elevates the community of survivors to claim a moral position and give agency to self and others to tell their experiences. Suffering and speech are thus connected, and both telling and listening are crucial to reconvene community that is glued together by shared memories, painful though they may be.

The year 1971 was a shared trauma on the subcontinent. Women, in particular, suffered the ravages of the war. Women's suffering, however, is not confined to individuals but is felt in communities as a whole in Pakistan, Bangladesh, and India. No doubt, the violence that preceded the suffering was intended to dehumanize the other, but having suffered in the war, the people of the subcontinent as a whole have been humanized and made aware of the power of tyranny and oppression. In this context sufferers are now charged with an explosive energy as well as an emotional need to claim their selves

Figure 3. Protest poster showing a family brutalized and killed in 1971.
Liberation War Museum, Dhaka.

beyond the act of violence and the trauma it produced. I agree with Renan
that telling their sufferings can "serve the common task of humanity" and
open up a space for creating a new history that is far more powerful than the
national stories in circulation now (155). The recognition of the suffering,
"ours" and "theirs," of women in Bangladesh can generate a new sense of an
unpartitioned community and undo the stultifying silence that has denied
a history of the violence in the war of 1971.

Many in South Asia may find the bitter effect of suffering in 1971 a ground
for revenge rather than a site for developing a language of understanding to
make a community of survivors and claim the history they have produced.
Nonetheless, I am persuaded to ask: Can we make the ethos of common suffering in 1971 a language of empathy to bond survivors in Bangladesh, Pakistan,
and India? Can this then become a site for women's speech and enable them to
claim a human dignity that has been denied to them? Through the exploration
of personal and collective memories of pain, the linked, though conflicting, experiences of suffering of the survivors of 1971 would become evident and
expose the multiple meanings that the war suggests to a variety of people to
enable them to come to terms with what happened and thus move beyond.

NOTES

1. Personal conversation with Ashok Mitra, who served as economic adviser to then–Prime Minister Indira Gandhi (Calcutta, 2005). General Lakshman Singh Lehl and General Jacobs reconfirmed this (Delhi, 2005).

2. To teach them a lesson, their Bengali neighbors raped them. I met several women during my stay in Bangladesh who confided that they were raped by neighbors who had tried to court them in the past. War provided an opportunity to vindicate the rejection.

3. Based on private conversation with a Bengali journalist whose identity must be protected because he is a political refugee in the United States.

4. Stories of the violence committed by Bihari men were revealed to me by many Bengali women in Bangladesh who witnessed the violence firsthand. While one may dismiss Bengali women's accounts as biased, it is not possible to discount them when similar evidence is provided by Bihari men themselves. Similar stories of violence were told to me by Bihari men during my stay in Pakistan in 2004.

5. Personal interviews with Drs. A. Dutta, Rangpur, February 2001; and N. Begum, Chittagong, November 2001.

6. Through embodiment people are sexed and men who cannot fight are shunned as weak and effeminate. This was definitely the outlook of the British colonial administrators toward Bengali men, who were used as clerks and pen-pushers but were not deemed capable to perform the manly duties required of soldiers. The shame of effeminization felt by Bengali men was overcome in 1971 when they went to war and committed extreme acts of violence against women, who were deemed a hindrance to carrying out the modern masculine national agenda. It seems that Bengali men, by raping, torturing, and killing women, entered the world of universal "manliness."

7. Dina Siddiqui explained this to me and corrected my use of Bihari women as "other" in a presentation titled "Bengali, Bihari and the War of Liberation of 1971: Speaking Silence and Displacement" at the Asian Studies Conference, New York, March 28, 2003.

8. I know from reliable sources that there are a few documents about women's experiences in the museum. Professor Enayat Rahim, who served as the Bangabandhu chair at Dhaka University in 2000–2001, shared with me some of the information available in these papers.

9. This is her real name. Often when I suggested to women that I would protect their identities and not disclose the source of my information, they requested that I tell their stories with their names so that they could claim their experience and memories, which have been denied to them for such a long time. There were many instances, too, when women asked that I use pseudonyms. Unless indicated otherwise, the actual names of the survivors are provided in the text.

Part II

Resisting Terror

Women, Agency, and the Micropolitics of Sri Lankan Life

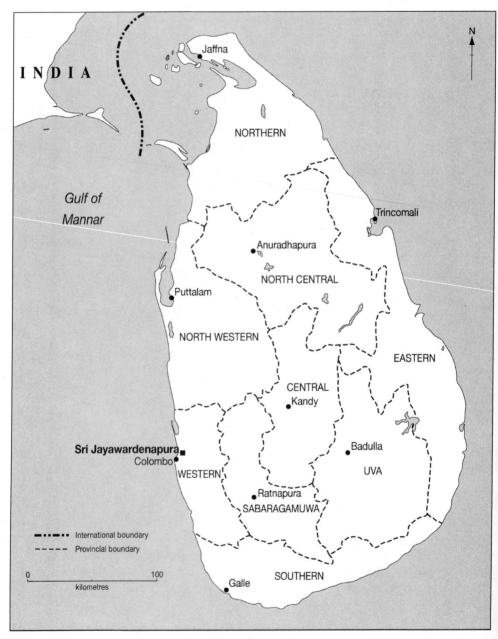

Map 3. Sri Lanka

The predominantly Theravada Buddhist Sinhalese make up approximately three-fourths of Sri Lanka's population of 18.6 million. The militant members of the Liberation Tigers of Tamil Eelam have emerged from the island's largest minority, the mostly Saivite Hindu Tamil people, who number approximately 3.2 million. Religious affiliations in Sri Lanka at present are approximately 69.3 percent Buddhist (Sinhalese speaking), 15.4 percent Saivite Hindu (Tamil speaking), 7.6 percent Muslim (Tamil and Sinhalese speaking), 6.0 percent Christian (Tamil and Sinhalese speaking), and 6 percent other. Collective identities on the island are more complex, especially from the perspective of religion. For example, most Tamil speakers are Saivite Hindus, but there are also Christian and Muslim communities of Tamil speakers. Sri Lanka's fragmented multiethnic society includes several small minorities such as the Catholic Portuguese burghers. Certain religious traditions, such as the worship of permutations of the goddess Kannaki or Pattini and the god Kataragama, are shared by Sinhalese Buddhists and Tamil Hindus.

British colonial policies resulted in the transformation and hardening of ethnic identity in Sri Lanka (Nissan and Stirrat 1990; Rajasingham-Senanayake 1999; Rogers 1995; Somasundaram 1998, 2003). The people of the island, which was then known as Ceylon, were categorized as distinct "races," in part on the basis of their spoken language. Racial-cum-ethnic categories were formally recognized in legal procedures, and political power was linked to racial criteria. Sri Lanka's present-day polarized ethnic identities—Tamil speakers versus Sinhala speakers—are, however, a recent historical development resulting from the failure of British policy to establish protective provisions for minorities in the multiethnic society. Citizens of Sri Lanka are required by law to carry national identity cards, eliminating individual choice on ethnic identity.

At independence in 1948 the new constitution enabled the Sinhala majority to assume control of legislative and executive powers democratically (Nissan 1996). The Tamil minority was increasingly alienated during the post-independence period, when Sinhala Buddhist revivalism developed into a political Buddhism that was inextricably interwoven with Sinhala nationalism (Tambiah [1986], 1991). The establishment of Sinhala as the sole official language of the state in 1956 was a pivotal point in the alienation of the Tamil minority, and in 1972 primacy was given to Buddhism as the state religion. University admission for Tamil minority students was then restricted, and Tamil armed resistance against the government began. Separatist sentiment grew as internationally funded irrigation projects resettled Sinhala farmers in areas of the island that Tamils considered their historic homelands.

In the early 1970s a spirit of defiance and resistance to the state's practices of discrimination arose in the Tamil populace. Following the violence of the Sinhala-Tamil riots in 1983, thousands of Tamils were trained in guerrilla warfare and the use of explosives in India, and by the late 1980s more than thirty armed Tamil organizations had formed to fight for a separate Tamil nation (Gunaratna 1987; Taraki 1992). Numbering over ten thousand today, the Liberation Tigers are the sole Tamil opposition group engaged in armed struggle with the Sri Lankan security forces for greater autonomy in the northern and eastern regions of the country. Their ranks include the elite Black Tigers cadre, known in 2003 for more suicide missions than any other militant group in the world.

Throughout Sri Lanka's civil war and its nascent peace process, women have exerted pressure on militarism and the perpetuation of violence. The chapters in Part II examine ethnographic research on women's disruption of cycles of violence in the island's Buddhist, Hindu, and Muslim communities. They explore how women mediate violence in the micropolitics of everyday life and how they contest militarism, disappearances of husbands and sons, and state-making projects. These chapters bring an ethnographic perspective to bear on the political and cultural complexity of agency, beginning with Patricia Lawrence's analysis of women's agentive acts in social conditions of collective trauma. She presents case studies of two groups of women in Sri Lanka's terrain of torture and disappearances: women activists in a local NGO and women who embody the Amman, or goddess, as oracles at Saivite Hindu temples. Lawrence explains that these Tamil women must live with what they cannot control, yet find ways to mediate and protest violence in a terrain where violence is most immediate and difficult: the everyday lived reality of the war zone.

Local female activists place themselves at risk as they challenge asymmetrical relations and publicly protest unspeakable violence through collective acts of conscious intention. At local Amman temples and shrines the oracles assist recovery from war trauma, sustain relationships, and resist the entry of violence into local support networks through the borrowed agency of the Amman. Throughout this provocative chapter we see how women's imagination, commentary, and protest emerges in a public domain and daily challenges the complicity of Tamil women with the political power of the state and the armed Liberation Tigers of Tamil Eelam.

In "Mothers and Wives of the Disappeared in Southern Sri Lanka: Fragmented Geographies of Moral Discomfort," Alexandra Argenti-Pillen focuses on the notion of distress, *dosa,* in the social world of female casual laborers on tea plantations in the Matara district of southern Sri Lanka. She examines the way in which national mental health NGOs liaise with state bureaucracy on behalf of women from rural slums who are searching for husbands and sons lost during the civil war of the late 1980s and disappeared sons who were sent to war against the armed Tamil minority. Argenti-Pillen's conclusion has important consequences for the field of peace studies. In this part of Sri Lanka there is no public outcry about the atrocities committed by counterinsurgency forces. Instead, postwar identities and accusations are based on highly individualized and specific accounts of violence. A female-kin-based moral consciousness has emerged that engenders social fragmentation. This is a protective mechanism, a form of marginality that protects these women and their families from the gaze of the state and its modernist state violence.

In her examination of the micropolitics of the Sri Lankan everyday, Mangalika de Silva captures the quotidian spaces in which social antagonisms among Sinhala, Tamil, and Muslim communities are played out. She describes those conjunctures in which practices of self and subjectivity engage projects of everyday politics of power. Throughout her chapter the notion of agency is problematized through an examination of contemporary postcolonial forms of women's mobilization, activism, and discourse within a variety of specific local and territorial contexts. These case studies allow her to map knowledge of self and other and the convergence of state and community onto the ongoing women's project of negotiating, reworking, and sustaining relations of domination and subordination in contemporary Sri Lanka.

The immense disaster of the tsunami on December 26, 2004, has deepened political fault lines and complicated the peace process with disputes about equitable distribution of international aid. With rising human rights abuses, criminality, and impunity in the eastern districts, the task of managing a failed ceasefire has replaced advancing the peace process.

5

The Watch of Tamil Women

Women's Acts in a Transitional Warscape

PATRICIA LAWRENCE

The women of Sri Lanka's Tamil minority confront life on a contested terrain where torture, disappearances, displacement, and politically motivated murder persist. Cycles of violence in the Tamil Homelands in the north and east of the island trace a series of failed ceasefire agreements between the government of Sri Lanka (GOSL) and the Liberation Tigers of Tamil Eelam (LTTE) since the 1980s. The eastern district of Batticaloa, the epicenter of the island's violence, is the setting of this chapter. Preservation of the integrated eastern and northern districts of the Tamil Homelands is crucial to the goals of Tamil nationalism.[1] The present moment finds a shadow war being fought over GOSL-LTTE control of the contested Tamil-speaking eastern district, with continuous abductions and killings and increased government military control over the people living there. The questions I want to address are how women are responding to the violent disfiguration of everyday life in Batticaloa where decades of contestation over state governance has produced expendable lives; and whether divergent forms of women's agency shaped by violent circumstances are working at cross purposes. I investigate the ways in which Tamil women are demanding social justice and seeking to protect women under a fractured majoritarian state government that is reluctant to enter into power-sharing agreements with the Tamil minority. Tamil women living in this warscape are forming organizations and convening meetings where they speak confidently about overcoming discriminatory relationships. Whether they are speaking out about social reform as members of the LTTE, as members of

Figure 4.
Female cadre
with gun.
Photo by
Dominic Sansoni.

women's civil society organizations, or as oracles in local Tamil Hindu temples
who borrow the agency of the Amman (a divine epithet meaning "Mother"
and a term of address for Tamil goddesses), women in Batticaloa have replaced
earlier networks shattered in the course of war and are empowering women's
agency as a social force in both the secular and religious spheres.

Women whose Tamilness has been strengthened through decades of state
violation of their collective cultural identity have chosen different paths
of response to their everyday lived experience. I do not presume to present
the voices of all Tamil women in Batticaloa; women there are engaged in
the educational, medical, and legal infrastructure. Some women have chosen
to take up weapons with the LTTE to fight against the GOSL for Tamil self-
governance, other women view the violence of war as the enemy, and still

others have experienced such severe personal disabilities and loss that a sense of agency in relation to the war is unavailable to them. Thousands of Tamil women have undergone military training with the LTTE and have sacrificed their lives in the separatist movement's front lines since the 1980s.[2]

Tamil women's relationships that have arisen out of war are founded in pre-existing support networks and a sense of strong collective responsibility. In Sri Lanka war has provided the ground for reshaping women's roles and relationships. The prolonged violent conflict between the GOSL and the LTTE over the Tamil-speaking region has motivated many Tamil women to engage in violence or to mediate, protest, and expose violation where it is most difficult—in the midst of war's lived realities.

Setting

As a postcolonial state struggling with internal ethnic conflict, Sri Lanka exemplifies a state that does not provide equal security for its multiethnic, multilingual citizenry. It is increasingly militarized, with security forces drawn primarily from its majority Sinhalese population. These forces expanded from 12,000 members in the early 1980s to more than 175,000 in the 1990s. Even before the tsunami disaster of December 26, 2004, the government of Sri Lanka turned to international assistance to meet the needs of its citizens during the decades of war.

Eastern Sri Lanka is perceived in the language of the state as a region of "high security," as a threat to the state's sovereignty. "Security" in its most common usage in the language of the Sri Lankan state does not refer to the protection of the citizenry but to the protection of the state (Wickramasinghe 2001). Among the 1.6 million Tamils who have been displaced on the island, there are 250,000 children. In the early 1990s approximately 80 percent of the population of the eastern district of Batticaloa was displaced during government security forces operations. According to the most thorough report at present, 90 percent of the thousands of disappearance cases in Batticaloa District were members of the Tamil minority, and 88 percent are recorded as victims of the government's security forces and paramilitary allies; 2 percent were attributed to the LTTE (Government Publications Bureau 1997). Commissions of inquiry documented more than 27,000 disappearances in the 1987–90 armed conflict in southern Sri Lanka between the People's Liberation Front and government security forces and also between the LTTE and government security forces in northern and eastern Sri Lanka, which intensified in 1990.

The war in Sri Lanka, Asia's longest, has taken the lives of 65,000 to 70,000 people on the island. The decades of violence and oppression have left a legacy of humanitarian disasters: loss of social infrastructure, malnourishment, illness, communal schisms, massive displacement, increased domestic violence, grinding poverty, and trauma. People in Batticaloa have suffered entrapment in this region of contested governance. The manner in which lives are destroyed is illustrated by the following entry from my fieldnotes of 1991:

> Friday afternoon Amma (the mother of a family I was staying with) and I were walking by the edge of the paddy fields near the house on our way to a nearby Kannakaiymman temple. She said the growing rice used to be very green and beautiful there this time of the year before the war (now the fields are barren). As we walked she said in her quiet way, without gesturing in any manner, that we were passing just then a spot where ten bodies were burned a few months earlier. She spoke as though someone would overhear her, without looking at me, adding that after they set the bodies alight with burning tires, people came running to the spot from the neighborhood houses, so desperate were they to see if they could recognize their "disappeared" loved ones. We walked on in the heaviness of the dumb condition that thousands of "disappearances" have left upon Batticaola, a muteness which had just then ever so slightly been transgressed, an immense silence that needed to be burst wide open for healing to happen but could not be. Most of the time her silence, like her patience, is something to be counted on.

A Warscape with Women's Support Networks

A Tamil grandmother once explained to me the difference between the prewar period of her life and her years of endurance and survival after Sri Lanka's eastern coastal plain became a landscape of war. In her village the matriclan membership of each person was common knowledge and kinship support was strong, although only about a third of its earlier population remained. "Before the problems," she said, "there was no fear." She was a *cumankali,* a married woman with a living husband and children and many grandchildren. She used to say that she hoped the war would end in her grandchildren's lives. Tamil culture is well known for the respect accorded the *cumankali,* to whom powers of protecting and ensuring the well-being of family members are attributed (Reynolds 1980; Wadley 1980). It is a Tamil understanding that both the *cumankali* and the local goddess have the capacity to provide protection. Similarly, rituals surrounding Tamil goddesses in hamlets, villages, and towns of the eastern region center on the protection of the local goddess. In the eastern district of Batticaloa, the worship of local goddesses during annual propitiation ceremonies requires the cooperative effort of Tamil women with close kinship ties who live within calling distance of one another and who assist one another with child care, cooking, and other aspects of women's work. Stories about the origin of these local goddesses often have themes about women who suffered greatly in their human lives before transcending the human realm. A distinctive east coast residence pattern of matrilocal household clusters has been described in prewar ethnographic studies (McGilvray 1982, 1989, 2008), and close groupings of sisters' houses can be found where displacement during the war has not disrupted this regional practice. Annual propitiation ceremonies for local goddesses also require the cooperation of each family's household, clusters of households, and the village as a whole.

In many places these female-centered aspects of life on the east coast of the island have been brutally reconfigured: some villages that were attacked simultaneously by ground and by air were transformed into state security forces camps; temples and homes became barracks for government soldiers; kinship circles were shattered by displacement; close family relationships were severed by disappearances or death and the refugees' exodus into what has become a global Tamil diaspora. Nevertheless, Tamil women's networking is resilient. There were women who remained in the wartorn Tamil Homelands and continued to engender relationships of support in the face of abductions during house-to-house searches, strafing of rice fields by helicopter gunships, and the collaboration of state security forces and paramilitaries in massacres and mass disappearances of Tamils.

Women's support networks were mobilized to provide protection and to alleviate fear. In a period when the violence was intense, roads were closed, and communication was severed, one Tamil woman whose husband had "disappeared" decided to take her family members to live in the interior mountains near Pulipainchakal. Prior to the trek she was traumatized to the extent that she had frequent nightmares of shooting, running with many people, planes dropping bombs, and dead bodies. They lived in the mountains as a family group of twelve: her four children, her elder and younger sisters and their five children, and her. Her younger sister's husband had recently been shot and her elder sister was also widowed when they went into the mountains. Active combat between the LTTE and the Sri Lankan army, navy, air force, special forces, special units, and paramilitary allies resulted in complete displacement of a number of Tamil coastal villages in Batticaloa. In the mountains there were no roads, only sandy paths; and displaced families constructed huts for shelter in the mountain jungles. They lived there for the next year. As she tells it:

> We had no salt, oil, or coconuts, but we had rice and milk from cows. We had wild greens. There were fish in some of the ponds there. Sometimes we would shoot a cow and roast it over the fire. There were wild elephants and we were scared of them. In Pulipainchakal, all the people were sick with malaria, cholera, dengue fever, and typhoid. My daughter almost died from malaria. Some died from snakebites. While I was there I became a midwife and helped in the delivery of six children. All of the people had to run for their lives when the helicopters were strafing the area or planes were bombing. Some of the children were killed. Once when I was with my younger sister and our children, a helicopter began firing at us at close range. I could see the pilot's face while he was shooting at us. After that we were terrified of helicopters. (Lawrence 2003b: 5)

This Tamil woman continues to care for her sisters and their children. In addition, she cares for a sister and a brother who have lost limbs while fighting on the front lines. She now works in an organization engaged in peace education (Lawrence 2003b).

Women's Response to Mass Arrests

In the early 1990s travel on the roads was extremely difficult. A friend and I were recalling that period when she stated, "We had to light a torch of *pantam* [dry palm fronds] in the night and wave the flames at the military checkpoints to get past the soldiers at the time of childbirth when a woman needed to go to the hospital." The military checkpoints on the roads were dangerous, especially after nightfall when the soldiers would drink alcohol and fire guns randomly. And in the daylight Tamils were arrested at the checkpoints. On the basis of suspicion alone Tamil people were arrested by the state security forces under the draconian Prevention of Terrorism Act and Emergency Regulations. Tamils were required to show national identity cards at checkpoints, and village names on the identity cards were sufficient grounds for arrest. Those who were arrested were often selected on the basis of skin color: darker skin was associated with the LTTE fighters, who were exposed to the sun for long periods. In the eastern region this meant that fishermen, agricultural laborers, and others who labored in the sun or who had darker skin were discriminated against under the act. Government soldiers pocketed extra money from bribes at checkpoints, and those who were too poor to pay the bribes were more vulnerable to arrest.

At military checkpoints elbows and knees were checked for scarring, which was perceived as evidence of military engagement as an LTTE fighter. One Tamil woman who had attempted suicide by pouring kerosene on her body was arrested under the assumption that her burn scars were the result of fighting on the front lines. Government soldiers hideously scarred a young student's face during torture; because he had no way of hiding these scars, he was arrested again and again at the checkpoints. Finally, his family arranged for him to travel to Canada via illegal networks.

In the late 1980s and early 1990s in Batticaloa, it was commonplace for Tamils who were arrested by the government forces not to survive detention. The bodies of murdered Tamils were burned to ashes in detention camps, in rice fields, and on roadsides; dumped offshore into the Bay of Bengal; or thrown into the Batticaloa lagoon. People came to understand that every hour counted in ascertaining where among the hundreds of detention areas a loved one was imprisoned. Some detention areas were "unlisted," though they might be in central locations as well as in remote places. If an arrested family member could be located before the first nightfall, his or her chances of survival were significantly improved.

After mass arrests, women of the villages and neighborhoods responded by forming groups to follow the government forces' trucks to the places of detention. There were often large groups of women sitting, sleeping, and cooking in the streets around the main Batticaloa prison, around the temporary detention camps on the main coastal road, at police stations, at other main prisons, and at the so-called Forestry Camp on Koddaimunai's Pioneer Road. The women sat as close as they could get to their loved ones, planting themselves there and refusing to leave. The women's presence in the streets for days made public the large numbers of Tamils who were blindfolded, forced into government trucks, ill treated during detention, and frequently killed. Most of the women who came to sit at the detention facilities were mothers. When their presence and the public statement their presence made became an embarrassment, the prison or detention camp authorities would attempt to encourage them to leave by giving them a form on which was written each woman's name, her relationship to the detainee, and the detainee's name. I was sometimes present when the forms were given out, and most women said they were the mothers of those imprisoned. The way some women slapped their mouths with their open palms in their inner battle to voice the word "Mother" (Taay) is indelibly inscribed in my memory. Military authorities had a legal duty to record the name of each person in a register of arrests and detention and to give forms to family members that served as records of detention, but the procedure was not followed consistently. Human rights organizations were unable to locate in the registers those who had been arrested and those who had been transferred from one prison to another. Forms were only issued to family members when authorities were under pressure to clear the streets of the crowd of Tamil women rooted in place near prison and detention camp entrances. Negligence in the issuance of forms continues to be a problem (Gunasalingam 2004).

Shattered Kinship

The widowhood of at least 8,500 women and the loss of a generation of men through enlistment in the LTTE cadres, death, disappearance, and relocation abroad has had far-reaching effects in Batticaloa. Combined with other factors, the loss of men has meant the desirable *cumankali* status of Tamil culture is an impossibility for many of Batticaloa's young women. In the 1980s and 1990s government security forces' offensive operations produced waves of displacement, repeatedly reducing families of once-productive rice farming and fishing villages to refugees. Widespread displacement and economic paralysis have disrupted the women's support networks of the traditional matrilocal residence pattern. Where sisters' matrilocal houses were still clustered, widows' close female kin afforded advice and consolation, cooperation with child care, and the safety of companionship in public, as when

walking to the temple, hospital, or market. In contrast to the matrilineal kinship support offered to widowed women, relatives in the widows' husbands'
lineages had a tendency to abandon their relationship with their former
daughters-in-law (Thiruchandran 1999). The traditional duty of parents to
settle their children in marriage was frustrated by the inability to build houses
for their daughters' dowries. Several factors contributed to the difficulty of
constructing dowry houses, including the paralysis of the economy, loss of
family members, taxes imposed by the LTTE, and displacement.

Even where traditional matrilineal, matrilocal clusters of sisters remained,
violence affected every household and altered kinship and neighborhood
relations. This was especially in evidence during the harvest seasons. In one
village, when I initially asked the mother of the first matrilocal household
cluster where I lived if I could stay with them, she took me into the kitchen
and showed me the space underneath the waist-high concrete hearth. "We
stay here when there is shooting," she said. Her family had spent entire nights
crouched together under the hearth. In the center of the village many houses
had large chunks of plaster gouged from the inner walls during shelling.

One mother clearly expressed the changed nature of everyday relations
between sisters when she lamented, "Now there is no value for life here *(Ippo,
inkke oru perumatiyum illai)*. Now the people have a stone heart *(Ippo ur mak-
kalukkellam kal nencam)*. When there is crying and shouting next door in the
night, I can't go over and ask, 'Why are you crying?' because we don't know if
the LTTE or the army is there." One aspect of her experience that was most
difficult for her to bear was her inability to go next door and help calm her
sister's family. When there were clashes between the LTTE and the state security forces in this village, she lost her capacity to act as an influential woman
in the village as well as within a close circle of kinship relations. After government security forces had reestablished a camp on the perimeter of her village,
the places where there were friends or enemies were impossible to distinguish. Eventually, each of her children moved abroad, settling in four different countries. Now she has also abandoned the old family home.

Women Cadres

Batticaloa was already the main recruiting ground for the majority of
the LTTE's male frontline fighters in the late 1980s. Following massacres in

Figure 5.
Female cadre
with photograph
of deceased
friend. Photo by
Dominic Sansoni.

eastern Tamil villages in the beginning of the 1990s, more women were re-
cruited into the LTTE. As the number of widows and female-headed households increased, so did the number of young women who made the choice to
enlist in the ranks of the LTTE for military training. Separate training camps
for men and women were established. Most of the women who completed
military training and fought in the front lines were between the ages of fifteen and thirty-seven. The age of widowed women was generally between
eighteen and twenty-one.

During intensified recruitment drives, a rule is enforced that each Tamil
family must either give one child to the organization for military training or
support the LTTE financially. Some impoverished families make the choice to
give their property, their house and farmland, to the organization and refuse
to give a child. International human rights organizations have been monitor-
ing LTTE recruitment of underage fighters for several years, and while thou-

sands of underage fighters who joined the organization have been released, the proportion of children who are joining the LTTE in continuing recruitment efforts has sometimes been higher than the number released. The reasons for this are complex and include children joining of their own volition. Tamil women constitute approximately 35 percent of the LTTE's fighting ranks.

A new political discourse is emerging in Sri Lanka with more open lines of communication with the LTTE. It is easy to be struck by the obvious closeness of female fighters' bonds. Today's female fighters are too young to have known Batticaloa in peacetime, but they are still aware of ways they have diverged from gender norms set out for women in Tamil culture. For example, most Tamil women can easily recite the "Four Virtues" of Tamil women: modesty, charm, coyness, and fear (Maunaguru 1995)—now replaced by the new notions of courage, confidence, and thirst for liberation. Stronger still are the bonds that form as a result of their shared experiences on the front lines. It is easier than it used to be to meet openly with female fighters in Batticaloa, and certain female cadres are assigned to meet the local press, foreign journalists, and embassy officers. They are told what topics they can and cannot speak about, on orders from the higher chain of command. LTTE women are immersed in a disciplined militarized culture, and their complete commitment to it has narrowed their exposure to the nonmilitary world. Most female cadres have little experience of civilian life beyond the areas under LTTE control and conform to stricter gender segregation than is found in civilian life. Tamil civilians often comment on the focused discipline of LTTE cadres and contrast their behavior with the lack of discipline of pro-government militias and paramilitaries who are trained, protected, and paid by the Sri Lankan state.

When I asked a female fighter about her favorite films during an interview, she spontaneously talked about films made by the LTTE's video wing, Nitharsanam, about the history of the movement. Nitharsanam has produced several films about the Women's Unit of the Liberation Tigers of Tamil Eelam. The two-part film *Akkini Paravaikal* (Volcanic Birds), directed by female filmmakers of Nitharsanam, portrays the growth of the women's LTTE movement, the actual training of women's cadres, and frontline fighting and praises the contribution of the women's brigade in the Tamil minority's struggle against Sri Lanka's majoritarian government. Nitharsanam DVDs are available in London, Toronto, New York, Paris, and Sydney, among other international locations, and are avidly viewed by the Tamil diaspora in approximately sixty countries around the world.

Black Tigers Day, a day for honoring LTTE warriors who have sacrificed their lives in suicide missions, is celebrated in every village in Batticaloa. Early one morning I found a queue of Tamil schoolgirls in white government-issued uniforms waiting to hear a female soldier of the LTTE present a speech under the photograph of a local martyr. Because this area of the interior is now impoverished, many of the girls were barefoot. Those who wore shoes—rubber sandals—removed them outside the fenced area of the martyr's "shrine," which was decorated with strings of small red and yellow flags. Each girl took her turn placing white jasmine flowers in front of the image of the LTTE martyr, reminding me of Hindu religious holidays when the school-children walk collectively to the local temple to participate in religious ritu-als. After the girls filed back down the sandy road to continue the day's classes at school, the female LTTE cadres, sitting confidently astride motorcycles, left for the next village where they would give political speeches under fluttering red and yellow flags and larger-than-life portraits of Black Tigers who had enacted the supreme sacrifice for the LTTE. For women as for men, being selected for a suicide mission as a Black Tiger is a great honor. Many cadres apply; few are selected. Because the LTTE is a secular organization, the reward after death is a place in the history of the movement (Trawick 1997, 2007). There have been 242 deaths of Black Tigers.

Female LTTE cadres have unshakable confidence in the rightness of their struggle for liberation. "Confidence" is a popular theme in their speeches. Today LTTE nationalism is demanding women's confidence, as in the follow-ing speech by the head of the LTTE women's political wing, Thamilini:

> Our society has fashioned a web of discriminatory relationships based on gender. The gender distinctions, and cultural norms based on these dis-tinctions, the imposed stereotypes and prejudices are standing as obstacles to the equality of man and woman. Our liberation struggle has brought women's struggle to the forefront. We are successfully expelling supersti-tions ensconced in the dark recesses of our mind that portray women as secondary citizens. The women's liberation movement is forging ahead as an integral part of our greater struggle. The ideal of women's liberation is core to our national liberation movement. Our leadership demands us to turn into women with self-confidence. We should relentlessly seek social justice and work hard to learn new skills and trades that will release our inner energies. This will make us strong and independent, and make us ca-pable to uplift our society. (Kilinochchi, Vanni, October 3, 2004)

Figure 6.
Mother with
camphor pot at *puja.*
Author's photo.

Silencing

In Batticaloa, where the brutality of war is an intimately known experience and where loss of noncombatant, civilian lives has been immense, most women have no access to a public voice and instead endure many kinds of silences. There is the self-imposed silence that may ensure protection and safety, as well as the traumatized silence of intimidation, erasure, and loss. "Silencing" and denial are common coping practices widely reported in contexts of violence where there have been large numbers of disappearances and extrajudicial executions (Das 1996; Kordon et al. 1988; Schreiter 1992; Suarez-Orozco 1992; Taussig 1992). Most ordinary Tamil women caught in the violent conflict silently suffer the abuses of the security forces and the conflicting demands of the LTTE, for they are caught in between, and they know that knowing nothing about things that are politically sensitive in nature and "keeping quiet" is crucial for survival. Private remarks on political violence are spoken in whispers—as though walls have ears. The psychological effects of torture, the government's main weapon in the eastern war zone, are manifest in the careful self-censorship of speech and the breakdown of lines of communication among trusted networks of kinship and friendship.

It is widely accepted that for the survivors of torture and violence, telling one's story, giving testimony, or, alternatively, participating in rituals that acknowledge their lived experience will produce relief from the psychological effects of trauma such as anxiety, depression, and feelings of powerlessness (Jaranson and Poplin 1998). There are of course cultural variations on how stories are "told," how "testimony" is given, and how "truth" is said. In Batticaloa disclosure of information about violent events increases the vulnerability of local people to abduction, interrogation, and death. Women's fear is often so overwhelming that it disorients the shared trust between even the closest family members (Argenti-Pillen 2002; Butalia 2000; Felman and Laub 1992; Fink 2001; Skidmore 2003). Women lead lives oriented to strategies of survival, and many lack belief in their ability to plan their lives—and may lack a sense of any future.

In the 1990s the eastern region was completely cordoned off from the rest of the country by military checkpoints, and movement was so restricted that people were unable to obtain accurate information about circumstances in the next village. Following events of violence, the fear at checkpoints was palpable. When we moved on the roads my Tamil companions cautioned me, "Don't ask anything. Don't say anything you don't have to." We waited in long, slow lines for our bags to be searched at checkpoints sometimes positioned so closely that the next checkpoint was visible. At checkpoints most crucial to government forces' control, the soldiers sometimes made Tamil travelers tear up their identity cards, chew them, and spit the pieces on the roadside. Inside a region of such high military surveillance, styles of communication were recrafted in ways that incorporated extreme cautiousness.

It was largely Tamil women, not men, who traveled to the Sinhalese side of the island to search for arrested family members, often pawning their jewelry to cover the expenses of the dangerous excursion. I met Tamil women from Batticaloa in the capital of Colombo when they were visiting or still searching for family members in prisons. They stayed at the Pillaiyar Temple refugee camp off Galle Road in Colombo where they could sleep for a night or two. They could be found crowding the offices of human rights lawyers who filed habeas corpus briefs, notably wearing safety pins instead of gold and ruby earrings in their ears.

Women in the Religious Sphere

There was a dramatic rise in bhakti devotionalism throughout the Tamil Homelands in general and in particular at a small "Washerman" (Vannar) temple that belonged to just over one hundred Tamil families whose world was irrevocably altered by war. During the previous decade and a half, the temple enshrining Kali at Punnacholai had expanded and transformed into a site attracting thousands of devotees of all castes from throughout the war zone. In 1991 onlookers were astounded that 560 people crossed the long pit of burning coals. Attendees told me that less than a dozen people had performed the vow to walk over the fire there in the years before the intense violence of 1990. Pervasive ground fighting, air attacks, and massive displacement in 1990 curtailed or eliminated altogether annual festivals of worship in Batticaloa District's temples. Camps for the displaced were overflowing with refugees, while some villages and hamlets were completely vacated or destroyed. Once annual temple ceremonies resumed in the volatile eastern region, each year brought larger numbers of attendees and many forms of vows said to instill the Amman's grace *(varam)*, protection *(kappu, kaval)* and courage *(viram)*. Now more than 7,000 women, men, and children cross the red-hot embers.

In an examination of agency and resistance, Sherry Ortner (1995: 180) considers how "religion is always a rich repository of cultural beliefs and values and often has close affinities with resistance movements." The rise of religious devotionalism at Batticaloa's temples goes against the grain of the LTTE, a pragmatist, secular organization whose position is that religion is not part of the consciousness of the movement.

The organization is careful to avoid divisiveness within the Tamil minority population on the island. Most Tamils are Saivite Hindus, but there are also small Catholic and Protestant sectors. As an extension of its goals of autonomous governance, the LTTE administration pursues development, modernization, and elimination of the inequalities of caste. The LTTE espouses religious tolerance, but its notion of modern society is antagonistic to the ever greater numbers of the Tamil minority population concentrating on religious life. As a repository of cultural beliefs and values from which the local population in the war zone draws, religion is a source of solace and recovery for survivors. The LTTE's increasingly consolidated political power and social control is at times contested in the everyday micropolitics of religious practice.[3]

The pragmatist LTTE took advantage of the large gatherings of local people at temples by staging political speeches between *pujas* (worship ceremonies) or showing recruitment videos nearby. At the Punnacholai temple, the LTTE demanded exorbitant parking fees for the thousands of bicycles and motorbikes that brought people there, and people expressed bitterness about this. The LTTE also attempted to collect a fifty-rupee "tax" on each *kappu*, or red protection thread, tied on the wrists of those who crossed the fire, but Sinnithambi, an elderly, tenacious member of the temple's priesthood, staunchly refused, arguing that such an act would infuriate Pattirakaliyamman, the local form of the goddess Kali enshrined at Punnacholai.

"Truth-Telling"

Throughout the process of social breakdown, chaotic violence, long-term violence, long-term trauma, rebuilding, and renewed warfare, I returned numerous times to sit in the sand next to one particular oracle (*teyvam atumal*, or deity dancer) in Batticaloa while she served as a guide through social catastrophe for local people. At local temples and shrines for the Amman, the oracles of Batticaloa offer solace, prescribe religious practices that sustain relationships, and confront the entry of violence into local kinship and neighborhood support networks. They do this through the borrowed agency of the local Amman, who is the embodiment of *cakti*, the active, hot, sacred female energy of the Hindu universe.

Saktirani is one of hundreds of oracles in Sri Lanka's wartorn eastern region. During temple *pujas*, devotees form long lines waiting their turn to ask for guidance or listen to what the oracle will say to them during the hours of the *puja* reserved for truth-telling (*vakku colluratu*). As one oracle explained spontaneously, when people seek truth-telling the goddess "comes upon" her: "If they come for consolation and solace *(arutal)*, or for grief and calamity *(tuyaram)*—at that time she will come upon me. She will tell me to tell if there is going to be difficulty *(cikkal)*, then Amman will reveal it." In a real sense Batticaloa's oracles mediated violence. Temple *pujas* were among the few social spaces in which noncombatant civilians could exchange perspectives about events of the war. I and the women of the households where I

Figure 7. Woman in
trance possession.
Author's photo.

stayed slept on the sand at the temples with hundreds of other women and
children of the village because it was not safe to walk on the roads past
bunkers and military checkpoints at night. There was a strong sense of collective trauma, as many wept in these initial temple gatherings. At the temples
I visited in Batticaloa villagers stood before the inner sanctum, arms out-
stretched and palms open, imploring the deities for the whereabouts and
safety of missing family members. I observed sacred space being treated as
ground for unshielded truth.

Oracles receive empowerment of the Amman through profound identification with a particular goddess. This power is associated with *cakti,* the active
female energy of the Hindu universe. The phrase "assuming form" *(uruvaru-
tal)* refers to the moment of *cakti* possession, described as a painful experience
of heat and trembling that resembles the uncontrollable shivering of a fever.

Caktis also stress that the Amman selects them, compels them, to do this; it is not something that one can choose to engage in of one's own volition. They say that during possession, they do not remember their words or acts. In the words of Saktirani, "I forget myself completely while telling *(ennaiye marantu nan namankkontupecutal).*" The oracle's acts are presented in a particular genre of cultural discourse that requires dissolution of the self and therefore absolves personal responsibility when speaking against the structures of power that oppress the people who live in the region, as well as when urging accommodation when people are confronted with the coercive forces of militarism.

Saktirani tells *vakku* at the Pattirakaliyamman temple and every day at her house, which has been transformed into a place where urgent problems are addressed. As I watched her interactions in the shrine area at her home, where on some mornings more than ninety people gathered, I learned about the range and severity of social problems that ordinary people were facing. People came in small groups of family members, traveling with their uncertainties and anxieties through many military checkpoints. They entered a social space for collective commentary on crises such as displacement, disappearances, abductions, arrests by the state, and conscription by the LTTE.

As the form of culturally defined agency she enacts is drawn from popular cultural beliefs of ordinary people caught in the civil war, she became a well-known local figure who mediated and acknowledged violence, but at the same time she faced unavoidable complicity with the coercive state-building project of the LTTE fighting for the separate state of Tamil Eelam, as well as the government's project of protecting the Sri Lankan unitary state. The guidance she offered deflected complicity primarily by acknowledging pain, guiding people through experiences of suffering and of shattered kinship by offering ways to strengthen potential relationships that were still accessible in circles of kinship and community.

There were often government sweeps through neighborhoods during which hundreds of Tamil people were arrested. Men and women who were tortured and released were often brought to Saktirani for treatment of recent wounds and emotional distress. Wives whose husbands had just been arrested came to ask in which of the many detention camps and prisons they were being held. Saktirani sometimes insisted that they immediately return with a new shirt and sarong. The clothing was blessed with mantrams and *vibhuti* (sacred ash) and passed through the detention camp soldiers to the imprisoned men in the belief that the blessing would secure their release before they disappeared in the hands of the military regime.

The strength of Saktirani's reputation centered on her ability to speak about lost connections *(totarpu illai)* and a belief in her capacity to feel the pain of others. Many people came to her in a state of unresolved grief to learn the fate of loved ones who had disappeared. She often offered finality about death. When the disappeared family member was no longer living, she returned the offerings and was consoling. She specified particular religious rituals and practices, such as the construction of a guardian deity shrine by the gate of the family's house to protect remaining household members or the enactment of vows. In disappearance cases she often acted out the suffering and torture the person had experienced with her own body, writhing and sometimes vomiting. Sometimes there were no words, only the expressiveness of her body. She embodied the violent death and chaos of a certain historical moment. Sometimes she wrapped herself in a sheet as though it were a shroud, covering her head, and was silent. The gathered people seated on the veranda waited. Saktirani was at the end of meaning. At the end of language, her body became the agent, a site where truth is made public.

Saktirani cared for women who were severely disoriented after having been sexually violated by government soldiers in their homes. She scolded young people who wanted to join the fighting and warned those who were already in the ranks of fighters: "You should not travel. Don't go near the sea!" or "Don't cross the Kallady Bridge!" or "Don't travel by motorbike!" She regularly predicted that some family member would be visited by violence.

Of necessity, Saktirani sometimes accommodated the forces of exploitation and power at work in the region. She offered explicit advice to families whose members were abducted by the LTTE for ransom. Deeply distraught relatives often could not pay the amount demanded. She calmly advised them to return to the LTTE and specified a reduced amount that would be accepted. People sought strategies for survival and diminishment of painful dilemmas. Some brought letters written to family members already in the diaspora. Saktirani sprinkled *vibhuti* in the envelopes and chanted blessings over them at her shrine, offering reassurance that their connection would not be lost. People about to leave Batticaloa via illegal travel networks in order to live abroad would ask her to foresee their future. She gave them small copper sheets in which sacred *yantiram* designs were etched and gifts from the shrine to clear the path of travelers abroad.

On one recent visit I removed my sandals, washed my feet at the well, placed red and pink hibiscus and white jasmine flowers on the shrine around the heavy black stone statues of Kali, and sat quietly on a woven mat. Parents desperate to find their daughter, who disappeared with a classmate after school, were seeking advice. They believed the schoolgirls had been taken to military training camps by the LTTE, which had mounted a vigorous recruitment campaign during the months of ceasefire. Saktirani named a camp location, and if she was correct, it was crucial information for retrieving their conscripted daughter. She encouraged the parents to talk with the Tigers.

I have not observed this in Saktirani's exchanges, but with other oracles at the temples mothers with children engaged as LTTE fighters demanded reassurance that their children would be safe and eventually return to them. In the voice of the goddess, oracles have offered consolation and promised children's safety in exchange for the mothers' "pleasing acts" at the temple.

Such agency attributed to the Amman oracle is not individually constructed; it is surrounded by strong collective belief interwoven with collective trauma. Saktirani's agency is borrowed from locally expanding belief in the goddess Kali. The extent of Kali's and Saktirani's popularity in Batticaloa is a reflection of trauma, broken trust, loss, and the urgent need for safety and protection.

The Suriya Women's Development Organization

The emergence of women's organizations is one of the most positive signs of the recovery of Sri Lanka's beleaguered civil society (Coomaraswamy 2001). Among women's organizations on the island, the Suriya Women's Development Organization has an interesting history and impressive record of achievement. The women who formed Suriya in the early 1990s concentrated their work in refugee camps located in and around the capital of Colombo. Many of Suriya's first members were themselves displaced from Poorani, a women's community in the north where women learned leadership and self-sufficiency skills and organized numerous women's projects in northern villages. When LTTE military activity in Poorani's neighborhood forced its closure, some of Poorani's residents migrated to Colombo, where they founded the Suriya Women's Development Organization to assist others who were displaced from areas of ongoing warfare in the north and east. Over several decades, Suriya has become a model of women's activist networking capable of reaching the most isolated and endangered village populations.

At the outset Suriya staffed medical clinics and established schools for children in the refugee camps and offered vocational training classes, legal counseling, psychosocial support, and health education workshops. A core group of women in Suriya were arrested under the Prevention of Terrorism Act and Emergency Regulations and held in detention for ten days. This experience served as a catalyst, strengthening their motivation to challenge injustices perpetrated by the government under the rubric of "security."

Suriya lobbied to prevent government closure of refugee camps in Colombo because people from Batticaloa District were averse to returning to the region as long as active combat was continuing. Nevertheless, the refugees were forced to board buses in the middle of the night and were driven back into the eastern war zone. Over the next weeks, Suriya received many urgent telephone calls from the refugees begging them for continued assistance. A group of four women made the unusual decision to relocate their work in Batticaloa, where the dangers were greatest and where they felt they could be most effective. They lived together in a small rented wing of a house by the lagoon.

Once Suriya moved to Batticaloa, their work expanded to include cases of arbitrary arrest, abduction, disappearances, battering of women, and income generation for women who were widowed. Unlike women's organizations operating in Europe and North America, Suriya did not formulate a narrow mandate. As the only women's organization in the eastern war zone at that time, its development was a fluid and responsive process of addressing the problems that local women brought to them. In their newly established office in Batticaloa, a space first donated to them, they offered guidance to women in need of counseling. Family members of women arrested under the Prevention of Terrorism Act and Emergency Regulations sought their help. They met with women needing legal assistance and an increasing number of women struggling with domestic violence. They initiated a counseling program in the hospital's burn ward for women who were admitted after having attempted suicide.

As Suriya's networks expanded, it concentrated on outreach programs. Freedom from Fear was an early program that addressed the shattering of village and neighborhood support systems. It was the product of early meetings with women in outlying villages whose isolation and vulnerability during military attacks and inability to get help when someone was abducted or disappeared were a foremost concern. The villages had no electricity or telephones. The number of female-headed households had increased drastically. Suriya's initiative assisted village women to map out networks of communication together in the prevailing emergency. The outreach programs for personal safety and security established networks that continued to strengthen the interconnectedness of Tamil women in Batticaloa.

In the face of the Sri Lankan government's deliberate choice to use torture and disappearance in its regime of terror in Batticaloa, Suriya organized public protests. During their outreach work in villages and neighborhoods, their mode of work connected Suriya with many women who had lost family members in the war. Disappearances were still occurring. Expressing dissent meant endangering one's life or the lives of one's family members. In the meetings Suriya held with women struggling against their situations in vulnerable outlying villages, the desire arose to find a way to overcome silencing and state truths publicly. Eventually—in gatherings of women in the inner rooms of houses—female survivors and members of Suriya agreed to take public action in the form of silent vigils. They held a vigil on the esplanade in Batticaloa town that they called "a day of peace and prayer," and another vigil at a site on the main coastal road where the Sri Lankan army arrested Tamils in several sweeps in a refugee camp in 1990, all of whom had subsequently disappeared (Lawrence 2000, 2003a). The stretch of coastal road where the vigil was held holds many memories of mass arrests, disappearances, and killings.

As members of Suriya and local people gathered for vigils, their participation established a sense of collective agency. Together they found a way to make a public statement about peace and the need to bring an end to disappearances as one collective body in dangerously sensitive political circumstances. Daya Somasundaram (2003: 11) describes the Tamil social environment as a "controlled, closed society, whether at the family, group, village or regional level." Somasundaram emphasizes that among Tamils there are strong "social pressures to conform, consent and speak in one voice" (11). When Suriya organized silent vigils, the organization was determined to mediate local-level violence in whatever ways they could. In these circumstances of collective social trauma, their silent vigils must be appreciated as a bold form of grassroots public protest. They exemplify the assertion of collective agency in conditions of threat to life. Their enactment of a public prayer for human rights was a form of protest that avoided further social fragmentation in Batticaloa's cultural and political environment.

The women of Suriya, along with poets and storytellers, organized public cultural events during a lull in political violence in the mid-1990s. Suriya's performances presented commentary on experiences of war, such as the following verses about widowhood that use a traditional form of "cooling" songs to the local goddess Kannakaiyamman:

Cool the thoughts of people living in Batticaloa
where the lagoon is all around,
cool down.
Thaaye! Who walked in the proper way
hearing the voice of the crane, dove and cuckoo,
cool down.
Ammah! Do you feel grief,
trembling each time you see the place where your husband died,
cool down.
Live with self-courage though you hear words as arrows.
Live well with good souls to stand with you in any state.

The last phrase, "in any state," implies the state of widowhood.

During the last half of the 1990s, Suriya began to engage more intensively in transnational networking, attending conferences for female activists in India, Pakistan, South Africa, the Netherlands, Ireland, the United Kingdom, and the United States. Crossing over into global feminist culture produced heightened activity in Batticaloa. Suriya expanded its staff and office space and equipped the offices with computers. Members developed analytic skills, organized workshops, and built a library containing literature on development, trauma counseling, gender studies, domestic violence, women's rights, and feminist perspectives on a range of topics. The organization expanded its outreach work and responded to the large number of cases of sexual violation and abuse that were brought to its attention now that it was well known in the region. Working relations with local police and judicial medical officers were often difficult. Suriya raised awareness of the need for police and judiciary education on women's rights and shared ideas with other women's groups based in Colombo, Kandy, and Jaffna (Coomaraswamy 2001).

Suriya's transnational networking sparked the idea for the clothesline project that was first imagined in a conversation between a member of Suriya and an activist in the Netherlands. The clothesline of women's saree blouses that Suriya created was strikingly colorful: parrot greens, like the green of young rice fields, hibiscus red, rose, yellow, burnt orange, blue, and the white of widowhood. It was a sharp statement of protest challenging the lack of accountability for criminal acts perpetrated by the military and a response to the crisis of leadership in the Tamil community, placed for passersby to see in the middle of Arasady junction, one of Batticaloa town's busiest intersections and most public places. Surviving female relatives of victims of

Figure 8. Women preparing rice at a Pattiraikali temple. Photo by Dennis McGilvray.

violent death and sexual violation—sisters, mothers, aunts, and daughters—gathered together to work on the clothesline project in village homes and in Suriya's office. Each woman brought a saree blouse that belonged to a female family member who had been killed, and together the women inscribed the blouses with the names, dates, and descriptions of the women's deaths. The clothesline was placed where tanks and military vehicles rumble through the public landscape, near bunkers, barricades, and military checkpoints. Public roads and streets were dangerous militarized spaces during this act of protest. The truth that they insisted be made public was that women's domestic space is no safer than the streets of the war zone. The local women who worked with Suriya on this were women with experience in militarized terrain. They were among the women who filled the streets around the prison and detention camps, who sat as close as they could to the bunker entrances when family members were arrested by the security forces, so for them the risk entailed in the clothesline project was not new. The clothesline was a statement about rape made by women living in a war zone who had to live with the threat of violation every day, whose loved ones had been raped and murdered, and who were determined to protest publicly.

Sometimes the women of Suriya expressed their protest quietly, as in the case of one woman whose paintings powerfully expressed themes of resistance to torture and rape by security forces, child conscription by the LTTE, and militarism. She felt it was too dangerous to exhibit her paintings in public at that time, yet painting was a carefully guarded part of her everyday life.

Suriya gained local credibility and trust, and the organization's counselors began to work longer hours. Because the civil war has brought violence into the family, the staff was soon overwhelmed with cases of abusive treatment of women and girls. Fortunately, the judicial medical officer in the Batticaloa hospital at that time was exceptionally cooperative. Suriya staff and the officer discussed links between the brutality of some cases and the systematic use of torture against the Tamil population. Occasionally, when there was no time to set up alternative arrangements, Suriya members brought battered or sexually violated women into their own homes when they were severely traumatized and afraid to return home. Counseling and sheltering women who were sexually violated by government security forces put Suriya members in danger. Women who were raped by soldiers sometimes left their homes and took their children to hide with relatives in distant villages. Because rape is viewed as an extreme form of violation causing permanent damage in Tamil culture, victims and family members attempt to conceal the crime. Suriya began to explore the idea of organizing a women's shelter after two separate cases in which women who were receiving counseling from Suriya staff returned to their homes and were murdered.

There were only two women's shelters in the country, in Colombo and Kandy. Suriya discussed the pros and cons with the women who ran those shelters. In 2000 Suriya presented its project at the annual conference of the National Coalition against Domestic Violence in Portland, Oregon, which was attended by 1,300 safe-house directors from Canada and the United States.

At that time one of their concerns about establishing a shelter was that security forces frequently conducted cordon and search operations at any hour of the day or night, and under the Emergency Regulations and the Prevention of Terrorism Act Tamil people have no protection from arbitrary arrest.

There were other concerns as well. For the protection of women seeking safety, a safehouse is usually set up in an unidentified location, and it would be impossible to keep the shelter's location secret in Batticaloa. There was no guarantee that Suriya could convince the LTTE not to appropriate the safehouse as a shelter from the security forces in instances of renewed violence. Also, if perpetrators of violence were to follow women to a shelter, Suriya would not be able to turn to the police for assistance because there is still a crucial need to educate police about women's rights and treatment of rape cases. Responses to politically sensitive cases of rape by government security forces and paramilitary forces would place Suriya members at risk. Suriya is continuing to work on the idea of shelters.

Penn Urimaikal Kannoddam (A View on Women's Rights) was the first of Suriya's publications. Voices from Suriya on violence against women were also broadcast on national radio. The organization composed and publicly performed songs protesting violence, continued to counsel women, and strengthened its educational outreach. Educational efforts include discussions of unsafe abortion practices, an issue the staff takes out to gatherings in the villages.

A coalition of female peace activists that includes the women of Suriya prepared a document on women's issues and the peace process. The following short excerpt exemplifies the manner in which women's organizations in Sri Lanka are working as a sector of civil society:

> As women, we are deeply concerned about the militarization of society due to armed conflict. The high levels of domestic violence and rape . . . are directly related to a climate of impunity encouraged by the war. We recognize that women in particular have been victimized by war and conflict in Sri Lanka, that they have been subject to the worst forms of violence, been displaced, made into refugees, and compelled to live as war widows. . . . Women have watched their family members disappear and their children conscripted into the fighting forces. They have suffered physical disabilities and psychosocial trauma because of the war. Therefore, women's realities and women's voices must be an essential part of the peace process in Sri Lanka.

Conclusion

Tamil women's strong sense of collective responsibility is reflected in the meetings of the Subcommittee on Gender Issues, an integral part of the peace process. Sustaining the peace process was given priority in their agreed-upon collective efforts. Resettlement of refugees and personal security and safety are the next crucial issues women's organizations must focus on. Educational programs for women in Tamil villages have been stepped up with encouragement to increase confidence and awareness while developing new livelihoods for women. Both the LTTE and civil society now support these goals.

Suriya's effectiveness as a grassroots organization has engaged members in discussion with LTTE political wing leaders. Suriya is aware that it needs to maintain an independent voice, continue to present alternative viewpoints, and share its informed opinions and understanding to educate other groups, including international NGOs, the LTTE, and engaged governmental bodies (Anderson 1999). Suriya has been active in opposing violence, oppression, and militarization.

Female cadres, activists, and oracles are engaged in projects of social recovery that are often interwoven at the local level. Both Suriya and the oracles of the religious sphere have strengthened local networks and assisted survivors. What is especially effective about Suriya is its close connection to far-reaching women's networks. The LTTE is also tied to local women's networks to mobilize women for social change, to choose a life with purpose, and to serve in a movement dedicated to a better life for the Tamil minority.

The divergent roles of Batticaloa women in the secular organization of the LTTE, in civil society's women's activist groups, and in the religious sphere have grown increasingly interconnected. In response to prolonged conflict and discrimination, divergent forms of women's agency are increasingly overlapping and women's networks are producing shared understandings. For example, a woman working in peace education cares for siblings maimed in battle. Widowed women who have gained new livelihoods through Suriya's support participate in temple rituals. Oracles at temples encourage women to discuss their concerns with the LTTE. LTTE female cadres have developed new interests in women's education and liberation and seek out the skills learned by longtime Suriya activists in civil society. As women's agency is reshaped by the shared experiences of war and its consequences, women are increasingly overcoming political silencing and speaking out in both religious gatherings and secular public meetings.

How local female activists, cadres, and oracles have become who they are in Batticaloa is a story of complexity and ambiguity, of resources for solidarity that women draw on to strengthen networks in a landscape of devastating social catastrophe, in a time of extreme change in women's lives. The very lives of Tamil minority women survivors in this asymmetrical war are crucibles of change as they perpetuate and revitalize Tamil women's support systems. New women's networks have emerged from the ashes of Batticaloa's war-ravaged matrilineal, matrilocal kinship networks, increasingly overlapping as years of prolonged violence continue, both constraining and informing Tamil women's agency. In the epicenter of the island's violence, their interwoven acts and understandings are central to the alleviation of discrimination, social suffering, and the future sustainability of the island's peace process.

NOTES

1. This chapter is based on a presentation given at the Joan B. Kroc Institute for International Peace Studies during a Rockefeller Visiting Fellowship in the Program in Religion, Conflict, and Peacebuilding. The ethnographic research is drawn from periods in eastern Sri Lanka made possible by the SSRC-MacArthur Foundation, the American Philosophical Society, the International Peace Research Association, and the Stichting Humanistisch Instituut Voor Ontwikkelingssamenwerking (Institute for Humanist Development), the Netherlands. I have deemed it necessary to alter personal names, place-names, and in some cases time sequences in order to protect people who live in the region. The names of individuals who collaborated with this research or who were sources of information are withheld whenever I thought that anonymity was required and whenever confidentiality was requested. I bear sole responsibility for any shortcomings in the presentation of these ethnographic materials.

2. According to the Liberation Tigers of Tamil Eelam, of 17,648 cadres who have died, 3,766 have been female fighters and 241 have been suicide bombers (both men and women). These figures have appeared in LTTE Heroes Day speeches and are recorded on the organization's websites.

3. Religious nationalism and the appropriation of the religious symbolism of Saivite Hinduism goes against the grain of the LTTE's secular identity and the definition of their struggle as one articulated in political and linguistic terms. It would also alienate sectors of the Tamil minority that are members of Catholic, Protestant, and the newer charismatic churches. Increased social focus in the religious sphere has provoked interference from the LTTE. The organization now uses temple events to extract taxes; it also controls cultivation of rice fields considered temple agricultural lands and has altered the administrative structure of some village temples.

6

Mothers and Wives of the Disappeared in Southern Sri Lanka

Fragmented Geographies of Moral Discomfort

ALEXANDRA ARGENTI-PILLEN

On my first day in the village in southern Sri Lanka where I planned to live and conduct participant observation, an elderly lady took me aside. She warned, "There are many killers *(marana kārayo)* in this area, aren't you afraid?" A year went by, and I never heard similar comments. The civil war (1987–89), marked by summary executions, cordon and search operations, disappearances, and public displays of tortured bodies, had ended nearly a decade earlier, yet I did not find the public outcry and moral outrage I had expected. Eventually a friend took me to a diviner, and through her the goddess Kali addressed me. She spoke of a problem with my blood, which got worse after I came to Sri Lanka, because of "the heat caused by the way the country is." These were the few occasions when I heard women utter general conclusions about the political situation. Most of the time women in the remote village that I will call Udahenagama expressed their suffering as related to specific illnesses and misfortunes or incidents of violence.

Beyond Patronage

In this chapter I focus on one notion of distress, *dosa,* which women in Udahenagama use to talk about war-related suffering. In the anthropological literature *dosa* is given two complementary meanings. Ayurvedic medicine defines it as a fault of the organism, an imbalance of the three humors (wind, bile, and phlegm). The other, wider definition is "troubles" (Obeyesekere 1976: 202).[1] The concept is used by Ayurvedic medical practitioners and shamans *(äduro)* alike.[2] Gananath Obeyesekere (1984: 40, 44) disentangles the historical development of the meaning of *dosa*, arguing that its original, ancient meaning has been superseded by its very specific medical meaning in classic Ayurvedic medicine. However, he stresses the meta-medical extension of Ayurvedic concepts such as *dosa* into Sinhalese popular culture (Obeyesekere 1976: 223). The broader meaning of *dosa* as "faults" or "misfortune," used by contemporary laypeople in everyday life, leads Obeyesekere (1984: 44) to question similarities to the ancient meaning, used before it became incorporated into the Sanskrit, Ayurvedic medical lexicon and received its more specific Ayurvedic meaning (1984, 44).[3] It is precisely this broader notion of *dosa*—misfortune, faults—used on an everyday basis by women in Udahenagama that I want to subject to further scrutiny. I introduce a third dimension and possible translation of *dosa* on the basis of my informants' everyday *dosa*-related practices. Further, I analyze how a shadow of this dimension emerges in my informants' culture-specific strategies of postwar social reconstruction and their relationship to centralized power structures.

My analysis is based on research in one subculture, the social world of women who work as casual laborers on the tea plantations of the Udahenagama area, in the Matara district of southern Sri Lanka.[4] Many mothers send their sons to the war against the Tamil minority in the north and east of the country. Others have lost husbands or sons during the civil war of the late 1980s, when communist insurgents (JVP) and counterinsurgency forces committed widespread atrocities against the civilian population and an estimated forty thousand people disappeared (Amnesty International 1993). During the 1990s, approximately thirty mental health NGOs emerged in Colombo.[5] These NGOs focus on the treatment of traumatized victims and the rehabilitation of torture victims and families of the disappeared. I use my observations of the activities of one such NGO in the village of Udahenagama as a case study to begin to question the interaction between women from the rural slums of southern Sri Lanka and national mental health NGOs.[6] Such "national" mental health NGO activity is a crucial aspect of the state's relation with communities that have a history of insurgency and counterinsurgency violence and, in particular, with mothers and wives of the disappeared.[7] Mental health NGOs offer a variety of services, including individual and group trauma counseling sessions, training of "befrienders," and liaison with the state bureaucracy. This last aspect was considered the most important by women in Udahenagama: NGOs facilitated transactions with state officials in the search for the disappeared, in the acquisition of death certificates, or in the filing of compensation claims. Mental health NGOs thus participate in local state making and play a key role in "the imagined state" (Gupta 1995) of relatives of the disappeared.[8]

Professionals from mental health NGOs whom I interviewed in Colombo sometimes complained of the limited outreach and impact at grassroot level. Often grassroots participation and connections to "remote" areas were used competitively by NGOs that offer trauma counseling. However, it was easy to observe in the southern villages that the mothers of the disappeared have not been able to develop a full-fledged social movement in rural areas.[9] Urban-based NGOs have been able to establish contact with individual clients in rural areas, but their organizational structure or group identity has not been replicated among rural families of the disappeared. The social organization of survivors is dominated by vertical alliances with NGO workers or powerful state officials and politicians. Nancy Scheper-Hughes (1992: 516) has called this a "social psychology of patronage" that results in highly individualistic strategies of survival and jeopardizes much-needed forms of collective action. I do not deny that a heritage of patronage politics plays an important role in contemporary forms of postwar social organization (also see Amarasinghe 1989; Gamage and Hettige 1997; Orjuela 2003; Dixon 1982; Spencer 1990). Nevertheless, the social fragmentation of the NGOs' outreach programs in rural areas such as Udahenagama cannot be fully explained on the basis of a study of patronage politics.[10] My analysis therefore aims to offer a glimpse "beyond patronage," at other cultural factors that compound the organization of a rural grassroots women's movement.

Dosa as Transferable Moral Essence

In this chapter I move away from a focus on the highly visible instances of conflict and illness in the community: the crisis moments of spirit possession, sorcery accusations, and healing rituals. Many women in Udahenagama use the word *dosa* to talk about their houses and households. They only occasionally specify the type of *dosa* or define whether the affliction is caused by ancestral spirits *(preta)*, wild spirits *(yaksha)*, earth godlings *(bahirava)*, or people *(vas dos)*. *Dosa* is used as a general term and has become a gloss for many types of affliction, including poverty and family strife, illnesses, and the effects of wartime disappearances.

On the basis of interviews with shamans and afflicted women in Uda-henagama as well as observations of numerous healing rituals, I provide a supplementary understanding of the dual translation of *dosa* as humoral imbalance and trouble. This third meaning qualifies *dosa* as a faulty moral essence that can be transferred and contained. Women's evocation of *dosa* suggests a fault in the moral economy of the household, its relations with humans, ancestors, or spirits. Suffering caused by illness, poverty, or political violence is thus understood in relation to the general moral status of the household. A sudden drop in this moral status or deterioration of relation-ships between the household and beings of the Sinhala Buddhist pantheon is expressed as *dosa*. What is important here is that *dosa* is not only a physi-cal, moral, and spiritual state; it is transferable.

During healing or cleansing rituals, ritual specialists transfer the *dosa* to a variety of ritual objects, for example, small offering trays, limes, lamps, a rooster, or an ash pumpkin.[11] These objects are moved in circles in front of the patient and thereby attract the *dosa*.[12] In some cases the shaman uses the sword of the god Isvara *(īgaha)*, moving it over the body of the afflicted to make the *dosa* descend *(dosa bassanavā)*. An important moment in a variety of rituals is a personal act of cleansing, when the afflicted person performs *mūna at piya gahanavā*.[13] The afflicted moves her hands from her head to a sacrificial object while the ritual specialist recites, "The ten great *dosa* are cured, the eighty great *dosa* are cured, the million *dosa* are cured. *Tīnduva*. It is over." The objects that attract and contain the *dosa* are said to have *ākar-shana*.[14] Such ritual containers are subsequently infused with smoke, cut into pieces, burned, or made to float away in a river.[15]

Cleansing acts are not only performed for sick people, however, but also for houses and gardens. Just like the *dosa* can be transferred out of a sick body, it can be removed from an afflicted place.[16] Shamans bury *yantra* underground where the foundations of a new house will be built,[17] limes are cut near door-ways, sea sand or mustard seeds are spread in the garden—all to attract (and remove) the *dosa*.[18] Moral decay and misfortune are addressed as a trans-ferable essence residing both in the body and in human dwellings.

Obeyesekere (1984) has argued that it is impossible to prove that the cur-rent popular notion of *dosa* as misfortune or fault is *identical* to the ancient Indian meaning before its incorporation into Ayurvedic medicine. He notes

Figure 9. A mother transferring misfortune *(dosa)* to a rooster *(mūna at piya gahanavā)*. Author's photo.

it is proven that current techniques of ritual healing are derived from folk traditions going as far back as the *Atharvaveda,* itself a compilation of pre-existing curing techniques (44). On the basis of Obeyesekere's conclusions, I postulate that the practice of transferring *dosa* is linked to a potentially ancient shamanic ideology.

I hereby take care not to apply a context-free model of shamanism. Humphrey (1994) rejects static models of shamanism and instead sees it as reactive and constitutive in relation to other forms of power (192), changing over time.[19] In contemporary Sri Lanka shamanic practice is a contested terrain. Many people of higher status in the Udahenagama area, living in closer proximity to roads, do not enlist the services of shamans but prefer to use Ayurvedic or English medicine.[20] Moreover, many women from marginal and poorer areas in Udahenagama claim to have become fearless in the aftermath of the civil war and immune to both spirits and shamanic healing (Argenti-Pillen 2003: 161–70). Both higher-status and fearless women do not participate in shamanic healing ceremonies. Inspired by Humphrey's (1994) analysis,[21] however, I argue that shamanism in Sri Lanka is not limited to actual shamanic practice, to "an object to be pushed around" by other forms of power (195). Rather shamanism constitutes a fluid set of attitudes that permeate many social contexts, including sometimes the associational culture of women who contest shamanic authority in Udahenagama.

Bearing in mind both Obeyesekere's and Humphrey's work—the premodern origins of Sinhala shamanic ideology, as well as the impact of premodern forms of centralized power on shamanism—the concept of *dosa* emerges as a memory trace of an earlier form of sociopolitical organization. This shamanic ideology now permeates contemporary social life in war-torn communities at the margins of a weak postcolonial state. Throughout this chapter I refer to the attitudes and practices based on the notion of *dosa* as Sinhalese shamanic political ideology.

I experienced the implications of this ideology when I visited a sick person in an area far removed from the road, after a two-hour hike up a steep hill. The family was anxiously awaiting the arrival of the shaman, and I suggested it might have been easier to take the afflicted to the healer's hamlet at the foot of the hill. My suggestion was met with consternation. It would be impossible to contemplate the idea of an afflicted person crossing rivers or passing crossroads. This would not only further endanger the sick person, but also endanger the wider kin group. In shamanic discourse, faults *(dosa)* within the family or kin group make individuals more vulnerable to illness, misfortune, and spirit possession. Spirits residing near rivers and crossroads could readily attack a person or a person's family weakened by *dosa*.

This simple anecdote elucidates the culture-specific way in which people in Udahenagama deal with such faults and by extension the moral status of families. Sick people from afflicted households would never visit shamans; shamans or ritual specialists always travel to their patients' houses.

In this sense the moral geography of suffering remains dispersed, imprinted on a landscape segmented by rivers and roads.[22] The social organization revealed in the shamanic treatment of *dosa* is one where a low-status outsider is called in to deal with the pollution and danger inherent in affliction.[23] People repeatedly told me that in this way the wider neighborhood is protected from the danger inherent in illness and moral decay and the afflicted household becomes effectively isolated and contained. This is especially the case when a neighborhood deals with households suffering from incurable diseases. I now turn to the role played by this shamanic ideology when a

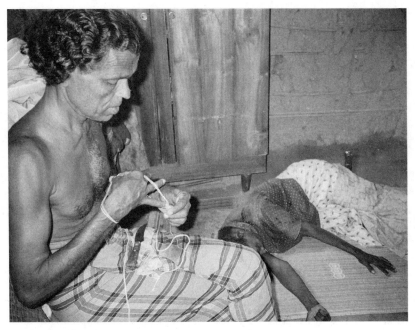

Figure 10. Possessed widow in her home with a visiting shaman *(äduro)*. Author's photo.

household suffers from the effects of counterinsurgency violence, torture, or disappearances.

A Village NGO

Women from Udahenagama who had used the services of a mental health NGO or had been trained by an NGO did not readily divulge information about this engagement to fellow survivors. This secretiveness cannot be fully explained by the lack of trust and the competition for limited resources within a social fabric damaged by war. The relative isolation of NGO participants in the village can be related to a wider cultural dynamic and Sinhalese shamanic ideology.

One of the main problems women from Udahenagama face when they want to participate in NGO programs is finding a chaperone who will accompany them on the journey to town.[24] A decade after the war, family members are often not very keen to continue to act as chaperones for women who intend to travel to the NGO's outreach center in the provincial capital, Matara, and continue the long search for disappeared family members as well as the battle for compensation. Some women were therefore forced to give up participation in rehabilitation programs. None of the women of Udahenagama would seek the company of other women in the village who participated in the NGO programs or travel to town with other NGO participants. In other words, women who have suffered similar forms of political violence during the civil war and are helped by the same national NGO do not necessarily support one another.

There is no taken for granted solidarity, friendship, trust, or common identity among women who suffered most during the civil war of the late 1980s and lost family members.[25] The danger inherent in moral faults traditionally is contained and diluted within the community, extracted from specific households, and burned or sent away along streams and rivers. Bringing afflicted people together and attempting to create a group of, for example, "families of the disappeared" at the grassroots level would, within shamanic discourse, amount to making potentially *dosa*-afflicted people or families travel across rivers and crossroads and create a *concentrated* pool of moral suffering.[26]

The ways in which people traditionally understand moral faults has further implications for the relationship between war-affected women and NGOs attempting to organize victims at the grassroots level. According to shamanic ideology, an individual's illness is often related to the faults of her entire family or household. The entire household participates in a cleansing ritual and needs to be ritually healed. Visitors attending cleansing rituals are themselves at risk of affliction and attack by spirits, unless they are protected by charmed oil applied by the shaman. Whether people suffer from illness, misfortune, or wartime atrocities, a kin-based sense of belonging is primary. This active sense of belonging and empathy is expressed and reinforced by traditional domestic cleansing rituals that mobilize a large, usually kin-based group one can trust.

Such a kin-based sense of belonging depends on many individual contingencies but does not involve the universalizing categories of groups defined by modernist elites involved in state formation and nation building. A shared moral essence, which goes along with trust and common strategies in kin-based groups, is related to very specific, individualized life histories (e.g., narratives about *dosa*) and cannot simply be experienced in relation to an abstract belonging to modern party or political formations or wartime factions. This results in a lack of cooperation and support among widows of the disappeared who do not belong to the same extended family.

In the current political climate national mental health and community rehabilitation NGOs have defined a specific target group in the rural slums of southern Sri Lanka: families of the people who disappeared during the civil war at the hands of either counterinsurgency forces or JVP insurgents. This target group that emerged from an urban peace-building and rehabilitation effort does not correspond, however, to a group identity rural women experience at the grassroots level. From a Western, modernist perspective, the geography of suffering in the village is fragmented and diffuse. Families whose sons have committed suicide, families whose sons have been tortured during military training in the Sri Lankan national army, families whose sons have been disappeared by counterinsurgency commandos in the late 1980s, families whose sons deserted and were arrested by the special forces in recent years, families who sent their daughters to free trade zones or the Middle East— all struggle to regain their dignity and manage *dosa*. Shamanic discourses on *dosa* provide strong spatial metaphors evoking a spatial confinement and individualization of suffering, resulting in a fragmented geography of affliction. A predominantly kin-based moral essence and sense of belonging characterizes survivorhood in the rural slums, and this cultural dynamic plays a major role in the relative absence of a full-fledged women's movement, with links to national mental health NGOs, in Udahenagama.[27]

Party Politics of the Drunk

This debate leads me to further questions about the degree to which women from marginal rural areas have been exposed to both modernist political and peace discourses. What is striking is that during the many conversations I recorded (see Argenti-Pillen 2003), political discourse or vocabulary was remarkably absent. Instead rural women use traditional idioms of suffering, such as, for example, the discourse on *dosa*, to talk about torture, disappearances, and political or domestic violence.

When asked why they did not speak about party politics the women would invariably say that this was a male affair, a topic of conversation for men in drinking groups.[28] Indeed, women liked to portray political talk as an exclusive activity of men who meet at illegal breweries on the outskirts of neighborhoods. Drunken brawls and fights characterize these meetings, often noisy affairs that can be heard over great distances.[29] Drinking groups are viewed with contempt by rural women because they are considered a major cause of the increase in domestic violence. By linking political speech to this context, women effectively remove it from their life-worlds and pressure other women not to be vulgar and allow political vocabulary to enter traditional discourses on suffering.

Political speech nevertheless emerges in the social context of shamanic performances in which both men and women participate—in the speech of wild, unsocialized spirits during cleansing rituals. Sex-crazed or drunk spirits engaging in ritualized comic dialogue *(daha ata pāliya)* in the early hours of the morning just before sunrise (see Kapferer 1983: 285–319; Obeyesekere 1969) often try to seduce the drummers, insult or attack them, and use political vocabulary and jokes. I quote the spirit Kenti Pāliya (S), on this occasion dressed in a Western man's suit jacket, in conversation with the drummer (D):[30]

> *S:* Oh, shit, the words are not coming out properly. The wind is escaping from between my teeth. . . . No fellow, something has happened to my whole face!
>
> *D:* What? What?
>
> *S:* Here, there is a spot/penis coming up here [play on the words *kurullo* (penis) and *kurullä* (spot)].
>
> *D:* No, a spot, a spot!
>
> *S:* Look!
>
> *D:* That is why your face is so swollen. You were getting a spot.
>
> *S:* Oh Buddha/father, what a large penis I have.
>
> *D:* Come on, how can a filthy old fellow become spotty?
>
> *S:* Why [not]?
>
> *D:* How can you get spots? [Implying he is too old for that.]
>
> *S:* Filthy old men, is it not good for old men to get a penis?
>
> *D:* A penis?
>
> *S:* So?
>
> *D:* No, you don't get spots.
>
> *S:* Don't I get them?
>
> *D:* No, it's us [the young ones] who are getting spots.
>
> *S:* Why is that?

D: We have a lot of oil! [*telē tiyanō:* to have oil in your body or skin, meaning to be flirtatious, to chase girls.]

S: Right! You [disrespectful pronoun] look at this. What is the color of the branch of the coconut tree?

D: Green [the color of the United National Party].[31]

S: No! Those on the edge, at the end of the branch.

D: Ah, those are young coconut branches no?

S: Yes!

D: Those are white. [Laughter]

S: Which ones have the most oil, old or young coconuts?

D: Now that is a question.

S: No, no. Which one has more oil?

D: It might be in the old coconut.

S: Look, look, now you have been insulted! Let's sing another song. Coffee shop—I am cutting bread. . . . I am pissing. . . .

(December 20, 1997, approx. 5:00 A.M.,
lower Hendolakana, Udahenagama)

Sexual innuendo and satire suddenly turn into a political joke. The fact that political language is a standard ingredient of such ritualized comic dialogues implicitly confirms women's perspective on political speech. Wild unsocialized spirits, who represent the antithesis of proper Sinhala Buddhist behavior, feel and act like ardent lovers and speak about political parties. Both men and women attend such performances and enjoy the vulgar jokes and bad behavior of the spirits.

In everyday life, though, even if prompted, women in Udahenagama were not keen to engage in political discourse. They would inform me matter-of-factly which households were "green" (pro–United National Party [UNP]) or "blue" (pro–Sri Lanka Freedom Party [SLFP]), but political vocabulary did not appear in everyday gossip among women or feature in discourses on political violence and the effects of the civil war. Instead women used traditional idioms of moral discomfort such as possession by spirits, sorcery, and the discourse on *dosa*.

There is one exception, though. Women used the personal names of politicians in the village (e.g., young supporters of the People's Alliance, 1994–2001) and eagerly gossiped about specific incidents involving young local politicians.[32] This discursive style however differs from traditional

Figure 11.
Women
watching the
comedy of the
eighteen Sanni
demons *(daha
ata pāliya).*
Author's photo.

women's discourses. Usually, women avoid the use of personal names (Argenti-Pillen 2003: 117–21), and the careless use of a personal name expresses a lack of respect. Many young politicians in the village are controversial figures.[33] Elders argue that, unlike they did at the age of nineteen, youngsters who grew up during the civil war do not enter "society" *(samādjaya)* but become "rowdies" *(rastiyādu pätte vätilā).* Elders, still shocked by war crimes committed by local youths during the civil war, thereby effectively challenge the youngsters' membership in Sinhala Buddhist society. Women, by addressing certain youths and politicians by their personal names, exclude them from the morality of the household in which the avoidance of personal names is a rule of respect. The way in which rural women have adopted some of the discursive strategies of political discourse—gossip about politicians—thereby reveals how they distinguish their social world[34] from the world of young party activists in the village.[35]

Party moral leadership, as well as party formation at the village level, contains contradictions that resemble aspects of shamanic ideology. Shamans belong to a caste of low social status and operate through wide, loose networks of affiliated people. This is comparable to the low status of young local politicians as well as the diffuse nature of party networks. Meetings of village-level organizations do not occur regularly, and there are quite a number of organizations that exist largely on paper.[36] Within this organizational culture one can see the blueprint of both kin-based and patronage-style forms of social organization. The cultural component reminiscent of shamanic ideology consists of social fragmentation as well as reference to low-status outsiders who operate at the fringes of the moral framework of respectable members of Sinhala Buddhist society. It is this organizational culture that is sustained and reinforced by women's subculture, in which suffering in the aftermath of the civil war is conceptualized as *dosa* and a fragmented geography of moral discomfort precludes the establishment in Udahenagama of centralized women's associations.

Conclusion: No Plaza de Mayo [37]

The work of urban-based peace movements and national mental health NGOs is made difficult at the grassroots level by the lack of ties between families who lost family members during the civil war.[38] Contrary to what Euro-Americans might expect, there is no public outcry among women in Udahenagama about the atrocities committed by counterinsurgency forces. Women's accusations are based on very specific incidents—who killed whom where and for what reason—and women's postwar identities are built around such highly individualized accounts. Moreover, the long-term effects of the civil war are discussed using a vocabulary imbued with shamanic ideology.

The discourse on *dosa* permeates everyday conversations and consciousness about the moral economy of households.[39] As such, it denotes an awareness of the potentially sickening effects of conflict—a moral discomfort that increases vulnerability to possession by spirits. In its translation as both humoral imbalance and trouble *dosa* denotes women's preoccupation with their well-being in a sometimes sickening social and political world. I highlight the fact that *dosa* is not an individualized moral consciousness or a bodily emotional state but is essentially transferable. The trajectory of *dosa* as it leaves a kin-based social group via streams and rivers evokes strong spatial metaphòrs,[40] reflecting an ancient water cosmology but more importantly a fragmented geography of moral discomfort.[41]

This study focuses on a key idiom of morality employed by women working as casual laborers on the tea plantations at the margins of Sri Lankan society. If asked to look for Habermasian parameters to convey my informants' participation in civil society's public sphere,[42] I would begin my search by focusing on the constant murmur about *dosa* pervading Udahenagama neighborhoods. As moral consciousness is the point of origin for the emergence of public opinion and the public sphere in the West, I view *dosa* as women's kinbased *moral consciousness* (see also Baker 1990; Koselleck [1959] 1988; Landes 1988). This moral discourse has an experiential depth beyond male-dominated prestige or reputation systems or the moral parameters of orthodox or state-sponsored Buddhism.[43] *Dosa* concerns family strife, mourning, relations with ancestral spirits, poverty, hunger, and aloneness and is used frequently to refer to war-related suffering. *Dosa*-based moral consciousness has a very different character from "opinion" or the secularized morality of liberal citizens (Habermas 1991: 91; see also Poovey 2002). What is most relevant in my analysis is not so much its shamanic dimension but the spatial geography associated with the experience and expulsion of *dosa*. While the cultural construction of a public sphere is based on an ever-expanding horizon based on stranger sociability (Warner 2002: 56–57), *dosa* morality engenders social fragmentation.

Shamanic ideology and the discourses on violence and its effects lead to a distinctly nonbourgeois associational culture (see Argenti-Pillen 2003: 151–52). It is village women rather than men who are at the heart of such contested cultural processes that reveal aspects of a nonmodern organizational system. This shamanic ideology exists side by side with the image of community politics projected onto such communities by elites and the state (e.g., village headmen, party factions, insurgents). This image of community politics projected by the state onto rural slums is shattered at moments when women occupy the center of the discursive sphere.[44] This sphere at the margins is produced through gossip, illness narratives, organization of ritual cleansing, and discourse on *dosa*.[45]

Critics of traditional forms of postwar community rehabilitation would remark that such survival strategies increase the social fragmentation of the community and lead to the isolation of the most vulnerable families.[46] Urban-based mental health NGOs are faced with fragmented groups that do not operate along the predictable lines of a bourgeois public sphere and social movements.[47] While marginal rural women certainly do not facilitate the work of national rehabilitation NGOs, they nevertheless protect their communities from the worst excesses of modern, neocolonial state formation: political polarization (UNP-SLFP), electoral violence, and counterinsurgency violence. Marginal, fragmented communities do not provide a ready-made social arena organized along the lines of modernist categories (pro-SLFP, pro-UNP, pro-JVP, pro-army, deserter) that can be galvanized through political propaganda or used for identification during counterinsurgency operations (e.g., concealed apprehension technique, or CAT commandos; see also Sluka 2000).[48]

During the civil war of the late 1980s, women and children in Udahenagama were threatened but not killed and men were killed or denounced to counterinsurgency commandos only when they had been involved in very specific, individual incidents or enmities (see Argenti-Pillen 2003). Local people from Udahenagama did not eliminate people solely on the basis of their categorical identities such as membership in a certain political party or wartime faction.[49] Rural women's idiosyncratic relationship to urban-based social movements as well as their disrespect for political discourses protect their communities from a modernist cycle of violence in which people become targets merely because of the categories in which they have been placed. In the rural slums of southern Sri Lanka social fragmentation therefore provides a form of protection against modernist state violence. It could therefore be said that if mothers of the disappeared were better "organized" in a Western bourgeois sense and adopt a distinct group identity, the community's vulnerability to an escalation of violence would increase.

Women's moral consciousness—awareness of the ever present possibility of *dosa*—grounds them firmly in a household morality, even when they are involved in a search for the disappeared in the modernizing public sphere.[50] While the veil in Islamic societies offers women a way to express their adherence to a kin-based morality, Sinhala Buddhist women's household-based moral consciousness *(dosa)* is invisible and constitutes an invisible contestation of the forms of sociability imagined by state-building elites. The fragmented geography of moral discomfort is perhaps only acknowledged by humanitarian elites as "marginality," "lack of education," "superstition, and "need for empowerment." Marginal women's moral engagement and the social fragmentation they support become more palpable as mental health NGOs and trauma counseling services find it difficult to get a foothold in marginal communities.[51] The image of a "contested state" emerges when *dosa*-related moralities are seen not only as a cultural barrier against stranger solidarity promoted by trauma NGOs but also as protecting marginal communities against possible state-led counterinsurgency strategies in the future.[52]

An understanding of the effects of the civil war on the basis of *dosa* challenges the notion of a deepening of democracy (e.g., Alvarez 1992; Appadurai 2002)[53] and "transnational governmentality" (see Ferguson and Gupta 2002) in the format of trauma counseling programs in war zones. As part of this "democratic" package, women at the margins in Udahenagama are invited to convert moral consciousness into opinion,[54] join a violent and polarized civil society,[55] enjoy stranger sociability, and participate as liberal citizens in a petty bourgeois public sphere. Such conversion would require an *in-depth* cultural modification of the present shamanic ideology of *dosa* and of the fragmented moral geography of suffering. Women in Udahenagama should not be seen as retreating into a remote shamanic past or as prey to an essentialized transhistorical consciousness but as successfully maintaining the fabric of their communities in the aftermath of devastating state violence. In view of the excesses of democratic politics in Sri Lanka, the question is not so much how civil society[56] can include mothers and wives of the disappeared—how democracy might be extended—but how marginal women's moral consciousness, disrespect for party politics, and celebration of social fragmentation might inform the postdemocracy period. A key defining element of postdemocracy would be the *absence* of proselytization of the notion of public opinion, as well as strategies to convert women's kin-based moral consciousness into opinion, or household moralities into categorical identities. Only in the aftermath of devastating insurgency, counterinsurgency, interethnic and electoral violence, and a consideration of Sinhalese women's role in the maintenance of civilizational moral values, does this culture-specific image of postdemocracy emerge.

NOTES

1. These include troubles caused by ancestral spirits *(prēta dosa)*, wild spirits *(yaksha dosa)*, evil eye or evil mouth *(äsvaha* and *katavaha dosa*, or *vas dosa)*, deities *(deiyanne dosa)*, and planetary influences *(graha dosa)* (Obeyesekere 1976: 206). Another category of *dosa* often used in everyday discourse is *tanikam dosa*, "the trouble caused by being alone."

2. The ritual techniques *äduro* use to cure affliction by spirits were a subdiscipline of Ayurvedic medicine in antiquity (Obeyesekere 1976: 205) but are now practiced exclusively by shamanic healers or ritual specialists. One ritual healer I worked with attempted to bridge this historical gap or appropriate the concept of *dosa* by asserting that the *dosa* belongs to Vessamuni, king of the wild spirits *(yaksha)*.

3. There are various translations and understandings of *dosa* in the ethnographic literature. Wirz (1954) translates *dosa* as "illness," "pain" (10), "lack of success," "disaster" (178). Basham (1976: 22) says the literal translation of *dosa* is "defect." According to Kapferer, it is illness caused by humoral imbalance (1983: 71) or as "faults" (1997: 353). Scott (1994: 280) translates *dosa* as "misfortune, troubles, ill effects."

4. This area consists of five loosely structured neighborhoods that I will call Hendolakanda, Galkanda, Beragama, Puvakdeniya, and Kalubowatta. The total population of the area was three thousand, according to the 1993 census (Resource Survey of the Integrated Rural Development Project of the Southern Provincial Council). Residents belong to the cultivators' caste, the jaggery makers' caste, or the drummers' caste.

5. In 1998 these included Association for Health and Counseling, Center for Family Services, Communication Center for Mental Health, Family Planning Association, Family Rehabilitation Center, Family Studies and Services Institute, Institute of Human Rights, Life, Muslim Women's Conference, National Council of YMCAs of Sri Lanka, National Christian Counsel Counseling Center, NEST, Sahan Sevana Psycho Therapy Center, Salvation Army, Family Counseling Center Sarvodaya Movement, Survivors Associated, Tamil Women's Union, Women's Development Center, Women for Peace, Women in Need, Young Women's Christian Organization, National Council for Mental Health Sahanaya, Sri Lanka Sumithrayo (Branch of Befrienders International), Alokaya Youth Counseling Center, SEDEC Relief and Rehabilitation, and Sri Lanka National Association of Counselors. All of these organizations are members of the Federation of NGOs on Mental Health and Well-Being.

6. In the Udahenagama area a total of twenty-two women had been in contact with the mental health NGO I studied. I was given their addresses at the outreach center of a national NGO and interviewed them during the later stages of my fieldwork, when my identity as an independent anthropologist had been firmly established in the village.

7. Also see Argenti-Pillen 2003: chap. 7. Two additional aspects need to be considered. First, the Sri Lankan state has acquiesced to the burgeoning development of trauma counseling and mental health NGOs but has not been open to human rights movements. In this sense mental health NGOs are not completely independent of the state sector. Second, the state's relationship with poverty-stricken rural women has been mediated by their status as a resource for sending sons to the Sri Lankan national army to fight Tamil separatists in the north and east.

8. Here I am very much indebted to Mosse's (2003) ethnography, which argues that the idea of the state needs to be released from its colonial representations and that we should pay attention to the multiple modes in which the state is experienced locally (23).

9. Here I follow the identity-centered focus of new social movement approaches (Escobar and Alvarez 1992: 5). Escobar and Alvarez (1992: 10) argue that cultural factors have

been given little theoretical attention compared to economic and political forms of social movement analysis. This question concerns the cultural makeup of social movements—"how people can be brought together in a group" and a collective identity can be constructed (11). This chapter precisely concerns the cultural elements that inhibit such group formation among the relatives of the disappeared in Udahenagama.

10. However, I do not deny that this is a fruitful entry point for the study of women's groups (see Beck 2003; Tripp 2001).

11. As Mercier (1993: 70) points out, exorcisms not only exorcise the spirit but also transfer the illness from one body to another, from the body of the sick person to a sacrificial substitute. He thereby argues that there is an efficacy of transfer of illness even before the sacrificial substitute is consumed by the spirits (71). This is the process I refer to when I talk about *dosa* as a transferable moral essence.

12. It is clear that *dosa* and *distiya* (the gaze of spirits possessing a patient) are removed at different ritual moments and with different techniques. Ritual specialists had different ideas about this distinction, but most agreed that to remove the *distiya* one needs large offering trays, limes, or vines.

13. This ritual segment occurs during large-scale cleansing rituals that last up to thirty hours *(tovil)* but also features in small-scale cleansing rites, which take place more often (*pidenna* or *gurukam; ädurukam* in general).

14. Obeseyesekere (1984: 108) translates *ākarshana* as "magnetism." This term is also used to describe the shaman's trance when infused with the essence of the deity *(distiya)* (14); a shaman's power to attract this essence is *ākarshana balaya,* "the power of divine magnetism" (18). The notion of *ākarshana* was also used in ancient Sanskrit grammar (see Renou 1941–42). Many grammatical terms derived from ritual practice (Renou 1941–42: 143). Renou defines *ākarshana* as a word's capacity to attract meaning from a preceding sentence (e.g., referential pronouns such as *this* or *that* acquiring their meaning from preceding statements) (125). In this sense *ākarshana* represents less of a material force than a transfer of meaning. Hence I conceive of *dosa* not so much as a moral substance but as a set of moral meanings or essences that can be relocated through the transfer *(ākarshana)* of shamanic practice.

15. Interestingly, the same popular discourse exists regarding fear *(baya),* which at times is conceptualized as a removable essence, which shamans extract by startling the afflicted (see Argenti-Pillen 2003: 165). One ritual specialist argued that humoral imbalance *(dosa)* actually feels like fear. I postulate that in the lay cultural understanding fear and *dosa* partially overlap or are understood by means of the same experiential mechanisms. Both can be extracted and transferred, and they both make the person vulnerable to attack by wild unsocialized spirits.

16. Women who suffer from social isolation or political victimization often complain that their houses feel dark, that there is a lack of light as well as *dosa* in the house. Another common instance of *dosa* is when people have financial difficulties and do not manage to continue with building. Then they say the house is afflicted by *dosa.*

17. One of the ritual specialists I interviewed was upset about the fact that the current generation buries their *yantra* in glass containers. Glass blocks the power of transfer *(ākarshana)* of the *yantra,* and they thereby fail to attract the *dosa.* According to this ritual specialist, clay containers should be used instead.

18. As well as the *distiya* (gaze of the wild spirits) when sorcery is involved.

19. Similarly, Gibson (1986: 203) questions the effects of a changing political environment on Buid shamanism. Recently Buid society moved away from limited economic interdependence between households to joint landownership, whereby land is considered corporate property of the community and disputes are aired in political meetings. With the emergence of a corporate community, Buid religion has been able to transform itself to take account of a corporate unit larger than the household. Large-scale shamanic séances emerged that parallel political meetings (215). In contrast, Sinhala shamanic ideology continues to promote a household-based, fragmented form of social organization.

20. For a wider consideration of the contemporary precarious position of shamans, see Simpson 1997.

21. Humphrey (1994) defines the history of shamanic discourse in northern Asia in relation to the political phases of state formation; "unsupervised" shamanism (197) occurs during periods of state decline and disintegration, revealing memory traces of previous active discourses (194). She challenges the accepted view that "the Inner Asian states were built up in a context of shamanism. Once a ruling dynasty had been established it introduced and propagated Buddhism. Shamanism was pushed to the margins and interstices. With the collapse of these states, Buddhism retreated, and shamanic practices, which had never entirely disappeared, re-emerged" (195). In Humphrey's perspective shamanism is not merely defined by retreating or expanding shamanic activities but by a more "fluid set of attitudes and practices" permeating a society (195).

22. Here I am indebted to Thomas's (2002) work on the spatial imageries involved in the experience and expression of moral geographies.

23. Most shamans, or *äduro*, belong to the *berava* (drummers') caste, a low-ranking service caste (also see Kapferer 1983: 52–67).

24. On the issue of chaperones, see Argenti-Pillen 2003: 24. Leaving the house without a chaperone puts women at risk of *tanikam dosa,* the fault of being alone.

25. This is the kind of "social imagery" (see definitions in Calhoun 2002; Taylor 2002), "stranger sociability" (see Warner 2002), and solidarity promoted by national mental health NGOs training "befrienders" to approach members of vulnerable households.

26. Fifteen percent of the households in Udahenagama are single headed (according to the Resource Survey of the Integrated Rural Development Project, Southern Provincial Council, June 1993). Meeting other families of the disappeared and learning to understand war-related suffering as "trauma" in the context of mental health NGO meetings is intended to create friendships and a sense of belonging based on specific wartime memories and the secular morality of "traumatization."

27. Also see Houtzager and Kurtz's (2000: 396) analysis of the critical dimensions of collective action and popular mobilization, one of the criteria of which is "bases for group solidarity and identity formation." What is clear is that in Udahenagama memories of the civil war are not a basis for solidarity among families of the disappeared, and a "community of memories"—a distinct group based on joint memories (cf. Weber 1978: 903)—did not emerge.

28. For a discussion of drinking groups as an increasingly influential axis of power over the past twenty years, see Gamburd 1995: 11.

29. Spencer (1990: 184, 170) makes similar observations. He relates that people attending political meetings take a few drinks to justify shouting during meetings and that "electoral politics represent both the most concentrated and the most pervasive moments of licence and ridicule in contemporary Sinhala life."

30. The system of transliteration used to write down this colloquial Sinhalese is inspired by Gombrich (1971: xiii–xiv). However, to avoid difficulties in typesetting, I have not distinguished retroflex, dental, palatal, or nasalized pronunciations.

31. This party was in the opposition to the People's Alliance government of President Chandrika Kumaratunga at the time of my field research (1996–98).

32. In view of the fact that there are few ideological differences between the major political parties (both at the national and local levels), it is perhaps not surprising that women focus on specific incidents in the personal lives of local politicians (see also Spencer 1990: 210).

33. This is true not only at the local level but also in a certain sense within national politics. Gamage and Hettige (1997: 144) argue that in the past parliamentary candidates were well-to-do professionals or propertied people, but "today the vast majority are lower middle class. Most have achieved a high standard of living only after becoming *professional politicians*. . . . [T]his is the main reason why many politicians resort to corrupt practices and accumulate wealth while they are in power" (my emphasis). It is the image of the antisocial behavior of such "professional politicians" that emerges today in the ritual comedy described above.

34. This is not unique to the practices of women in Udahenagama. Hirschmann's (1998) study of nonelite associational life among poor women in South Africa and its relation to state-focused definitions of civil society concludes, "probably their preference would be to stay clear of what they see as politics" (236).

35. This brings to mind Weber's (1978: 938) depiction of modern political domination through parties: "Their means of attaining power may be quite varied, ranging from naked violence of any sort to canvassing for votes with coarse and subtle means: money, social influence, the force of speech, suggestion, clumsy hoax, and so on to the rougher."

36. Interviews with headmen in the Udahenagama area revealed the remarkable absence of *flourishing* grassroots political/social organizations. About fifteen organizations had been established in Udahenagama, but they convened sporadically. The organizations that were most active were the Funeral Aid Societies, organized at the level of neighborhood or hamlet, rather than village level.

37. I evoke here the cultural context of grassroots women's movements of relatives of the disappeared in Latin America, exemplified by the Mothers of the Plaza de Mayo in Argentina (e.g., Schirmer 1994). Stephen (1995) describes the involvement of rural women in a social movement of the relatives of the disappeared in El Salvador (CO-MADRES), as well as ties with other rural or peasant social movements (815). However, she comments on the changing history of merging *household religion* with civic government, as the institution of ritual kinship *(compadrazgo)* serves as a basis to extend family ties within and between communities for political and other ends (822). What I argue here is that "household religion," which governs women's suffering related to disappearances and war in Udahenagama, does not lend itself particularly well to establishing ties among families of the disappeared.

38. Compare this with the very different grassroots associational cultural context discussed in Scarpaci 1991. His work discusses how NGO-led shantytown health care in Argentina, Uruguay, and Chile emerged as a new autonomous social movement that avoided co-optation by political parties and the state's stigmatized public health system. The described forms of collective action emerge, however, from neighborhood-based activities in urban contexts (121).

39. As such the discourse on *dosa* is an important component of Scott's (1976) "moral conscience" in small-scale peasant communities.

40. These include a conceptualization of rivers and crossroads as a locus for spirits (*yaksha*), as well as a place for humans to make offerings to the spirits. However, a consideration of the transfer of *dosa* onto such offerings adds a dimension to these spatial metaphors and conceptualizes crossroads and rivers as routes of transfer and outer boundaries for moral segments of neighborhoods.

41. Taylor's (2002: 108) discussion of modern and nonmodern social imageries mentions that the implicit map of social space can have deep fissures, "which are profoundly anchored in culture and imagery, beyond the reach of correction" by theory. He furthermore asserts, "The public sphere is a central feature of modern society. . . . What is this common space? It's actually a rather strange thing" (112).

42. Habermas (1991) celebrates the key moment in European political history when conscience and consciousness became *opinion*. Guided by the experience of the religious civil war, Hobbes's *Leviathan* (1651) projected a state authority neutralized in religious matters, based on public opinion, rather than religious conscience (Habermas 1991: 90).

For a wider consideration of the possibilities of cultural assimilation of the notion of a public sphere, see Abedi and Fischer 1993; Beck 2003; Graham 1993; Hui and Fischer 1994; Sivaramakrishnan 2000; Uribe-Uran 2000.

43. Herein I include women's supplications and offerings to the deities (e.g., *bodhi puja*) to receive help finding disappeared relatives or to take revenge.

44. This echoes Brow's (1988, 1996) work on alternative moralities. He asserts that "the dominant ideology has not colonized the whole terrain on which villagers construct their understanding of authority and justice" (1988: 322).

45. This follows Harcourt and Escobar's (2002) focus on women's place-based politics and their role in "shifting cultural codes" (11).

46. Also see Jean-Klein's (2003) comments on the trend in Western social science to treat social fragmentation in a derogatory manner as the outside observer can see no obvious pragmatic reasons for "a system's disposition toward apparently uncontrolled and pointless fragmentation" (568).

De Mel's (2002) data on Tamil women's recruitment by the LTTE adds another dimension to the issue of the fragmentation and isolation of the afflicted. Although she is writing about a different Sri Lankan cultural context, she nevertheless comments that "communities are reluctant to come forward to help the bereaved" (103). This makes women vulnerable to LTTE recruitment strategies.

47. This is an aspect that would fall under the notion "endogenous community imperfection" used in the development literature (see Platteau and Abraham 2002).

48. In fact, a higher proportion of wives and mothers of the disappeared belong to marginal communities since insurgency and counterinsurgency operations were most

concentrated in marginal areas, near district and divisional boundaries (see Argenti-Pillen 2003: 81–82).

49. For a discussion of categorical identities and indirect social relations as an essential attribute of "the infrastructure of modernity," see Calhoun 2002: 161–62.

50. Jean-Klein's (2003: 562) notion of "housescape" lends itself well to qualifying the moral space Udahenagama women inhabit when venturing into the national arena. For a further discussion of this "private-public" dynamic and the effect of war on such competing social formations, see Joseph 1991, 1997. Her analysis of the relationship among women, families, religion, and states in Iraq and Lebanon questions the impact of war on competing social imaginaries (1991: 196). In Ba'thist Iraq, women were an important tool for state construction. Freed from their family networks and socialized into loyalty vis-à-vis the party and the state, they became socialized into the worldview of the state leadership (1991: 179–81). However, "the Ba'th may have been working against themselves" as war and economic instability forced certain sections of the population back into their families (1991: 187).

51. Here I bear in mind Jean-Klein's (2000: 122) assertion, "Statism and kinship are not principally conflicting, mutually displacing processes and sets of practices. . . . [h]owever, historically specific statist movements connect more productively with *some* familial relationships than with others" (original emphasis). I do not want to reduce *dosa*-based moral consciousness to kinship morality but would like to expand Jean-Klein's thesis to include the relationship between specific state-building efforts and prevalent shamanic ideologies, as remnants of interactions with earlier forms of centralized power.

52. The criteria I use for this evaluation conform to Starn's (1992: 108) call for "a new appreciation of the politics of the possible," where success is not merely evaluated in relation to the "grand standards of modernization theory or orthodox Marxism."

53. Appadurai (2002: 38), for example, qualifies this deepening of democracy through "guerrilla exercises in capturing civic space and the areas of the public sphere hitherto denied" to marginal groups. This however presumes that subordinate groups have an elementary understanding of the concept of the public sphere.

54. I consider the conversion from moral consciousness based on household religion to opinion one of the key cultural roles played by the global trauma counseling movement. Inspired by Escobar's (1992) work, I conceive of trauma counseling not only as psychological comfort for the traumatized but also as part of a "Western cultural-political technology" (66) to challenge tradition, restructure war-torn societies, and facilitate inclusion of marginalized communities into a bourgeois public sphere.

55. Here I follow Hirschmann's (1998: 235) critique of male-centric positive political assessments of civil society failing to confront violence as a fundamental aspect of civil society.

56. This question is often framed as a quest to expand our notion of civil society to include women from nondominant sectors or nonelite associational life (e.g., Hirschmann 1998; Tripp 1998; Werbner 1999).

7

The Other Body and the Body Politic

Contingency and Dissonance in Narratives of Violence

MANGALIKA DE SILVA

This chapter delineates historically specific practices of violence in everyday life in Sri Lanka. These practices are socially and culturally constituted. They are contingently produced and reproduced in multiple regimes of power. In paying particular attention to marginal and subjugated phenomena, that is, the microphysics[1] of violence or the microtechnologies of subjectivization, I want to make visible specific modalities of power that enunciate gendered relations, identifications, and subjectivities. For a critique of state and community practices to emerge, it is necessary to capture the minute, local articulations of intimate knowledge of politically marginalized subjects, histories, and social locations. Unveiling specific forms of discrete and naturalized violence produced under the sign of the political will provide an understanding of how authoritative state practices or the ideological state apparatuses might be implicated in the production and perpetuation of gender power and violence.

By "gender power," I mean the production of masculinities and femininities, bodies, subjectivities, and selves inflected by other power axes such as class, ethnicity, and religion. I argue that the very paradoxical doubleness of being a subject and being subject to relations of power of hierarchy, hegemony, and inequality is a coercive product of the coincidence of the dominant sociality and morality of the nation and authority of the state. I suggest that such violence has its own genealogy and epistemology. The political and historical conditions that enable different practices of violence are central to the constitution of the subject and construction of identities. Such conditions are also historical contexts in which political contestations aspire for dominance where the struggle for community is located. My contention, however, is that both the community and the state collude in organizing regimes of order and constituents of power.

A variety of submerged and (un)conscious political motivations come into play in quotidian formations of violence. In writing "uncelebratory" and "unedifying" accounts of violence, I am also concerned with the semiotic and the performative, elements that produce the startling effects of a public spectacle. Such signifying features of hierarchical practice have the capacity to bewilder and are produced in the interstices of local micropolitics. In certain social configurations, violence as spectacle is conferred legitimacy, authority, prestige, and power. In everyday hierarchical negotiations, violence is deployed under the sign of a contested politics, "nationalist," "communal," "fundamentalist," acquiring discursive authority and hegemony.

Sinhalaness, Muslimness, or Tamilness, enmeshed as each is in intersecting fields of structure and meaning, is constitutive of and constituted by the field of hegemonic nationalisms. Violence justified ideologically in the name of politics structures social relations and colonizes social space, enabling conditions of its possibility/impossibility. Violence in the name of politics, albeit of a hegemonic kind, is implicated in practices that seek to ghettoize and depoliticize subaltern forms of counterprotest and resistance. Violent practice produces oppositional and binary bodies, heroic and aggressive, criminal and communal, which are hierarchized and celebrated, minoritized and humiliated.

Through a reading of the Sinhala cultural practice of *lajja-baya,* glossed by Gananath Obeyesekere (1984) as "shame-fear," I wish to explore how different communities at various historical junctures advance their hegemonic politics and struggle for community, producing and reproducing relations of inequality and hierarchy. In so doing, I want to interrogate the minute, contingent ways in which the Sinhala cultural idiom of power, *lajja-baya,* is projected to the other/marginalized/minoritized community, producing subjects bearing a radical otherness. A critical site, which continues to be conquered and colonized in struggles of community, is the female body, the naturalized, gendered body of modernity. Given the physics of (gender) power in the archaeology of the nation where the prostitute/whore is differentiated and excluded from the virgin/mother only to be silenced by erasure, the prostitute occupies a position of disruptiveness, shame, and anarchy in the moral social order of the dominant national imaginary. Hence the Sinhala nation's ignominious stripping of Sriyalatha.

Body as Shield, Battlefield, and Territory

Twenty-nine-year-old Manchanayaka Appuhamilage Sriyalatha, widow, single mother, and sex worker, was strip-searched by ministerial security division (MSD) officers on March 19, 2000, after they observed her ostensibly suspicious movement, covert mobility, dressed in a *shalwar khameez*—"a dress many female suicide bombers wore" (*Sunday Times,* March 19, 2000)—in a high security zone (HSZ) in Colombo, that isolated, closed-off territory, the den of security for the rich and powerful, nationally, commercially, and socially, linked to local, global, and transnational domains of capital. The security men stripped Sriyalatha at gunpoint, fearing she could be a potential suicide bomber, the disgruntled subject of modernity committed to undoing, unmaking the (modern) project of the (Sinhala) nation. "With guns pointed at me from a distance," she told the *Times,* "they ordered me to raise my blouse. Similarly they asked me to take off my undergarments. They simply stared at me while I stood seminaked on the street." The strip searches served to strip the veil of feminine modesty, disciplinary femininity, keeping loose, defiant, stubborn women in their "rightful" place, the place of the hearth, the ideological means by which (gender) power is produced and sustained in patriarchal cultures of shame. But more important, the act of stripping unveiled the postcolonial state's war of sexual terror and violence waged against its female "citizens."

The military high command and the air force were then alerted to avert a national security threat, real, alleged, or imagined, by launching a "preemptive strike" on the alleged suicide bomber, since each suicide mission is aimed at deconstructing the legitimacy of the postcolonial Sinhala state—its authority, political agency, and sovereignty. In the aporia of (ethnic) enmity and conflict, the ideological state enacted a series of institutional arrangements to prevent "disorder," preserve "order," and prescribe disciplinary and surveillance strategies. These institutional mechanisms were primarily aimed at symbolizing or forestalling risk and harm to the nation, to institutions of the state, the consequences of which on the Sri Lankan socius are incalculable.

But the Sri Lankan everyday is a space/place of instabilities, reversals, possibilities, and accidents where the imperceptible is missed and fails to be objectified (Feldman 1995). The extraordinary military logistics being read-ied to preempt one woman's deadly suicide attack on the capital city lent cre-dence to the presence of actual female terror in a "forbidden" zone. In the military scheme of things, a woman had turned herself into a mobile war machine, timing her final blow-up moment, the hidden female agency lurk-ing in the body politic. To the men's utter horror, that moment of collective annihilation—the woman's body devouring and engulfing the (Sinhala) na-tion and blown to smithereens—did not seem to materialize. Worse, Sriya-latha failed to comply with military protocol and discipline (that of individu-alized surveillance and normalization) by not putting her hands up and by not producing her national identification card (NIC). Her refusal to raise her hands and submit to military commands heightened doubt and terror. Female terror threatening other bodies (the social body of the Sinhalas), the military men threatened to shoot her. She screamed, *"Mata veditiyanna epa, mata lamayek innawa"* (Don't shoot me, I have a child). The "I" is a fragmented and shifting one. Sriyalatha refused to identify, declined to name, and *resisted* being authorized. Her interiority was one of indifference, indifference to the men whose mark of presence is asserted in terms of opposition, itself a differ-ence, opposition to difference marked by her presence. In the dialectics of veiling and unveiling of "danger," her body is mapped and resignified as a battlefield, a policed zone, and a site of dread, danger, and terror, a space of "duplicitous surface and structural subversion." Sriyalatha, the constitutive outside of the sovereign national (secure) body, the "safe" body (the Sinhala body politic) versus the "unsafe" (pornographic) body that refuses to abjure risk. Sriyalatha represents a site of originality, circulating risk and threat. The differential effects of the body produced through such uneven positing un-mask the excess of state power. And yet in the enunciation of defiance could be seen a site of "ambivalent agency." Still, the language of her refusal assimi-lates the very terms of sovereignty, the gender norms of maternity and her fa-milial attachments.

Literacy, communicability, and decipherability are forms of symbolic and cultural capital. Language, like memory, is part of the power of conscious-ness (Derrida 2001). They form part of the markers of an individual's cul-tural makeup, the tropes of community. They constitute rationalities inform-ing practices of governmentality, that imperative to govern political subjects, the exercise of political sovereignty by the state over subjects, that cut across and intersect the fields of discursivity/nondiscursivity and impinge on how a subject gets constructed and excluded/included in the community and nation. The moment of violence captures poignantly her linguistic vulnerability and injury in the historical context of ethnic prejudice and criminal impunity of the Sri Lankan state. Judith Butler (1997) usefully reminds us how the power of language to injure stems from its "interpellative" power and how linguistic agency enables vulnerability. Sriyalatha blurs all distinctions of identification, thereby not enabling pigeonholing. Her identity confuses, shifts, and dissolves. She seems out of the depths, endless and unfathomable. She engulfs and enveils any essentiality, identity, and properness. The hegemonic nationalist militarist discourse invoked by the patriotic sons of the nation of the Sinhala state sought to "crack open" her ethnicity, her ethnically symbolized body overdetermined as Tamil, yet not determinable.

Sriyalatha had gone to Union Place to meet a client. In this very localized, globalized urbanity and postcoloniality, intimacy, be it social or sexual, comes into conflict with ideologies of sovereignty. With no sign of her client, she began to stroll down Jinarathana Road. Sriyalatha was unaware of the new urban militarized zones, geographies and maps ethnic antagonisms had produced. These ethnically informed zones and landscapes are themselves the conditions of possibility of specific minor and major wars of purification, cleansing, and defilement. For Sinhala men, bearers of "national security," burdened by the national(ist) angst to defend the motherland, the land of the Sinhalas, Sriyalatha embodied the actual terror of a suicide bomber, a dominant representation of the Tamil woman in the Sri Lankan sociality. Terror-inducing space represents risk, danger, and violation. Her intrusion into public space is construed as "contagious" and "offensive" conduct. Nation is inviolable. Spatial forms of authority and hierarchy are embedded in notions of "purity," "sacrality," and "sovereignty." But as a woman, a discrete margin, and as a subject constituting herself in history, not as an abstract fantasy, Sriyalatha was vulnerable to being objectified, sexualized, and shamed, heightened by her inability to establish her "ethnic identity," her mark of ethnicity signifying the undecidable mark. Her experiential angst was being mediated and challenged through specific means. In honor/shame cultures, male honor resides in the sexual probity of women. A woman without shame dishonors men, the nation.

As potentially and speculatively Tamil, she inhabits a space of immanent death and destruction. Impervious to the ambiguities of identity, she unconsciously, indignantly transgresses and subverts the divide between permeable/impermeable by stepping into Colombo's HSZ. It is a division that separates life from death, an enclosed space of anticipated, feared if not actual violence, a constricted place, a circumscribed space where one's ethnicity, Tamilness, is a singular determinant of conditions of possibility/impossibility. The zone, then, is a space of death where life is reduced to an abstraction or effacement of difference; social, sexual, political, and economic forms of the differentiation of subjects. Military imperatives override social and sexual integrity, bodily dignity.

The ritualized humiliation of Sriyalatha enables a hegemonic moment to inflict a collective sense of humiliation on women, the other. Her mistaken identity of Tamilness is an effect of power induced by ethnic and cultural stereotypes; her dark complexion and the specific dress she wore are produced as indigenized ethnic symbols of Tamil women. The ontological argument is implicitly made here predicated on a cultural essentialism and scientific classification of individuals: all Tamil women are dark skinned and wear *shalwar khameez*. Bundled into a military jeep, Sriyalatha was whisked away to the Slave Island police where she was incarcerated and interrogated for several days. During interrogation, she was repeatedly, summarily assaulted for her singular "failure" to convincingly respond to queries of the military high command. In the local policing of economic, racial, and class margins, the deviant (othered) body further adds to localized insecurity. The discourse of national(ist) security is invariably structured by the logic of exclusionary practices, the need to identify and define who belongs and where. The promises of modernity had granted women like Sriyalatha a different weight and resonance. By unknowingly daring to trespass on territory of exclusivity and luxury preserved and secured for Colombo's political elite, she inverted power relations. Authority is collectively made when bodies simulate power, remaking meaning.

Sriyalatha is originally from the remote farming village of Thelambiyawa off Kurunegala in the northwestern province of Sri Lanka. Married to a soldier but without a marriage certificate, she could not claim the wages of her deceased partner because she lacked "substantial proof." The dominant sexual morality that prescribes and inscribes Sinhala women posits them in the rigid binary wife/whore. In the operation of this dualism premised on sexual hierarchy in the semiotics of the nation space, Sriyalatha could not establish her identity claims as wife; neither could she claim to be a mother. Her status of being a widow is a disabling possibility, a negative normativity for women who carry the stigma of being seen as "inauspicious" and "unlucky," yet have the potential to disrupt the symbolic order given the field of "unregulated sexuality" they inhabit. Her *ressentiment* is an index, not just of the failure of the nation, but of its criminal complicity with the physics of power. An ordinary soldier's death might have enabled certain claims, but not in Sriyalatha's case. A widow's claim to entitlement is founded on a juridical notion of matrimony endorsed by the benevolent patriarchal state. A privileged widow, of a major general or brigadier, is a recipient of military glamour valorized by the state.

Positioned and posited by her class, gender, and location, Sriyalatha is a widow of no consequence (to the nation): her marriage never entered the marriage registry and was therefore not legally constituted. Her motherhood was not (state or community) sanctioned, and her ostensible male offspring remains illegitimate in a culture of male bravado and bourgeois marriage. Her demeaned body deciphers the discriminatory structures of the body politic. One's insertion into political citizenship must be negotiated in national and statist terms. The patriarchal Sinhala state, in recognition of its fallen heroes'/husbands' fearless feats and sacrifices in the front lines in defense of the nation, accords military privileges to bourgeois widows by bestowing the glamour and glory of memorials, foundations, and special funds, state privileges denied to Sriyalatha because she is the widow of no consequential effect.

Sriyalatha possessed no NIC, a bureaucratic procedure that cancels out the multiplicity of identification making uniform and national one's ethnic identity, a necessary condition to establish one's claims to citizenship and political community. While a colonial category, the postcolonial imposition of the NIC was actualized especially under the repressive rule of the Emergency and Prevention of Terrorism Act. The need for the NIC was validated in terms of an ideological imperative at the height of the (internal) threat to the state from the south and from the north and east. Rationalized in the name of "political stability" and "state sovereignty," the NIC was forced on the subject population. Sriyalatha could make no allegiance to a place of her own. Living on the fringes of marginality, she could not, *did not* belong.

Her refuge was not the gendered space of the brothel, the space of sexual transgression and expropriation. Every night, she slept in a ghetto, that urban condom near the squalid Pettah bus stand, a place of duplicity, immorality, and evil, the ubiquitous space of "degenerate" men and women, the masculinized community of the "criminal underclass," beyond Sinhala civility and bereft of any sense of *lajja* and *baya*. Sriyalatha was a destitute, displaced woman. Induced by the burden of economic misery and destitution to part with her only child, she sent him to a child care center in Kurunegala, her way of averting herself (the indignity of motherhood) from herself (woman-hood). Her everyday life was one of strenuous, bitter struggle just to survive. While in Colombo she was thrown into the perilous world of prostitution and, testing her tryst with historical contingency. The hideous "trade of criminals" was legislated by the colonial state and actively vindicated by the Sinhala Buddhist nationalists. Each happening in her life was marked by uncertainty, instability, and discontinuity. By unconsciously or subconsciously resisting the norms of circulation instigated and enforced by the state/community and by actively practicing "illicit" forms of economic/sexual/political/social exchange and transaction, Sriyalatha was affirming a sense of belonging, however precarious, that might be deemed infrapolitical; she was a woman in between—between modernity and its aftermath, humanity and inhumanity, citizenship and its denial (Rancière 1992). There is a sense of immediacy to her daily struggles, even the struggle to just get by that involved a stubborn indifference to all norms, of civility, sociality, and womanhood. She regained a sense of self and subjectivity through indifference, by transgressing dominant, oppressive modes of fashioning community, by repudiating a community constructed around national affiliation and sexual attachment (Parker et al. 1992).

The event generated salacious diatribes in the sensationalist, chauvinist print media. Writing to the daily *Island* newspaper, a reader pilloried Sriyalatha for her act of "criminality" and "deviance." He justified the armed forces strip search by saying, "As a sex worker, that was her living anyway." Her subject position is assigned, to use a Foucauldian formulation. Oppressive language does more than violence; it *is* violence (Morrison 1993). The scrutinizing, paternalist gaze was fixated on her sexuality, not on the military/sexual assault of a woman's body, not on state violence, not on police brutality, signifying her ethnicity and class. By vulgarizing state power and military valor in his hate speech, the reader reinvigorated contexts of hate and injury (Butler 1997). The terror-induced violence inflicted on Sriyalatha was quickly turned into a source of slander. Such are moments when power vulgarizes itself. The reader lauded the state for "proper" and "swift" action merely to glamorize his own (and the Sinhalas') brutal forms of the vulgar. In the exemplary nationalist discourse of military security, her body signified the indissociability of sexual affront and racial frontier. Women's groups voiced their outrage and condemnation. The stripping was seen in a continuum of extreme violence against women. Feminists attributed the "offensive" and "invasive" security procedures, such as strip searches, to the degree of brutality and militarization in Sri Lankan society. Yet in the women's invariably obtuse critiques of state militarism and the military, the repressive arm of the state, eminently political questions of the modalities and governing instrumentalities rationalized and legitimated in stripping women in the service of national security were left unaddressed.

Sriyalatha's class and its constitutive gendered oppressions were glossed over and the nationalist justification for violence in the name of public security was unquestioned. Crucially and paradoxically, feminists located the core problematic in a liberal discourse of rights, asserting women's inalienable "right to dignity" and freedom from harassment, with varying degrees of emphasis on "respectful," "humane" behavior in future searches, instead of subjecting the conceptual conceits of national security to hermeneutic suspicion. The object of "feminist" critique was not the ideological presuppositions of national security that increasingly hinged on a discourse of militarism. Nor did they rigorously question the protocols of violence under regimes of impunity and how such regimes constantly sought to rework power relations—inequalities among and between genders, classes, and ethnicities—in the quest for hegemony. The uncritical, nonthreatening, and problematic recourse to a universal language of rights amorphously predicated on the "free subject free to decide" circumvented the inevitable recognition of power differentials in assertions of community, identity, and difference. However, as Butler (1997) has argued, words wound, representations offend. The feminist critique was not adequately honed to enabling women to move beyond the textuality of discourse toward the texturality of the (ethnic) body, for the mime in which bodies collectively make authority and remake meaning drowns out the larger, more structural din of sexuality. The discursive strategy of rights adopted by women's groups thwarted crucial primary political insights, i.e., the tactical and obverse ways of articulating relations of domination and thereby effectively undermining the ambiguous and dangerous rationality of security—the Sri Lankan state's hegemonic impulse to militarize and criminalize women's bodies.

What intensified power relations among women was the hasty decision by women's groups to arbitrarily call off a public *shalwar khameez* demonstration planned near Liberty Plaza, located on the border of the HSZ. The decision to defer the protest interminably was incited by an assemblage of spatial, temporal, and subjective constraints of memory and history, the fear of a possible police and/or military assault on the protesters that would result in arrests, detention, and further strip searches. Such expressions of fear were shared by individual women who originally conceived the idea of protest. It was also argued that the women's action might be construed as a "grave provocation," with the protest itself transforming into a site of (state) violence. However, the women's nonaction, their action of indefinitely suspending the protest, in the wake of Sriyalatha's stripping, arrest, detention, and assault provoked angry reactions from some activists who signed up for the protest in earnest and a minority MP representing the Tamil plantation community who despairingly caviled about middle-class Colombo women's pretensions to fighting oppression and violence and their feigned commitment to women's rights.

The women's resistance to *shalwar*-clad public protest against oppressive security made visible the confluence of internal power relations in the construction of privileged identifications, techniques of coercion, and oppressive and disabling notions of self vis-à-vis self and self vis-à-vis other. The point here is not that female activists are conscious accomplices to ideologies of militarism and nationalism but that, by failing to problematize state violence and violence against Sriyalatha, they reinscribed the conceptual presuppositions and problematic of national security discourse through which the state continued to justify criminalization and militarization of specific spaces, bodies, and practices. What Sriyalatha's experience exemplifies is the very banality of violence against women in the Sri Lankan everyday.

Given the discursive salience of social morality (organically linked to the "libidinous economies" of Sinhala community) that authorizes stripping of women, it was *not* the bodily violation in the form of the stripping of Sriyalatha that was seen as savage and obscene but her *materiality* as a prostitute, a site of moral ambiguity marked by desire/tension in the nationalist semiotics of Sinhala sexuality. The moment of production of woman as prostitute locates gender identifications in a larger field of contested significations. The resignification of Sriyalatha as prostitute and therefore as promiscuous and sexually immoral figure opens to interrogation discourses of Sinhala Buddhist militarism and bourgeois hypocrisy through which notions of collective selfhood have been mediated in Sri Lankan modernity. In the mediatized representations of the "sensational stripping," her body is projected as oversexualized, commodified and criminalized in a field of a particular kind of politics—sexual, communal, and national.

Sexual politics denies prostitutes the possibility of community. There is a body, female Sinhala, operating in a discursive silence. Yet it is not empty but full of density, itself offering a discrete corporeality. For men of "honor,"

Sriyalatha had irreverently and obstinately deviated from the masculinist ideological norm of *lajja-baya,* a signifier of feminine charm and public modesty,
a woman without, unrepentantly incapable of, *lajja* and *baya.* A body declared
not to be in the "national interest." The Sinhala nation's "respectability" (embodied in the deified mother/bourgeois wife) was thus marred, stained by
her antinational "debauchery." Her "sexually charged" public presence was
both a "disgrace" to the nation's prestige and emblematic of "national decay."
The microphysics of power determines, in fact legislates, which bodies can
appropriate and inhabit which bodies/spaces. While Sriyalatha, because she
is a woman and a sex worker, was pathologized, vulgarized, and demonized,
the regular, persistent, and permissive state violence that maims, mutilates,
and murders was represented as rational, moral, and necessary. Her body was
configured as a site of danger and doom, both gender and geography conniv-
ing to instrumentalize her as an object and as a potential agent of violence,
failing to incriminate the state as the actual perpetrator. The seductive state
fired by a moral purpose remains as the unmarked, unalloyed provider and
protector of its subjects. Its use of violence to govern is justified through in-
vocations of varying notions of democracy, security, and stability. The state
was not seen as an accomplice in criminalizing her femininity and endangering her broken life; rather her defiant intrusion into "sovereign" space was
seen as threatening morality, order, and security. Sriyalatha was made into a
"spectacle," the object/target/tactic in which both the state and the community aided and abetted in the authorization of violence, in the consolida-
tion and concealment of authority, turning power into a carnal fetish.

In this normalization of the spectacle of violence, the spectacle of the
violated body, which invoked laughter, bemusement, and revulsion in the
Sri Lankan social, official values are not desecrated or inverted, to use a
Bhaktinian formulation. Rather, in this gendered enjoyment of violence the
community confers legitimacy, honor, and power on the state's capacity to
differentiate, discriminate, and dominate. State as instrument and as agent of
violence can be selectively panoptic. Gender power is made into a performative fetish in the phantasmagoria of political struggles for dominance. Power
as fetish is thus sacralized and hierarchized. The performative space is a place
inscribed by hierarchies, institutions, and techniques. Feldman's (1991: 30)
insight is useful here: "Violence symbolized or practiced in this performative
context is identified as the appropriate medium for colonizing the outer margins of community space, while kinship and residential structures are reserved
as the central ordering apparatuses of the internal community proper." Gender

power's excess, masculinist violence is aestheticized in the form of routine stripping of women in ordinary situations, during spousal rows, at elaborate electoral campaigns, and at mass protests. Hence the location of *lajja-baya* in the Sri Lankan social field: its normalization in the socialization of Sinhala girls, a Nietzschean authority that submits the body to a regime of indignity and pain. In practices of everyday life, gender power, then, is derived from the productive effect of *lajja-baya*. The state as the monopolizer, as the authoritative agent of violence, invaded Sriyalatha's body to strip her of socially sanctioned *lajja-baya* by strip-searching, the imperative of "national security," while implicating her in offensive (lack of *lajja-baya*) and criminal conduct (being antinational by walking into the HSZ).

It is in opposition to the loss of *lajja-baya* that Sinhala civilities are then posited and defined. Feldman (1991) has argued that power is embedded in the body, which becomes an instrument of agency when politicized. But politicization is neither singular nor uniform nor even. In postcolonial social formations, the socialized body is early on also the politicized body reconstituted through a variety of signifying practices. Interlocking and overlapping ideologies of class, caste, gender, and ethnicity impinge on processes of politicization and signification in the constitution of the subject. How bodies are produced and practiced in the social field is critical to enabling/disabling conditions of possibility.

Here I take a detour to engage in a discussion of the different modes of politicization that precede the making of identity. The process of politicization is fraught with violent struggle. Identities are "forged," in a double sense, through "convivial tensions" (Mbembe 2001) in struggles of community seeking hegemony. To capture moments of contest regarding the different conditions of such politicization is to emphasize their force and visibility within contested relations of power. The implications of their violent consequences are central to a radical critique of community politics.

Belonging Recast in a Totalizing Religious Idiom

This ethnography is drawn from the multireligious geographic space, itself a product of colonialism and internal colonization; a process unleashed by decolonization with forces of Sinhala chauvinism, entrenched in the postcolonial state threatening to correct wrongs of the past. This space encompasses the three villages of Sivapuram, Dehiwatte, and Periyapalam, which stand adjacent to each other and have histories of animosity and revenge. Neelapola, which lies between the Tamil village of Sivapuram and the Sinhala village of Dehiwatte, was filled with fields whose cultivation was disrupted when the Liberation Tigers of Tamil Eelam (LTTE) captured the agricultural lands, bringing the ethnically cleansed village under its hegemonic control and surveillance. The place became inscribed as "uncleared" in the state-sponsored discourse of militarism and national security.

During spiraling ethnic violence, Dehiwatte came under severe LTTE attack during which scores of Sinhalese peasants were massacred. Dehiwatte farmlands were subsequently recolonized by the LTTE, with the surviving community of Sinhalese abruptly halting their agricultural activities and abandoning the only material resource, paddy fields, on which their families depended. Their subsistence economy ruined, the Sinhala peasants were left with memories of unspeakable violence visited on their relatives and neighbors.

Women in Sivapuram who have long suffered under prolonged and chronic ethnic war had been sustained by needs-based safety nets of external support in terms of income-generating activities and by their contingent use of strategies to negotiate recalcitrant patriarchal structures and institutions. As women, their use of and control over meager resources previously unavailable or denied to them were being resisted by the Tamil patriarchy. But as Tamil, they were at the receiving end of ethnic hatred mutually instigated through acts of violence and counterviolence. Culturally, Tamil women's honor and sexual purity are held sacrosanct to community order and stability.

Against the backdrop of regional deprivations, inequalities, competing forms of historical consciousness, and ethnic and nationalist sentiments, communities became collectively or individually marked and pitted against each other. In the highly charged, polarized political context, where the commerce of ethnicity advantaged the group capable of negotiating from a position of dominance, Sinhalese began to resent the privileging of Sivapuram Tamils in the distribution of infrastructure facilities. In the delivery of electricity to the communities, for instance, Dehiwatte village was excluded, fueling hostility and antagonism.

In Periyapalam, where livelihoods were sustained primarily by rice cultivation, Muslims suffered disproportionately when water supplies were blocked from going into Muslim areas. Muslim cultivators charged the Tamils in Sivapuram of avenging the violence visited on them by denying Muslims access to the vital resource of free river water, which had run through the villages unimpeded for decades. Sivapuram Tamils had disrupted the river's flow into

Periyapalam, which affected large tracts of cultivable land owned by Muslims. Included in the category of the worse-affected areas in the humanitarian discourse, Sivapuram and Dehiwatte, and curiously not Periyapalam, continue to receive community relief and psychosocial support services. It is against this historical background of reciprocal antagonisms and politicized ethnic relations that new communal claims over territory were being made.

Muttur, located in the eastern district of Trincomalee, has had its enduring moments of rupture, which affect social relations among Tamils, Muslims, and Sinhalese. Muttur town is populated largely by Muslims who run their mercantile establishments and trade with Tamils and Sinhalese in the villages. There is a great deal of economic interdependence as each community seeks to buy or sell their produce to the other.

In the months before the ceasefire between the government and the LTTE in April 2003, Muttur was turned into a virtual battleground of ethnicity-driven politics of regional power blocs—the sole regional politicomilitary hegemon being the LTTE—competing for dominance. Abductions became frequent, disappearances numerous, and extortion routine. In the violence that visited Muttur during the uneasy lull of "peace," several Muslims were gruesomely killed, some abducted, tortured, and executed, others gunned down where they bathed or worked. Commercial buildings and homes in and around Muttur, belonging mostly to Muslims, were set ablaze. So were Tamil shops and homes.

Muslims, driven from their dwellings and their town reduced to charcoal, have been steadily streaming to Kantale, while Tamils in fear of Muslim reprisals have been moving into Trincomalee. There is a great deal of anticipation of events, bloody and brutal, yet more horrendous in their ramifications. But more disturbingly, there is an unquestioning allusion to a new "Muslim menace" threatening to derail the fragile ethnic peace. Fiction or rumor, it is intensifying the prevailing sense of insecurity and fear. The presence of various Muslim faction leaders in Muttur, some representing southern Muslim interests and not necessarily eastern Muslims' grievances, also aggravated Tamil-Muslim relations, fanning a mob mood among the besieged Muslims.

However, the site of violence that draws my attention here was located outside these mourning, melancholic villages, where a disputed hillock stood. It was the week leading up to Good Friday, 2001, six months after the signing of the Memorandum of Understanding between the government and the LTTE. A large number of Catholics inhabit this area, constituting one-third of the population. Christians began to make claims on the hilly region by posting crosses—fourteen of them altogether—inscribing the place with biblical meaning. The unoccupied and barren heap of earth had earlier been colonized and militarized by the Sinhala army, which erected bunkers and declared it a surveillance zone. The military did not consider the dry, empty mound a key strategic location. Given its topography and relative isolation, it could not be transformed into a base, even though in military calculations it constituted an important piece of territory. The unwarranted presence of the Sinhala army, however, did not provoke or incite violence. Its arbitrary rule was neither challenged nor undermined. There was no open resistance or hostility to the military administration of the area, though the army had plunged into a strategy of capturing territory in a relentless cycle of loss and gain of land—a primordial material resource of the imagined community, a vector of capital inscribed with notions of sovereignty—in their fight against the separatist LTTE.

The cleared/uncleared division had been institutionalized and naturalized in the battle over territory. The controversial mound, classified as cleared, had come under the physical control of the Sinhala army. Communal contestations over its symbolic and material control symbolized the webs of property and power in the community. But such local contestations are informed by an awareness of the "imagined community" (Anderson 1991) of belonging as a process and practice of minoritization (Bhabha and Comaroff 2002). Muslims, agitated and outraged by Christians' "aggressive conquest," mobilized the community, marched to the site, and began to remove the emblems of Jesus' crucifixion, one by one, claiming the territory as theirs, as belonging to the community of Islam. Catholics, furious that their religious space has been invaded and violated, demanded the return of the crosses to their original place. Muslims protested, and in the ensuing violence several small mosques were set upon. Although publicly peaceful, the angry protest elicited a violent response. As a consequence, Muslim religious property was systematically targeted. An invisible paramilitary "Osama group" had been active in Muttur around this time. Or so the buzz went around.

Tamils feared revenge killings. Their lives came under direct physical threat. The army was immediately deployed to arrest the spread of "religious discord," to stem the tide of "religious frenzy." The Catholic Church intervened and negotiated a "truce" cajoling the antagonistic groups to thrash out a settlement if not permanent at least provisional. No locally or regionally based political party was able, *allowed* to make capital out of simmering ethnic enmity. Agents involved on both sides of the religious divide showed stubborn resilience under pressure from religious and community leaders to desist from violence. Even after the more gruesome events of violence, a few weather-beaten, dilapidated, desolate gray-green crosses could be seen at the foothill where the former military camp had withered away, leaving in its wake only a police post.

It was argued that the Catholics' motivation for engraving Christian emblems was religious. Though ethnically Tamil, the Christians also define themselves in terms of their religious identity as they form a distinct minority within the larger collectivity of Tamils, the majority of whom are Hindus. There is a common perception of discontent among Tamils and Sinhalese in the east who view "Muslim prosperity" as a consequence of the ethnic conflict. Tamils thus construct their own memories and narratives of victimhood and discursively represent themselves as primarily victims, victims of Sinhala nationalism and "Muslim complicity" in the nationalist violence against them. In this discourse Muslims were construed as either passive witnesses of violence against Tamils or active collaborators, accomplices of Sinhala nationalism. "They had everything to gain from the Sinhala Tamil ethnic misery. Those who were displaced or forced to flee from their original places of abode have had to sell their property to entrepreneurial Muslims in order to invest in education and immigration," one Tamil lamented.

Muttur had traditionally been a place of cultural and religious diversity. Regional inequalities were compounded by ethnic inequalities, affecting the region's own communal and historical patterns of sharing and wiping out individual and collective histories of struggle, dissent, and suffering. Ethnicity, as the dominant marker of identification, came to signify and structure social relations across communities and between the state and its margins. Ethnicity was the sign under which suffering, victimhood, and pain were privileged and hierarchized. Expressions of anger and the rhetoric of revenge in the depths of grief were products of the twin histories of minoritization and marginalization, exacerbated by ethnic prejudice and discrimination. It is in these fantasized and imagined spaces where violence is anticipated but absent yet possible.

Moments of violence involving Catholics and Muslims throw open possibilities for redefining identity and community and recognizing the inevitable presence of the other in their midst. For Catholics and Muslims who were embroiled in a contest over space, local, communal, and regional—a space that is nevertheless multireligious, a contest made possible by that very space. If an adversarial religious encounter enabled the production of violence, it was by reworking the religious logic and symbolism that originally incited the violence that both communities were able to prevent it. While the violence visited on the community was seen as communal, politics necessitated its deployment in an unequal field of power where political claims, couched in overt religious idiom, over communal space were being constructed and contested.

Land historically has been a critical issue for local subaltern groups whose lands were snatched away by the Sinhala state under the elusive sign of democracy and development. The historical struggle for control over scarce resources is complex and deeply political. Even though the conflict was restricted to Tamil Christians and Muslims, it was immediately insinuated into the larger political context of Tamil-Muslim relations. Difference was established not only through the logic of religious identification but also contingently through the (ethnic) constitution of Tamilness/Muslimness. Violence is hence the name of the sign, fluid and arbitrary, under which authority, itself a product of history, is practiced by modern political communities.

The struggle for power among communities is navigated through political desire, enabling both the production of violence and its abatement (Jeganathan 2000). The political challenge is to displace their conditions of possibility, that is, the conditions of production of violence. But to argue thus is not to deny the possibility of antagonism and political agency so essential to the subject-making process as modern power is complexly and infinitely entangled with desire, making subjects yield to as well as resist violence. It is when competing political desires collude in contexts of contested historical fields, the fields of adversarial engagement and of oppositional ideological programs, that they give vent to acts of (violent) assertion and subversion. However, as the events in Muttur illustrate, it is also in the semantics of the language of incitement and religious iconography that political agency, at once disruptive and subversive of projects of community, must be located.

It is to the political and historical conjuncture of May 2001 in Mawanella in the Sabaragamuwa province involving Muslims and Sinhalese that my ethnographic focus shifts here—to the spectacle of the slashed and bleeding body of Anzar, the "impudent" minority held hostage by Kumara, the "alienated" lumpen of the majority who relies on Sinhala masculinist hubris and prowess for survival, the indomitable area thug and supporter of the ruling regime, the People's Alliance (PA) party cadre turned bodyguard.

The Thug: Capitalist Modernity's Ally and Alibi

In the months leading up to the events of May 2001, Mawanella, in southern Sri Lanka, had been a site of conflict and antagonism. It came under intense public scrutiny when the town went up in flames, resulting in the murder of a Muslim at the hands of the Sinhala police and the subsequent destruction of Muslim homes and businesses. In the narratives and recollections of these events, Sinhalas and Muslims posit themselves as victims and implicate each other in the production of violence. In politically contested sites of antagonism, majority-minority relations and identifications are constantly overturned, subverted, and reworked in response to fleeting historical conjunctures. While the specific violence against Anzar and the collective violence against Muslims have their micropolitical locations, in the targeting of Muslims for illegal taxation in the form of *kappam*, the events of May 2001 also reveal how local conflicts are framed, mapped, and constituted by national politics.

The two social formations, Muslims and Sinhalese, are polarized along the axis of party allegiance: United National Party (UNP) and Peoples Alliance. The local articulations of power were further compounded by the national emergence of the SLMC (Sri Lanka Muslim Congress), which constituted itself as a political organization contesting dominance of the Sinhala nationalist parties. The SLMC claimed to represent the material and ideological interests of all Muslims, not just the Muslims in the east. The entry of a political organization founded on the principle of religious difference, designed by eastern Muslims for the national collective Muslim selfhood, polarized issues of choice and allegiance. However, southern Muslims, including those concentrated in Mawanella, have been traditional UNP supporters. Even though fervently aligned with the center right conservative UNP, the organization that is best able to secure their material interests, southern Muslims are primarily seen in terms of their religious identity, a mode of identification Muslims find inevitable in the face of the "ethnic monopolies" maintained by both Sinhalese and Tamils. However, it is the Muslims' religious identity or identification that is often projected onto their political allegiance. Muslims' proclaimed faith in the Sinhala organization (UNP) is often seen as a "sly" move to insert themselves into a project of Muslim nationalism, which ultimately constitutes a political challenge to Sinhala nationalism. Hence Muslims are always already positioned in an adversarial relation to the Sinhalese, represented by the two ideological hegemons, the PA and the UNP.

But differences of class and ethnicity also inform and produce particular social relations and identifications. Against the pulls and pressures of nationalist currents and ethnic politics, minute daily battles were fought in the marketplace—Muslims in a stand-off against groups led by Prasanna, who, having access to institutions of state power such as the Pradeeshiya Sabha and the local police, wielded political power. Intimidation and harassment became the order of the day. The harassers were bands of local men, but henchmen from outside moved to the town and engaged in strong-arm tactics. Their "show of force" consisted of reminding the Muslim community who they actually were and what they were capable of: men backed by local political bosses and the police. But beneath the (locally specific) contextual battle against *kappam* could be seen ideological rivalries between PA and UNP constituencies, heightened by the governmentalization of ethnic politics with real effects at the national, regional, and local levels.

Muslims refused to be cowed, resisted being subjugated as a minority by the majority Sinhalese, and sought to reassert their presence in the public realm as a community of Muslims different from Sinhalas, as followers of Islam. In asserting their religious faith, they were also asserting their presence as a community of traders, as a majority concentrated in the town, the domain of capital accumulation where Muslims enjoyed "disproportionate" economic wealth and power. But the Sinhalas resented their "majority" status and hence their hold on the local economy, which, they argued, left Sinhala peasants in rampant misery and poverty.

In hegemonic narratives of violence, purges of rivals and violence in the Sinhala polity are not defined in communal and ethnic terms, whereas violence among and between Muslims and Tamils is often represented under the sign of communalism, fundamentalism, or fascism. Benedict Anderson, in *Imagined Communities* (1991), argued that people were willing to kill and die for the nation, but the implication of their fanatical allegiance to the postcolonial (nation) state was left unproblematized. The colluding yet dissonant narratives of violence reveal the impossibility of maintaining a neat polarity between the state as a site of coercion and the community as a site of subversion, possibility, and resistance. Communal space is a place of antagonism with a multiplicity of invisible ties, an assemblage of irreconcilable, contradictory forces struggling to majoritize competing ideological projects by invoking the state, the political party, and social and religious affiliations, which, while implicating each other in the production of violence, also participate in each other's complicities in search of hegemony.

Allegiance to the political organization, a ploy put to strategic advantage, is contingent on specific interests. For example, if the political party in power as the national government fails to deliver or reneges on promises, opposition political parties that aspire to the status of national sovereignty will strengthen their power bases by making more pledges to their respective constituencies in the process of ethnic mobilization of their support, vowing to fulfill the undelivered promises only to discard all promises once voted in. With social and economic alleviation being relegated to secondary importance by the national parties, individual political activists such as Prasanna and his band of marauding thugs build political power around their local political master by stuffing ballot boxes and intimidating opposition-party voters with the sole intention of securing economic advantages while their regime is in power through jobs, new commercial ventures, and access to the market. To publicly invoke the party symbol and identify with the dominant political community is an expression of power, which creates a sense of identity, community and purpose.

The Muslim community in Mawanella, like elsewhere, is internally divided along party lines. The reason is clear: the party is good for business, and it is less "chauvinist" than the PA. The Sinhala community, too, is fragmented ideologically: UNP versus PA versus the People's Liberation Front (JVP) versus Sinhala Urumaya (SU; Heritage of the Sinhalese). But Sinhalas, unlike the Muslims, constitute a nation, argue men in the community, burdened by the historical limitations of Sinhalaness. Though a political entity designed exclusively for the Muslims, the SLMC has been unable to mobilize the substantial constituency in Mawanella solely on the basis of religion. In the region's electoral history by far, the highest number of preferential votes was won by a Muslim candidate, Kabir Hashim, on the UNP ticket, at the general elections in December 2001, seven months after the violent events in May. Hashim comes from a family of conservative UNPers who for decades have been committed to the party's ideological program, neoliberalism and transnational capital.

However, the May events of violence rocked the regime's wobbly alliance with the already disenchanted, uneasy Muslim Congress. The SLMC construed the events in terms of the "national humiliation" of Muslims. The PA, for its part, accused the UNP of staging a venal coup d'état against a defenseless electorate, which had no parliamentary representative. The "carnage," it alleged, *was* the coup d'état. The December 2001 general elections saw the

UNP ride to power because of the humiliated SLMC's dramatic desertion from the PA and the resultant shift of loyalty to the UNP.

Sinhalese outnumber Muslims in the electorate of Mawanella, though Muslims who own much of the urban land, form a majority in the town. Muslims had pushed for years for an urban council against the rising current of opposition from Sinhalese and rural Muslims. A few Tamil residents remained scattered, many of whom were displaced from the north and east in the aftermath of the ethnic war. The Black July 1983 pogrom had cost the Tamils their livelihood and homes. Tamil plantation labor, too, had gone into the construction of the town under British rule.

In the dominant narratives of the community, Mawanella had been a relatively peaceful place unsullied by dirty politics until intimidation and violence in the pursuit of hegemony made their entry in 1994. Local activists set up more than one hundred illegal kiosks backed by political patronage in and around the congested bus stand. These were political favors to party loyalists, professional robbers or thugs, who by day broke into homes and looted goods and by night worked for local politicos by putting up posters. The Mawanella Pradeshiya Sabha, the decentralized state administrative structure, known for corruption and nepotism, had endorsed state support of the venture. Local men such as Prasanna who lord themselves over others (i.e., Muslims) for pleasure, instituted the *kappam* system by means of which they extracted money for cigarettes and food. They were overlords of the market and CEOs of the lottery and *kassippu* (homemade illicit liquor) trade. For them, *kappam* was a way of exacting gratitude for the "benevolence" of the Sinhala nation accorded to Muslims, as a minority.

The survival of the Muslim trader was intertwined with the local Sinhala thug's supposed largesse, a derivative of the Sinhala nation, a product of his Sinhalaness. Corruption, which enabled new structures to emerge, has been institutionalized at every level of local government. Some of the kiosks were rented out to small business owners who paid *kappam* out of their meager daily earnings to keep the overlords at bay. Their control over market space thus established, gangs of thugs began to stalk the town day in and day out. They slipped into hotels to eat and drink, leaving without paying. In a climate of profound political cleavages, pressure was exerted on Muslims to support Sinhala-dominated political alliances. Intimidation strategically harnessed, men relied on arbitrary and routine acts of plunder to assert their dominance. The function of the differential logic of the demands was discernable in the semantics of violence: Muslim men were stripped of their headwear; the *hijabs* of women at the bus stand were lifted in the presence of their elderly relatives; and Muslims were interpellated as *thambiyo,* a racially coded derogatory word for Muslims.

In popular recollections of the May 2001 events, it is the specific forms of violence against Muslims as a community (constituted by religious difference) and the semantic sexual differential of that violence that are foregrounded: a woman was stripped of her headdress while walking on the road; a former reserve policeman who snapped at a local thug for removing his friend's fez was cut on his neck. With unwavering political patronage, the nation's men mark their presence in the community flaunting state vehicles, transporting illicit brew, and carrying weapons. Mawanella Muslims petitioned the local police for action in vain. Beyond the control of the police, who themselves had come under the command and control of local political elites, the men continued to hunt traders for money, and the pressure against Muslims was great. In this highly charged political environment, Ifran ran his boutique, acquired under the 1977 UNP regime and now a thriving business near the noisy central bus stand. Unlike most of his neighbors, he would close his shop only after all the buses left. He recounts:

> If there are people lingering, no matter how late it is, I would keep my shop open. It must have been around 10.30 P.M. when a vehicle screeched to a halt from nowhere. I saw three men approach my shop. I had closed the cash counter and [was] about to leave. Two of them stood outside; one walked in and demanded 100 rupees. I refused. He left and reappeared minutes after. This time he asked for some cigarettes. He held a 100-rupee note and I rushed to the cash box to get his balance. Spouting filthy language, he hit my forehead hard with a coarse club and then my leg. My cousin brother who was next door chatting with friends rushed to inquire what the matter was. One of the thugs punched in my brother's face, dragged him to the clock tower, tied him to the iron railing erected around the Buddha statue, and had his mouth slit with a knife. While Anzar was held on his knees with blood dripping from his mutilated mouth, Millangoda poured water on him, challenging Muslims in the vicinity to save his life. The gang was comprised of ten members, but only three men were seen throwing their weight around, flexing their muscles. There were policemen who saw the incident but did nothing to help the victim.

On the night of May Day, the key suspects had not yet been arrested and Muslims confronted the police. An altercation resulted in which a police jeep was attacked, breaking its windshield. Police then fired into the sky and the protesters dispersed. The Muslims organized a protest the next day, where they shouted slogans calling for justice to the victims and punishment to the perpetrators, demanding in particular the immediate arrest of the men responsible for the brutality against the innocent Muslim. A group of Sinhalese congregated near the Buddhist statue, their numbers swelling gradually. Aranayake MP Lalith Dissanayake (PA) and Pradeshiya Sabha member M. Zavahir (UNP) tried to pacify the Muslims, urging them to call off their protest. Earlier, and under pressure, the two politicians visited the jail to see if the culprits were actually in custody. The drunken men who had celebrated PA-sponsored May Day parades in Aheliyagoda had been caught by police at dawn on May 2, soon after their clandestine return to Mawanella. Dissanayake assured Muslims that justice would be done, that protest was futile, and insisted they disband and return home.

The demonstrators, unconvinced, did not budge. They were not persuaded by what seemed like empty platitudes and the familiar insincere rhetoric of politicians. Snubbed by the Muslims, Dissanayake dashed to his car, and the protesters wasted no time jeering his departure. Stones, bottles, and grenades rained down on the demonstrators, triggering a violent melee. The police, having failed to uphold due process of law and diffuse tension for two nights, did not hesitate to test their brute force in a situation of complete breakdown of trust, in the Theater of the Absurd, firing indiscriminately at a group of protesters running for their lives. One Muslim spectator who had come to the town from the village of Owatte to buy a few groceries on credit—and with little hope as he had no money and no business was possible owing to the general call of *hartal* (strike)—was gunned down. He died instantly, his head blown off. Grenades were lobbed into the fleeing crowds, who looked for cover to avoid tear-gas canisters and bullets. Men began to pillage and plunder.

Rumors spread like wildfire to all parts of Mawanella and beyond. Communal stories were churned out of how Muslims had attacked a Buddha statue, crushed it, and urinated on it; of how an influential monk was mutilated by Muslims and his mangled body put in a gunnysack before being dragged down the road. Others implicated Muslims as "marauders" on a "rampage to kill Sinhala Buddhists." Sinhala villagers—men, women, and children—carried axes, mamooties, knives, crowbars, hooklike weapons and swords and stood on the edge of the river or paddy field from where they could spot the "invading army of Muslims."

Muslims, increasingly targeted in towns, armed themselves, too, with knives, swords, and clubs. In small towns such as Ganetenna and Hingula, organized groups attacked mosques, destroying property. Religious texts, including old copies of the Qur'an, were pulled from shelves, thrown on the highway, and burned. Coins from the mosque till box were sprayed across the tarred road. The mobile "loot and burn to teach Muslims a fitting lesson" gang, uniting under the banner of Sinhalaness, chanted, "Burn! Destroy! No *thambiyas* can be trusted!"

Looting or burning, the rampaging mobs excelled in the craft of violence, perfecting it with masculine, libidinous gusto. Muslim homes on the Colombo–Kandy road were smashed and set ablaze, carefully leaving intact neighboring Sinhala shops and residences. In the resulting fires, however, Sinhala shops, too, were gutted. Some Muslims found the opportunity to loot profitably and to set fire to shops owned by Sinhalese. Violence spread as far as Rambukkana, Aranayake, and Kadugannawa on the Kandy road. Many in the community believed outsiders were brought in to besiege the Muslims. The Ceylon Transport Board played its own collaborative role, supplying tires and petrol in ample measure. In the fear-engulfed months that followed, Muslims lost six of their business buildings on the twenty-sixth of every month. In the targeting of one specific community for violent assault, in this case Muslims, Sinhalas, too, became victims of violence in specific locales where Muslims were dominant. Hence the violence cannot be elucidated solely in terms of structures of anticipation (Jeganathan 1998).

There were other everyday grievances specific to the locality that played a contingent role in the development of the May impasse. Muslims resented the Sinhalese-dominated local authorities who used political power to persecute their community. Prasanna, the former policeman turned Sinhala gang leader, chief among the perpetrators of violence against the shopkeeper, was found murdered in Nadeniya, his hometown, a few months after the May violence, his dead body left on the edge of the stream. Sinhala villagers claimed the killers came dressed as Muslims. The Muslims attributed the motive for murder to internecine Sinhala gang warfare. According to one middle-class Muslim, "The politicians make use of these thugs to do their dirty work, and when they get out of control, they kill them." Prasanna's real killers were later arrested, and their motives were said to have been revenge: they were onetime partners in crime. His funeral was attended and honored by a large number of Muslim villagers and influential Sinhala politicians in the government.

Shaken by the "riots" in Mawanella, the PA regime alleged the events had been a joint JVP-LTTE conspiracy to topple the government, thus assigning the violence to the other. Gyanendra Pandey (1994) writes that dualism in such representations of violence relegates history to the state and violence to the other. Muslims accused the PA cabinet minister and MP for Rambukkana, Mahipala Herath, and Lalith Dissanayake—though rivals in the preference vote game, united in the Sinhala cause—of an "excess" of state violence. A segment of the civilian population was concerned about the virulent anti-Muslim propaganda instigated by the Sinhala Urumaya Party (SU). Handouts were discovered in the aftermath of violence that exhorted the Sinhalese to boycott goods from Muslim shops and discontinue business dealings with them, reminiscent of the right-wing religious Vishwa Hindu Parishad's (VHP's) fascist campaigns in Gujarat in 2003.

The politicoeconomic strategy of the Sinhala Veera Vidana (SVV), the ideological wing of SU—economic boycott and political isolation of Muslims—ultimately proved futile. Yet the organization is as active in Mawanella as it is in ethnically mixed regions trying to "save Sinhala lands from 'rapacious' Muslims and Tamils." The Muslim as citizen is in perpetual motion to remake himself or herself in the realm of community and state institutions. In the act of assigning violence to the other, in this case the Muslims, the Sinhala state returned memories of shame and humiliation to the Muslims, absolving itself of any role in the violence against them. Posters began to appear before the attack. Some of them said in Sinhala *"api joli karamu"* (let us enjoy), *"me ape rata"* (this is our country). Violence incites and excites *joliya* (thrill) in men. There is fun (i.e., political enjoyment) to be derived from acts of violence. Politics enables the excitement and production of violence in contingent encounters between communities and the apparatuses of the state. In the cacophony of quotidian conflicts, there is mutual enjoyment of the other's humiliation and usurping of grief and outrage. Violent acts invoke a psychology of indulgence and pleasure among spectators and perpetrators. It is when the savagery of the state and the everyday cruelties in society converge that violence troped under dissonant signs unmakes and remakes projects of state and community. What counts as violence and what does not is always produced under the sign of politics, which contains differing meanings of the political for different groups mobilizing identifications in search of dominance. As the contingency of a territorial contestation involving Muslims and Catholics discussed in this chapter shows, social relations are irreducible to ethnicity or religion. In certain configurations, it is possible to see the development of conflict and violence, but such violence cannot be explained solely in terms of "ethnic" or religious" enmity. In others, violence is made impossible by a reworking of the logic and space of identity and difference.

NOTES

I wish to thank the Joan B. Kroc Institute for International Peace Studies, University of Notre Dame, for inviting me to present this paper at the conference "Women and the Contested State: Violence, Religion and Conflict in South Asia," held April 11–12, 2003. I gratefully acknowledge the comments and suggestions of participants on the Sri Lanka panel and on this chapter in particular. I am indebted to Patricia Lawrence, who originally proposed putting together a set of themes to be discussed empirically and conceptually. My grateful thanks also to Monique Skidmore for her patience and support. Material for this chapter was also drawn from my ongoing Ph.D. research on the anthropology of contemporary Sinhala-Muslim relations. Last but not least, my sincere thanks to Inoka Priyadharshini for an ethnographic description of the events that took place in Muttur.

1. By "microphysics," a Foucauldian formulation, I am referring to the different forms of embodiment and their effects in discursive formations and nondiscursive processes. Here, I want to make the link between gendered production of the body and practices of violence.

Part III

Encounters with the Mysterious

Alternative Power Structures in Authoritarian Burma

Map 4. Burma/Myanmar

Burma (Myanmar) is an example par excellence of Benedict Anderson's (1991) concept of the imagined community. It has been imagined, over time, as a Buddhist monarchical kingdom, a British addition to the Raj, an independent federated and democratic nation, a fundamentalist Theravada Buddhist state, a Marxist Buddhist state, a socialist Buddhist state, and a "united" nation ruled by ethnic Burman military generals. In fact, Burma has never been a unified state, not politically, ethnically, or religiously.

Burma's current military dictatorship traces its roots to General Ne Win's usurpation of power from Burma's fledgling postcolonial government in 1962. Ne Win ushered in the era of the "Burmese Way to Socialism." In 1988 a nationwide pro-democracy uprising was brutally crushed, and in 1989 a clique of generals created the State Law and Order Restoration Council (SLORC). Multiparty legislative elections were held in 1990, with the main opposition party, the National League for Democracy (NLD), winning decisively, but the SLORC refused to hand over power. Student demonstrations and continued appeals to democracy by the 1992 Nobel Peace Prize winner, Aung San Suu Kyi, and the NLD did nothing to loosen the armed forces' control. In 1997 the SLORC rearranged itself into the State Peace and Development Committee (SPDC) and in late 2005 moved the capital from Rangoon (Yangon) to Naypyidaw (Royal City) outside the village of Pyinmana in central Burma.

For Burma's fifty million inhabitants, almost all civil freedoms, including freedom of speech and assembly, are disallowed. The military regime remains in power through the use of force and the strategic use of political violence, propaganda, censorship, and surveillance to create an ongoing climate of fear. The formal economy is almost nonexistent, and the banking system exists almost solely to launder the profits of the heroin and various trafficking industries. Burma ranks 142 out of 145 countries on the world corruption index; it is the world's most conflict-prone country; and it ranks as the twelfth least secure in terms of core human rights abuses.

More than 10,000 people have died each year in Burma's civil war since 1962 when Ne Win came to power. At least one million people are forcibly displaced, with more than 650,000 reported in 2005 to be hiding in the jungle or forest or on the run from the Burmese army or in relocation sites. Currently 160,000 Burmese reside in seven refugee camps in Thailand, and other refugees flee over the western border into Bangladesh. The NLD has been continually harassed, and Aung San Suu Kyi remains under house arrest in Rangoon. The political future of Burma looks, in 2007, decidedly bleak.

Burma is an unusual site for examining the ways in which women engage with religion and the supernatural and the many reasons for these encounters. The authoritarian regime has effectively disappeared the role of women in public, except for the wives of the ruling junta members, who constitute the only visible sign of empowered women. The chapters in Part III present a range of women's encounters with the mysterious in the context of state terror, state violence, and forms of structural violence that affect women and men differently.

Monique Skidmore not only examines the ways in which women have disappeared from public space and discourse and from traditional female religious roles but also finds the places that women have disappeared to. As Betty Joseph argues earlier in this volume, in postcolonial Asian nations playing "catch-up" with the West, men are viewed as progressive leaders on the national stage, but there are no corresponding modern images of women. In Burma this is not only the case because women must "shore up" the cultural order by being private sphere managers and nurturers, but because of the shadow of Burma's most famous citizen, the democracy leader Aung San Suu Kyi, who epitomizes the worst imaginings of the generals when Burmese womanhood meets modernity and becomes a powerful political force for change.

Given the paucity of influential roles for women in this authoritarian nation, many women seek alternative forms of power in the mundane world, outside the military social structure, and they turn especially to religious institutions and roles and reinterpret religious roles in new ways. They thus engage with Buddhist mystic sects, Buddhist monasteries, meditation centers, and the Nat spirit cult, in the process sometimes appropriating traditionally male roles as spiritual leaders and healers, sheltered by the reverence for Buddhism afforded to citizens of central Burma.

Ingrid Jordt uses the case study of women who become Buddhist nuns and women who live in meditation centers to examine the forms of civil society they strive to create in order to reform the monastic order (Sangha), and ultimately also the military state, from below. Jordt begins by asking where the public sphere has disappeared to and finds an alternative public space in Burmese Buddhist institutions. Women engaging with Buddhist institutions do so "to coerce the government into partial compliance" with the demands of morality and justness from the population but also to be seen to be sustaining the demands of the junta. The mass lay meditation movement is overwhelmingly female, with no overt political goal, and it does not seek to threaten the state. Its power lies in the millions of Burmese adherents who, by supporting the Buddhist dispensation, provide a resounding assertion of the moral terms of public life. Such verification of certain values cannot be taken as a criticism of the state but as the political, collective, and psychological work of Burmese Buddhist women. Women's agency becomes manifest in a religious idiom that exerts palpable pressure for reform on the Burmese junta.

Bénédicte Brac de la Perrière draws on almost twenty years of research with Nat spirit mediums to examine women's changing participation in the Nat spirit cult during different periods of political unrest, fear, and economic crisis. Not only is the Nat spirit cult revealed as a site of increased activity during such times, but transsexual men are co-opting women's role as spirit mediums. In spirit cults around the world, mediums often give voice to political dissent and veiled resistance, but the Burmese Nat cult offers women no such respite from authoritarianism. The military regime has moved to standardize spirit festivals and thus control the symbolically subversive feminine aspects of the "spirit wives." The power women in Burma find in the spirit cult, however, emerges from the idea of marrying a spirit rather than a man.

Women can access a form of religious agency whereby they have space from the patriarchal norms of Burmese society as expressed through marriage and Buddhist doctrines regarding the superiority of men. These women are careful not to use the cult for purposes of resistance to this military state but instead resist their incorporation into its broader gendered structures. These three chapters thus survey the breadth of women's engagement with religion and the supernatural in central Burma as a quest for amelioration of fear and impoverishment and for sources of alternative personal and political power.

8

Buddha's Mother and the Billboard Queens

Moral Power in Contemporary Burma

MONIQUE SKIDMORE

Anthropologists have documented many examples of the increased regulation of women's bodies when the body politic is threatened. The desire to manage the subversive power of women while at the same time needing to shore up the state's or group's external defenses is a dilemma that has been faced by male leadership for millennia. In British colonial Burma and today in a nation recolonized by its own military, there is a certain kind of regulation and control of women's bodies mandated by the state in an attempt to satisfy this perennial quandary for male dictators. This chapter explores the juxtaposition of the body of the Burmese woman and the body of the state in the shadow of one woman, Aung San Suu Kyi, recipient of the Nobel Peace Prize. In Burmese cities we are newly besieged with images of orthodox women, but her image is too heretical, too hagiographic, to be seen, and so in living rooms throughout the country, her father's picture is proudly displayed. He, General Aung San, is the signifier of the political potential of wives and daughters of presidents and prime ministers in South and Southeast Asia. Her name is known but dangerous and therefore too powerful to speak aloud. She is, simply, in whispered voice, The Lady.

Women in Public Space

Using the popular, all-night dramatic-cum-rock star performance venue, the Burmese *zat pwe,* Ward Keeler (2005) argues that versions of masculinity are being contested, negotiated, and enacted in public performances, in contrast to the disappearance of women from them. The *zat pwe* performance concludes with a duet, in which a man and a woman, dressed in traditional court attire as prince and princess, sing and dance to and with each other. In marionette plays this duet still occurs, but in live performances the princess is replaced by a semicircle of background singers, a chorus that contrasts with the brilliance of the male star. He has adopted a crooning style, creating an intimacy not with the princess but with the audience. Keeler (2005: 223) argues that Burmese modernity is a masculine one and that the roles left to women in the public performances are the conventional stereotypes of Burmese women as "modest paragons of virtue, old shrews, or prostitutes." He concludes that at present there is no way for a Burmese woman to be represented in public as both feminine and modern.

In a culture long since converted to Buddhism and many times colonized, the key ways in which men gain social power and prestige are as government bureaucrats, military officers, or monks. Newer routes to power include becoming a drug lord or urban entrepreneur, but both are subsets of the category of military officers and reliant on the fortunes of the illegal and legal economies respectively. In contrast to these various male identities, Burma's authoritarian regime is carefully crafting the image of the female as it is depicted in urban public space. It allows women to be represented in advertisements as having modern and international awareness, but these depictions are generally subsumed by the avalanche of media images of docile military wives and other submissive patriotic women and girls waving flags, holding balloons, and fawning over the members of the armed services in general and the military council in particular. Not only must women fade into the background, but, as in the new incarnation of the *zat pwe,* they must be subordinate at all times to male power. In the first section of this chapter I discuss this recent phenomenon of the absence of multiple images of women in urban public space, then turn to the role of the powerful female archetype, the Medaw, or Grandmother, a representation that draws in part from the unspoken assumptions in contemporary political culture that link political with spiritual power. In particular, it links the political power of Burma's most important woman, Aung San Suu Kyi, with otherworldly spiritual power.

It is this very representation of the female as a powerful charismatic leader that is completely suppressed in Burmese society.

Billboard Queens

Kathypan: Myanmar Blood Purifier for Women
If this medicine is taken regularly every month, it will not only cure the user's menstrual diseases, but will also give her a beautiful complexion. The medicine is guaranteed free from harmful ingredients. (Myat Chan-Tha Medicinal Hall)

The full-page color advertisement for the emmenogogue Kathypan appears in the Myanmar telephone directory. It features a beautiful young Burmese woman in Western evening wear but with a traditional Burmese hairstyle. She is bedecked in rings, bracelets, and necklaces of rubies and diamonds. She clutches a handbag, wears cosmetics, and is seated in front of an Asian-style teak cabinet. The picture implies the continued strength of Burmese culture and Burmese products (such as teak and rubies), especially indigenous medicine.

This traditional way of life is suggested as fitting comfortably with the modern and material aspirations of Burmese city dwellers. Similar images of young women—billboard queens extolling an Asian modernity compatible with the use of traditional Burmese (and more broadly, Asian) medicines—line major intersections in Rangoon (Fig. 12).

Sometimes these young women wear Western clothes à la Scarlet O'Hara in *Gone with the Wind,* a hundred years out of date, but sometimes they are pictured in jeans or short skirts, posing with young men on motorbikes. These girls represent the modern Burmese teenager of Singaporean marketing dreams, and they sell Fantasy soda, beer, and other products marketed to the teenage middle-class demographic of the cities (Fig. 13). To flirt with modernity is to flirt with the loose morality of America and England, a fine line to walk in Burma but one that the mobile phone–toting, Internet-savvy, karaoke and fashion show groupies of the Rangoon social scene are increasingly comfortable doing (Fig. 14).

Judith Farquhar (2001: 106) notes a textual process of "both flattening and multiplying" images of the body in East Asian popular literature, a process repeated in contemporary films, festivals, and magazines, on the Internet, in

Figure 12. Hand-painted billboard on Sule Pagoda Road, Rangoon, advertising traditional medicines. Author's photo.

Figure 13. Mandalay Beer billboard, Rangoon. Author's photo.

Figure 14.
J'Donuts advertisement
featuring image of
Westernized modern
Burmese woman.
Author's photo.

Figure 15. Donor ceremony featuring members of the parastatal Myanmar Maternal and Child Welfare Association (MMCWA). Author's photo of MRTV image.

posters, and on billboards, of "Burmese beauties" who are visually multiply present but politically absent. Like other dominant modes of modernity, the modern woman is very young, barely more than a teenager. The billboard queens are among the primary ways in which women are being represented today in urban public space.

Taking up even more space in the urban media are the wives of the ruling council members. Organized into parastatal women's organizations such as the Myanmar Maternal and Child Welfare Association (MMCWA), these military wives have infiltrated and suborned women's groups that have sought to operate as nongovernmental organizations (Fig. 15). Accompanying their husbands, they donate robes to monks, smile at schoolchildren waving Union flags, and maintain a plump comportment and traditional dress and hairstyle. Like their counterparts who walk the dusty suburban roads, the *thilashin,* or Burmese nuns, these women are the face of contemporary orthodoxy.

An article in *Today,* an English-language tourism magazine published in Burma, calls the country "The Land of Virgins and Restful Nights." The executive editor, Thet Lwin, declared, "We want to convey how much we value

Figure 16. One of the numerous opening ceremonies aired by state television. Author's photo.

virginity. . . . [M]ost visitors go away highly satisfied with their visit to the Land of Pagodas" (quoted in Bleifuss 1997: 9). And, indeed, the third way in which women reappear in public space is as slaves—as sex workers in karaoke nightclubs and international hotel discos, as docile factory workers in the joint-venture sweatshops, and as servile manikins who hold balloons and ribbons aloft at official events, attendant on every whim of the military men (Fig. 16).

Appropriating Male Power

In the past few years I have been conducting fieldwork in towns and villages north of Rangoon, the former capital city. This is where much of the magical infrastructure that powers the illegal lottery, the astrology business, and the mystic Buddhist sects have relocated, and these satellite towns and large villages have strong links with the forcibly relocated northern Rangoon suburbs. As it has become connected to the metropolis with bridges and better roads, the area has become a loose conglomerate of linked satellites. The family groups in this large zone have members residing or working in Rangoon, in the paddy fields, in factories and industrial zones, in military areas, and in the area towns. Only a decade ago this mobile zone was a series of forested villages surrounded by paddy fields, with a few small and dusty towns straddling the road out of Rangoon.

During this time, I have also been visiting the area's garment factory sweatshops and furniture workshops. In stories and snatches of conversations, I kept hearing of women of influence: Natkadaw, spirit mediums who stop spirit attacks and decrease absenteeism in factories; Mae Wunna, guardian of Mount Popa whose extensive knowledge of magical and medicinal herbs is a powerful source of healing knowledge; Oukazoun, female treasure guardians who lure men away from their wives and city jobs; and a great increase in the phenomenon of Medaw worship.

The growing influence of spirit mediums in the area is attributable in part to the perceived need to civilize and Burmanize the natural world between the established cities, towns, and villages that are being remade as industrial sites. The spirits of the fields, rivers and creeks, dams and ponds, banyan trees, dead trees, and other topographic markers need to be placated, just as when residents were forcibly relocated to paddy fields on the outskirts of Mandalay and Rangoon after the failed 1988 pro-democracy uprising.

Other women are also called in to keep this newly constituted workforce of young men and women pliant. These include traditional masseuses who ameliorate blocked channels from bunched muscles and injuries caused by repetitive work and female healers who claim that the ancestry of their craft stems from Mae Wunna. The rumors about women or perhaps female sprites who live in the forests and lure men from their city wives have always been just that, rumors. Certainly, though, increasing numbers of young men are lured to the forest north of Rangoon in search of monks who predict the results of the Burmese lottery, *hna lon*.[1]

In Hmawby, the northern city that is the contemporary epicenter for religious and magical power, there is such a monk who has built a new monastery, dedicated to a *medaw*. He propitiates the female buffalo-headed Nat spirit whom he calls Pegu Medaw. He is about fifty years old, has been a monk for sixteen years, and is practicing *thamada* (concentration meditation). When he meditates magical numbers appear in his mind, and he reveals them to people in sermons and lectures. He sees his job as helping people by revealing the winning numbers of the Burmese lottery. It was his success at such predictions, a success he attributes to his propitiation of the *nat medaw*, that

Figure 17. Nat medaw image in Hmawby. Author's photo.

led him to relocate from the other side of town and build the new monastery. It contains an elaborate shrine for Medaw Gyi, as he calls the *nat medaw* (Fig. 17), and he has also commissioned a similar image for Burma's premier Buddhist site, the Shwedagon pagoda in Rangoon.

The proliferation of statues of different kinds of *medaw* interested me because their creation coincides with the towering images of the billboard queens in the downtown city areas and the image of the plump matrons of the MMCWA who rule the suburban streets. I was interested in talking to living *medaw* to understand how they are crafting their image and how they and their clients see the *medaw* archetype as fitting into the broader gendered and militarized social structure.

In July 2002, the day before the beginning of the Buddhist period of retreat, I drove out to interview a self-styled *medaw* in a northern relocated township of Rangoon. It was a difficult time to interview magical and religious healers as they were returning to their monasteries in the countryside to be ordained as monks, or in the case of Medaw, as a nun. Here is an excerpt from the interview:

Nine years ago, while I was sitting in the stationery shop in Pyin Oo Lwin, and I was praying at that time, the position of my hands changed into the

Buddha *ku-mu-dia*. Then the position of my hands changed into the various different positions of the Buddha's hands. I didn't know what [was] happening, and after that I was asked to go to the prayer room. The command came into my mind. I heard nothing. I saw nothing. It was just in my mind. I went upstairs and prayed and offered light to the Buddha. I was moving from the shop to the prayer room and vice versa. Gradually I began spending more time in the prayer room. I was asked to meditate, and so I meditated. I was taught in my mind. The position of my hands was always spontaneously changing into the position of the Buddha *mu-dra*. Later it appeared in my mind that I can treat people with my hands. At that moment, I was so happy. I spoke to the guardian spirit, "If I can save people, I will live whatever life you want me to." It is not easy to cure an illness. If I can save people, I will live whatever life Buddha wants me to live.

Since that day, various Buddha images have appeared in my mind. I can see them, and I can hear what Buddha wants me to do. Mostly, Buddha asks me to meditate. After six months, I asked, who is protecting me? I wanted to let people know that I can cure them, that their illness will really be gone. . . . So who is this person? I asked. . . . I asked Buddha while touching my forehead. At that moment, Buddha showed me everything and told me everything, opened everything. At that moment, that person was Buddha's mother, Mae-daw mi-nat-tha. Earlier Chit Chit [the Sayadaw (abbot) sitting next to me on the floor] heard this fact from a voice in his ear, that Buddha's mother, Mae-daw mi-nat-tha, gave me this great gift. I did not tell anyone about it.

It's been nine years last June. Now the treatment and curing time has gone from three hours to fifteen minutes per patient. . . . All of the patients here [gesturing to the crowd of people sitting in the doorway and backed up the stairwell], I cure. I recently cured Chit Chit.

The Rise of Grandparents

It would appear that in the past decade in Burma charismatic women have been appropriating forms of magical and religious power, previously almost exclusively the domain of men, and using it to achieve power in the mundane world. They style themselves as Medaw, the literal translation of which is "Grandmother" (Schober 1989: 302) or as deriving their powers from supernatural *medaw* (Fig. 18). The equivalent of the *medaw*, the Grandmother

Figure 18.
Another example
of a recently
created *medaw*
image. Author's
photo.

archetype, is the Grandfather archetype, known as Bo Bo Gyi. This is a class
or type of images that once may have been tree spirits or one of the pantheon
of thirty-seven Nat spirits, but these classifications are fluid in Burma. For example, in the past few decades sculptures depicting Bo Bo Gyi have taken on
a more benevolent, wise, and almost doting appearance. Bo Bo Gyi statues
have been brought within Buddhist pagoda grounds and removed by the military regime from important sites thought to have tourist appeal. The legend
of Bo Bo Gyi places him in the same category as Bo Bo Aung and Bo Min
Gaung, immortal wizards who were the subject of millenarian or antigovernment movements. In the process of being sculpted as a benevolent male elder,
Mandy Sadan (2005) argues, the Bo Bo Gyi archetype has become politically

neutral and urban residents increasingly call on Bo Bo Gyi to help ameliorate the ills of modern urban life, in a politically appropriate way.

Propitiation of images is serious business in Burma, and the regime is always trying to keep a lid on the simmering antigovernment sentiment that in the past has been expressed by monks and wizards *(weikza)*. That is why the billboard queens and their starchy cousins, the wives of the military men, are allowed to fill the urban space and legal media with their orthodox appeal and womanly concerns. There has been, as yet, no corresponding neutralization of the political potential of the *medaw* archetype as has happened with images of male *weikza*, but then, until now, there has been no living woman attributed with the revolutionary potential that living male wizards are believed to hold. It is my argument that the increase in power and popularity attributable to *medaw* in Burma is due in part to the shadow of Burma's most influential political *medaw,* made evident by her frequent house arrest since she led her party to victory in the disallowed 1990 elections.

The Rangoon Medaw whom I interviewed is an example of how urban women can successfully take on the mantle of Buddhist and spiritual power and have that power validated in the everyday world. They become recognized as having the kind of power usually only attributed to men or to *medaw* spirits and deities. This particular healer has adopted the rustic red robe of Buddhist ascetics or *zawgyi* and styled herself as well versed in ascetic Buddhist techniques *(dhutanga)* and therefore worthy of the respect of Buddhist Sayadaws. She possesses certain *abinyas,* special powers enabled through her mastery of meditation. Her power, she claims, derives from another *medaw,* Queen Maya, as Gautama Buddha's birth mother is known in Burma. The Rangoon Medaw is so powerful that a dwarf appeared at midnight when Chit Chit was living the life of a forest monk, in a clearing by his hut, and presented Chit Chit with two objects imbued with *dagó,* Buddhist force or power. Such magical objects *(rupakaya)* have the ability to fly through the air to the site where they will be venerated in the appropriate hands (Schober 1989). In a dream Chit Chit received a vision instructing him that he was to take the objects to Medaw.

What kind of religious person, then, is the living *medaw,* and what is the significance of the images and talk of *medaw* so common in the villages, towns, and suburbs north of Rangoon? Her power comes from and is legitimated by the Sayadaws who sit at her feet, the Buddhist objects that seek her proximity, and her benefactor, Buddha's mother, Queen Maya. *Maya,* "deception" or "illusion" in Sanskrit, means in effect that greatest illusion, "that which convinces us of existence" (Khandro 2002: 1). The linking of women with corporeality and the mundane world, or earthiness, is common to many Asian knowledge and belief systems. Maya allows humans to gain perception, the ability to understand and differentiate truth and reality from illusion, thus paving the way for right conduct and morality. In a negative sense, Maya grounds individuals in the mundane world, hindering their ascetic and otherworldly impulses (Khandro 2002: 1). Women in Burma are, according to monks interviewed by Ingrid Jordt (2001: 122–26), more numerous among the meditating laity because of their greater concentration skills, skills honed through childbirth and other forms of suffering occasioned by this grounding in the mundane world. This image of the suffering, nurturing, and, ultimately, stronger female is present in all of the varieties of *medaw* images, myths, and personages in Burma. Popa Medaw, for example, is "a demon mother who died of grief when her twin baby boys . . . were taken from her to be raised at King Anawratha's court. A touching character, she is always invoked at *nat pwes*—even though she is not one of the official 37" (Bekker 1994: 291).

Sarah Bekker (1994) describes a young male actor whose mother dies and a year later finds himself in a Burmese movie about Popa Medaw, who possesses him. Although psychological motivations for entering the Nat spirit cult vary over time for individuals, initially Bekker posits that "grief for a departed mother, perhaps along with guilt, has caused her re-creation in a form which can both be worshipped and depended upon for protection and comfort. . . . His dance for the Popa Meidaw usually leads into one for Khin Ma Tha, the foster mother of Popa Meidaw's infants; then into Thoun Ba Hla, the mother of little Ma Ne; then into Ma Ne. . . . [A]ll these dances revolve around mothers and their children" (291–92). And in a village a few hours north of Rangoon is a family of thirteen, of Indian ancestry, that maintains photographs and a shrine to Kali and in her name performs healings, cures bewitchings, and generally nurtures the health of the village inhabitants. Kali is yet another suffering, healing, and nurturing female (Fell McDermott and Kripal 2003) who in Burma is called the Kali Medaw.

Like Burmese nuns, it is the high mastery of meditation and ascetic practices that affords the Rangoon Medaw the respect of monks and laity alike. According to Jordt (1988: 34), "The Buddha was unequivocal on the point that women are as capable as men in the area of spiritual practice." Hiroko Kawanami (2000: 87–89) argues that in reality women have always been discouraged from becoming renunciates in Burma and that the male population much preferred women to remain lay households and donors. Although the lineage of Buddhist nuns has died out, in the nineteenth century it was decreed that women who are ordained as nuns may wear white or red robes, and *thilashin* in Burma wear salmon pink robes. *Thilashin* commonly take instruction from the monks, not the other way around and are "confined within a male authority structure" (Jordt 1988: 34). Although women who renounce the world cannot have the equivalent of a Sangha, or monastic order, in contemporary Burma, the emphasis is placed, according to Jordt, "on the qualities of a woman renunciate [rather] than on the technicalities of the proper ritual" (35). She argues that this is why we see the emerging trend that "*thilashin* are beginning to be recognized as a different kind of religious person" in Burma (36).

The Rangoon Medaw does not teach *dhamma*, the word of the Buddha, and she does not associate with monks so as to share their field of merit, but, like male mystics, she has the power to rescue other sentient beings from suffering (Schober 1989: 255). She dons the salmon pink robes of Burmese nuns during the Buddhist Lent and then reverts to her self-ordained *arahant* (saintlike) status. Unlike monks, she does not claim to rescue beings from their current position on the wheel of suffering but from the sufferings of their physical bodies. Once they are rescued, she shares in their merit, and they are then free to follow the Theravadin Path to Enlightenment (Schober 1989: 259). In this sense, she is a self-ordained ascetic, a *tapassi:* "one whose practice has led to the acquisition of tapas (power or energy)" (Schober 1989: 283–84). She is a leader of a healing sect *(gaing),* and her association with monks is, for the healer and monks alike, a dangerous one, as mystic sects have been declared illegal for more than twenty years. This situation persists even though contemporary *gaing* members and leaders I interviewed, like Schober's informants (1989), espoused no political ambitions, despite the history and legends of Burmese mysticism being replete with subversive and revolutionary tendencies.

To pull the threads of my argument together, then: women have traditionally gained power, in the time of the Buddhist kings, as queens and Nat spirit mediums, the wives of the spirits.[2] Both forms of power involve being married to someone more powerful; it is a form of *parampara,* or lineage of transmission of power, of the same order as that between Queen Maya and the Rangoon Medaw. This lineage of transmission of power is seen increasingly in female healers and spiritists in central Burma and in images of the *medaw* archetype who bestows healing power on her disciples. The Burmese military regime is acutely aware of the political potential of individuals holding spiritual power throughout Burmese history. This is why images of the Grandfather archetype, Bo Bo Gyi, have undergone a process of political neutralization in their sculpting and placement in recent years.

No such process has been possible with regard to the spiritual power of Grandmothers. In Asia this lineage of transmission applies equally for political and for spiritual power. It is, for example, common for the wives of murdered or deceased political leaders to come to power. In Burma, the daughter of the independence hero, Aung San, has come to political power as the leader of the democracy movement, but she is the only woman to do so. She is dangerous because of her skills in Buddhist techniques of meditation and her devout asceticism (Houtman 2005; Schober 2005). Her status and that of the head of the New York–based Burma project, Maureen Aung Thwin, are continually denigrated in the state media. Their images are not allowed to appear in public space. These prominent political women are equated with bad queens in Buddhist history and compared with evil and wild spirits, prostitutes, low-caste Indian groups, and other negative stereotypes active in the public domain (Skidmore 2004).

The images that are allowed to exist are those of the billboard queens and the military wives engaged in nation-building efforts. Burma is a country where women have acted as village headmen, have been rewarded by the government for their services in fighting crime, and have been editors of the major national newspapers and magazines and where *medaw* images are plentiful. It is strange, then, to see a new absence of images of politically and spiritually powerful women and the representation of public space as overwhelmingly male, where women melt into the background, a phenomenon that is at odds with the reality of women's prominence in public life.

Anauk Medaw: The Shadow of The Lady

In "The Cordon Sanitaire" (2002), Philippa Levine notes the distinction in British Burma between the visible street women and the sequestered, invisible prostitutes. She quotes an 1873 medical officer: "There are of prostitute women two distinct classes—the bona fide order, who live in a recognized quarter, and sit at their doors with painted faces, lanterns, and looking-glasses inviting all comers; and the secret set . . . who do not publicly confess prostitution, but are available when called upon" (51). In British society the body of the streetwalking prostitute embodied lawlessness, but in colonial domains, Levine argues, the very invisibility of these hidden prostitutes made painfully visible to British administrators the cracks in the moral, legal, and static definitions of the social world promulgated by the British. The territory of gender and efforts to govern it are central to Levine's colonial analysis but never more relevant than today in Burma when the territory of gender and the invisible, subversive power of the feminine are once again central to "proscriptive modes of justification and order" in the former British colony and throughout the former nations of the British Raj (54). Levine also notes the imperceptible melding of geography with gender as brothels remain "domestic spaces turned into commercial purposes" (54). This definition of brothels is equally applicable to public images of Burmese women as gender and geography merge in the scripted images of the billboard queens promulgated by the state media and transnational Asian marketing companies in the modern Burmese metropole.

Much of the discomfiture found in the letters and memos of British colonial administrators stems from the refusal of many prostitutes to confine themselves to Tackally, the traditionally enclosed sphere for Rangoon's prostitution trade.[3] The confining of female sexuality within the bounds of red-light districts and in the universally familiar tawdry dress of the street prostitute and brothel habitué gave, according to Levine (58–59), a measured sense of relief in the British Raj, because it marked these women as belonging to public space. It was the sundering of the distinction between public and private that Levine reads as the most powerful aspect of "hidden prostitution," and in Burma today similar contradictory problems are posed for the regime by the new visibility of female magical healers. Even as women adopt this male form of religious and charismatic power—nuns and female *rustic-robed* ascetics and cult leaders, for example—it is harnessed now as visible and therefore within the proscriptions of justification and order. This is the contradiction with the self-representations of women as ascetics and magical healers; they refuse to be the domestic turned into the commercial or to remain within the male authority structure.

By refusing to be spirit wives (Natkadaw) and instead being spiritually superior to Sayadaws, akin to Buddha's mother, they are closer to bodhisattva, or Buddhas-to-be; they are women beyond the control of the military council, answerable only to the Buddha, and deriving their power in this world from sources that are undeniable and untouchable by Buddhist generals. The political potential of such women is a source of new unease for the state, which contests such images with its own proliferation of politically neutral

Figure 19.
Aung San Suu Kyi.
By permission,
Panos Pictures and
Nic Dunlop.

female archetypes. All to no avail. Throughout the country one cannot help but hear the rumors that the democracy leader, The Lady, is a *nat thami*, the Guardian Nat of Democracy, the Goddess of University Avenue, a bodhisattva come to deliver the people from dictatorship (Houtman 1999: 282–84; 2005; Nemoto 1996). And in her tacit acceptance of the label political *medaw*, The Lady uses forms of both Buddhist and Nat spirit power to claim the moral authority necessary for political legitimacy in contemporary Burma (Fig. 19).

Billboard queens line the city streets and the military wives of the MMCWA own the streets of the suburbs, but looming over all these modern women is the shadow of The Lady: morally superior to mortal men, imbued with the strength of the nation and the people she inherited first from her father and then from her leadership of the pro-democracy movement, and completely cognizant of her fellowship with other powerful female presidents and prime ministers in South and Southeast Asia. Her towering shadow, the powerful significance of her absence in public space, is nothing but the fear of the military regime writ large and the awareness of their impotence to control or contain the power of the feminine in Burma.

NOTES

1. Guillaume Rozenberg (2005) has written of this particular expression of modernity that has come about with the collapse of the mini–economic boom of the early 1990s and the relaxation of rules regarding travel for Burmese citizens.

2. In the past decade this predominantly female form of power has been diminishing with the rise of male transvestites adopting the role of Natkadaw and forming *nat* troupes. Several of the female Natkadaw I interviewed now wish to be described as *achawzaw,* or spirit healers, to distinguish themselves from the transvestite spirit troupes that emphasize performance, dance, and costume as opposed to the healing and counseling aspects of the role when the medium intercedes with the Nat on behalf of the client.

3. In regional and Upper Burma, the English word *hotel (ho-teh)* is synonymous with "brothel," as Chinese and Burmese hoteliers retain a number of young women as in-house prostitutes, a tradition continued by most of the new international hotels in urban areas.

9

With Patience We Can Endure

INGRID JORDT

At present Burma is ruled by one of the world's most repressive regimes. However, those of us who conduct research here have been sharing the observation that our exposure to it has been minimal and indirect. We tend to witness little of the violence we know has been endemic during the time we have been in the country. I wish to comment on the reason for this by way of a beginning to this chapter. It is not, I think, because we happen to be located where or on occasions when the regime's repression is not exercised. Rather, there is a sense in which the violence, as well as any burgeoning forms of resistance to it, is best observed beneath the surface of what Habermas (1991) originally referred to as "the public sphere." For him, the public sphere (and here I refer to his notion of "bourgeois public sphere")[1] is ideally "a discursive arena that is home to citizen debate, deliberation, agreement and action" (Villa 1992: 712). In this chapter I consider the usefulness or lack thereof of this and related terms for considering the form the regime's suppression of political freedoms takes, as well as the spaces or spheres in which opposition to or accommodation of the regime take place.

I began by commenting on the position of the researcher relative to the suppression and violence of the military regime, and I wish to continue in that vein for a little longer. I do so because I believe that some of the same impulses that prompt us as outside researchers to avert our gaze from matters that are taboo from the regime's standpoint are shared also by Burmese people themselves living as subjects under these conditions. As a researcher, when a taboo subject comes into view, the tendency is to demonstrate to everyone around you that you are not seeing it. You might be inquiring along a certain track, when suddenly it seems that you are treading on uncomfortable ground. Your conversation partner begins to show apprehension, to avert her or his gaze, for fear of coming under the arbitrary surveillance of a highly controlling military apparatus.

There are of course other reasons for a researcher to avoid uncomfortable subjects, among them concern about being expelled from the country and having one's visitation rights revoked. I was thus expelled for four years following a brief and innocent meeting with the late prime minister U Nu in 1988. And so if I may continue with my own experience as a researcher in more recent visits, I believe the reader will gain some insight through my eyes into the nature of secrecy, suppression, and public discourse in Burma. In 1995, seven years after the military's brutal crackdown of pro-democracy demonstrations staged around Burma and focused on the capital of Rangoon, I returned to Rangoon and the meditation center Mahasi Thathana Yeiktha where I had first resided as a *thilashin,* or nun, in 1984–85. This was not my first return to Burma (as an anthropologist), but to my eyes the mark of time seemed to weigh more heavily on the city and its people. The unremittingly oppressive imprint of the State Law and Order Restoration Council (SLORC) was everywhere in evidence. Preparations for the Year of Tourism were under way. The junta busied itself with Burma's grand opening.[2] The whitewashed facade of the city, its sterile billboards proclaiming state propaganda, the absence of the little shanty rows that used to line the road leading to the heart of the city, the tawdry ocher-gold paint that blanketed ancient Buddhist monuments—everywhere the signs cried out that a different city lay somewhere beneath this dazzlingly vulgar, disciplined display. World-class hotels and Southeast Asian–style shopping complexes had been erected in numbers. Yet only the very smallest segment of the elite could afford to patronize such places. Military decree severely restricted individuals from assembling. Constant surveillance—open and secret—produced the palpable sensation of terror and suspiciousness in the population, a contagious feeling toward which I felt no immunity. State domination over the city's public space appeared absolute.

How did one encounter the surveillance? If I was speaking with someone even in private and touched on topics that did not seem suitable because they made some connection to the broad field of politically sensitive topics, he or she would immediately put a finger to the lips and point to different places in the room to suggest that we might be being bugged. I would then turn the conversation back toward an explicitly Buddhist discussion. As will become at least partly clear in this chapter, it is because of the fusion of political and religious spheres in Burma that one could easily traverse this divide. In any case, even if you were in a public place such as a market you would look around constantly because people would tell you, "This person is following you, he's military," or "That person over there is a spy here in the market. Watch out! Don't do anything in front of him." In my case, a monk, who the executives at the Mahasi center considered a government spy, was assigned to me as a tagalong, putatively as my helper but also my constant companion. Although I did not consider him a direct danger to me, my suspicions were reinforced by the fact that it was I who was careful not to be indiscreet in the matters discussed. Everywhere I went, people were extremely suspicious. And of course you have the obligation not to betray the people who are sponsoring you as their guest, in whatever circumstances. Your actions will rebound on them. So you are careful not to accept the wrong dinner invitation, to be seen somewhere you shouldn't be, and to constantly guard your speech—to speak only of the subjects you have told the government you have come to talk about, which in my case was doctrinal Buddhism.

It is fair, then, to conclude this introduction with a focus on precisely the question of the public sphere and what is regarded as appropriate, safe discourse or forms of discourse in such circumstances. The regime has sought to secure its authority in one respect by enforcing an oppressive silence on the public sphere. It will not tolerate free assembly or collective debate and consistently hands out long prison sentences to all those who seek to form associations without its direct permission. Yet if Burmese have been silenced in their critique of a repressive regime, where and how might they discuss these matters? How do they present an alternative position to the government when it is not allowed? Put more analytically for our purposes: To where has public space escaped? Have Burmese simply retreated to the private domain of their homes? Has a critique of the state become sublimated in some other fashion?

First, I want to discuss the latter possibility, in terms of a number of subjects or domains of inquiry. This entails allusion to Burmese Buddhism-specific notions of power, authority, and government legitimacy, and in these terms, the specific ways in which the military regime has gone about asserting its power. Once this framework is clear, I turn to the forms of resistance to the regime discernable in two spheres of action: the renunciate positioning of monks and the (largely) female devotees who engage in meditation and who participate in what I have elsewhere discussed as the mass lay meditation movement (Jordt 2007). I argue that an alternative moral social order based on right intentions and the assertion of a right society in Buddhist terms is invoked to coerce the government into partial compliance at the same time that Burmese themselves are seen to accommodate or at least sustain the awful demands of the military junta.

An Alternate Action Sphere

In her recent account of terror and oppression in Burma, Christina Fink (2001: 185) relates that students secretly circulate banned books in an effort to "use literature to educate people about the political situation and motivate them to consider taking action. . . . Once a person had read [a book], he or she would write a short comment and the name of his or her home town in the back and pass it on to another member." In this way students make explicit their common purpose and sense of community. In a society where it is impossible to have free and open conversation, Fink suggests, students have created a kind of public space in the interior of their private spheres. Individuals who may never have met in face-to-face relations in public spaces encounter one another through serial communication in an underground realm of public life. In this stunted political environment, communication thrives on the determination to secure an alternate space from which to communicate and exchange ideas that critique the state and escape its hegemonic control. In Fink's words, "For those who had developed political ideas, knowing they had similarly minded peers in other parts of the country was very important. They often felt isolated among their own school-mates, most of whom thought it pointless to question military control" (185).

It is this issue of how public space gets created in an interior sphere that I also wish to address. However, while it is probable that this sort of mechanical reconfiguration of public space in the interest of resisting the government is taking place in a number of situations, I believe the underlying model on which this siting builds in fact conceals from view a more profound and culturally particular process. This alternate process accomplishes some of the same ends, while its dynamics resonate more directly with a majority of Burmese because, as a form of social action, it satisfies cosmological criteria for validity.

Fink's notion of where to look for resistance conforms to where we would expect to find a nascent democracy movement in the West, were similar circumstances somehow to be in force. In this case, the "public sphere" is implicitly taken to be a synonym for democratic society itself. Indeed, in this model it is predictable that under circumstances of oppression, vox populi would simply find an alternate microphone with which to disseminate its views. This microphone is projected "underground," and its activists are often students, who the world over are enthusiastic in pursuit of freedoms and resistance to oppression, human rights violations, and so on. This is not to play down, or certainly not to discourage, the fact of this level of resistance in Burma. However, I argue that a more mature and by another measure far greater segment of the population is involved in what can be construed as antiregime discourse but which is not outwardly so.

To make my case, I wish to point to one further framework implicit to Fink's account. This is the Habermasian assumption that the "public sphere" is characterized by verbal and written communication, that is, rhetoric, conversation, debate, and so on. Fink (2001: 189) explains, "The generals understand that if people do not have concrete ideas about how to change Burma and are lacking leaders and organizations to spearhead a movement, they will remain quiescent." The public space, which as I earlier pointed out is analytically linked to (democratic) civil society, is supposed to be where citizens work out ideas known familiarly to us as "public opinion" and where grounds for agitation against the government are deliberated and established. The regime, for its part, acts out its role as the oppressive state by seeking to extinguish the opportunities for open discourse among its citizens. Thus we see the characteristic political scientific framework of state versus civil society emerge as the implicit model for analysis.

Two clues to the inadequacy of this model in Burma are as follows. First, there is the fact often raised by commentators of Burma that, as hard as one looks for activism, in the end what one mostly sees is an apparent apathy to the awful situation (Taylor 1987; Min Zin 2003). The origins of this apathy are traced, in this view, to a fatalistic interpretation of the doctrine of *kamma* (Sanskrit, karma). The minister of Home and Religious Affairs explained to me, giving voice to common wisdom, "The people have to realize that they have this relation with Ne Win[3] because of their past actions. How can they escape their own karma?" To take the point a bit further, in the West we have an idea about regime legitimacy that is based on regime performance, grounded in terms of whether there is slave labor, oppression, torture, imprisonment, and the delivery of various goods to the populace. In Burma those ideas of performance, at least from the perspective of a fatalistic assertion of *kamma,* are not determinative criteria for legitimate rule. A "king" who is brutal may nevertheless be legitimate.

From another perspective, however, traditional folk understanding has it that kings are to be counted among the five enemies or perils. In her book, *Freedom from Fear,* Noble Peace Prize–winner Aung San Suu Kyi reflects on traditional Burmese understandings of political legitimacy by recounting the moral duties of Buddhist kings:

> The Buddhist view of kingship does not invest the ruler with the divine right to govern the realm as he pleases. He is expected to observe the Ten Duties of Kings, the Seven Safeguards against Decline, the Four Assis-tances to the People, and to be guided by numerous other codes of con-duct such as the Twelve Practices of Rulers, the Six Attributes of Leaders, the Eight Virtues of Kings and the Four Ways to Overcome Peril. . . . In-tegrity *(ajjjava) [sic]* implies incorruptibility in the discharge of public duties as well as honesty and sincerity in personal relations. There is a Bur-mese saying: "With rulers, truth, with (ordinary) men, vows." While a pri-vate individual may be bound only by the formal vows that he makes, those who govern should be wholly bound by the truth in thought, word and deed. Truth is the very essence of the teachings of the Buddha, who re-ferred to himself as the Tathagata or "one who has come to the truth." The Buddhist king must therefore live and rule by truth, which is the perfect uniformity between nomenclature and nature. To deceive or to mislead the people in any way would be an occupational failing as well as a moral offence. (1991: 170–71)

However, interpretations of virtuous kingship according to a Buddhist moral framework are not easily or directly translatable into a theory of mod-ern democratic politics for Burma. Western criteria for regime performance and democratically informed ideas about popular sovereignty depend on other ideas about the origins of society and the proper relations obtaining between civil society and the state. In the context of the mass lay meditation commu-nity I studied, Aung San Suu Kyi was viewed first and foremost as the daugh-ter of the martyred independence leader Aung San and as a charismatic op-position to the military authorities in power. It was not democracy per se that compelled admiration and loyalty. I often heard gentle critiques of The Lady (at first she was called "the little girl") for what was viewed as her lack of understanding of Burmese Buddhist ideas on account of having been raised abroad. The conceptual apparatus for conceiving of power struggles as those between civil society and the state was strongest among students, although students also drew on cosmic symbols and took the names of Buddhist kings to signal their roles as "pretenders to the throne," for example, during the 1988 demonstrations against the government. In other words, resistance to the regime most widely resonates when these are framed as arguments about the *cosmic* legitimacy of the military. Whereas students are viewed as the most active and vocal opponents to the regime other forms of resistance can also be identified in the activities of the Sangha (monastic order) and the lay meditation community. It is here, in the ostensibly apolitical sphere of *sasana*[4] activity that political action may be detected and measured and where political legitimacy is ultimately defined and warranted. It is not primarily through political commentary that monks represent a threat to the legitimacy of rulers, though surely there are outspoken monks. Rather, it is the way monks assert a moral purity transcending the morality of kings that they are able to bring their influence to bear on the question of regime legitimacy. This is because Burmese Buddhist beliefs widely hold that merit (acquired through lifetimes of generosity and morality) is the cause for relations of domination and subordination. In this framework, monks actively produce the power-sustaining domination by transmuting acts of donation and reverence by members of the regime into worldly power and authority. For this reason monks are to be both venerated and supported by the government while at the same time they must be removed from the realm of everyday politics and contained in their domain as world renouncers—the antisociety. It is from this tension that we may explore the rich engagements of resistance located at the nexus of activities between the military, the Sangha, and the lay supporters of monks and members of lay meditation societies.

What my informants often said—and thus the title of this chapter—is, "With patience *(kanti)* we can endure." Is this the very soul of apathy? Or is it a window into a culturally specific way of bearing hardship that encompasses also a species of resistance that we can probe and investigate? Following James Scott's (1985) assertion that everyday resistance by subalterns show they have not consented to domination, I explore how practices of donation, reverence toward monks, and meditation are locations for identifying "hidden transcripts" critical of the legitimacy of the military regime.

More important, I wish to signal that these are not merely forms for voicing grumbling discontent but also active spheres that seek change not by operating directly on the body politic (i.e., political action) but by acting on the psychophysical body process (through such things as donation, moral adherence, and meditation) that is the grounds for ontology and being in the world. Precisely because these actions are apolitical they are tolerated by the government. At the same time there exists an unspoken but vigorous competitive engagement on the part of the government and ordinary citizens to participate in and control *sasana* activities since ideas about the sources of power and authority are shared by both members of the military regime and Buddhist citizens. What I wish to argue is that the ostensibly apolitical sphere in which political action may be detected and measured resides in the ubiquitous realm of Buddhist practice or *sasana* activity, which is why it is indecipherable to political scientists who search for answers only in the realm of overt political action and who therefore overemphasize state/civil society frameworks and the processes of democratic reform and authoritarian leadership's resistance to it.

Monks and the State

Monks, who are considered "world renouncers," are by definition the antithesis of polities. In 1995 an adviser at the Religious Affairs Department explained to me how important it is that the government control the Sangha. "Monks," he said, "are like kings. Whatever they say the people will do. The government doesn't want to purge [i.e., purify the religion of heterodoxy] during this period because they want the support of people, and monks have people's support." By this, he meant that monks stand at the head of moral communities, and should they turn their attention to political rather than just spiritual matters, they can pose a threat to the regime.

In the face of this threat, the regime monitors the monks and will disrobe (and then perhaps prosecute) any engaged in overt or covert political activity. In the latter case, the pretext for disrobing becomes the purported violation of the *viniya*, which define the proper behavior for monks. Thus the disrobing of monks, which is itself readily interpretable as sublimated political action, falls under the category of *sasana* purification, for which kings are granted traditional obligation and privilege (see Jordt 2007). And yet—and here is my conclusion foreshadowed in a nutshell—the way in which monks and their followers may ultimately come to have political impact is by assert-ing a moral convention for action that contains within it criteria for regime le-gitimacy, as well as the communal building blocks of political power. Monks pose a threat to the regime because they can claim a higher moral ground; they are the heads of moral communities that adjudicate on the question of potency and the legitimacy of rule. The regime is fearful of being widely deemed insincere in its efforts to support and protect the *sasana*, which is the will of the religious masses. This is true vis-à-vis the regime both on a collec-tive and an individual level, as many members of the regime are themselves observant Buddhists who do not wish to alienate themselves from their sources of merit: leading monks.

The principles of conversion from moral community to political power are too intricate to be described in the space permitted here. However, a re-counting of an empirical example of this procedure will bring us closer to understanding how religious communities, especially those dominated by the participation of women, exert their influence. I refer in the following ex-ample to an alternate sphere for political behavior. These are forms other than those identified by Habermas and Fink, for the case of Burma, in which one can locate a sublimated critique of the state.

A Revered Monk and the Regime's Attempt to Capture His Potency

Pilgrimage is a common means to religious piety in Burma. Widespread pilgrimage to the venerable monk, Thamanya Sayadaw, alleged by many to be a fully enlightened saint, or *arahat*, is noteworthy in several respects. For years, until his death in December 2003, busloads of devotees departed daily from Rangoon on a ten-hour ride to Karen state where Thamanya Sayadaw resided atop a mountain ringed at the base by three Pa-O villages. They came to offer their respects and donations *(dana)*, to hear him discourse on the *dhamma* (Buddha's teachings), and to bask in his radiant presence for a short while.

Thamanya Sayadaw's presence, moreover, is in evidence all over Rangoon. His picture functions as protective amulet on the dashboards of cars and buses, around the necks of women and children, in the glass cases of gem and jewelry dealers in the marketplaces, among the paraphernalia and Bud-dha *rupas* (images) in public and private shrines. The typical response to the question, "Have you been to see Thamanya Sayadaw?" is either "Of course" or "Not yet." People often recount the number of times they have undertaken the pilgrimage, adding wistfully that they hope to go again if the Sayadaw (who was in fragile health in his final years) "lasts."

This example already shows how people are communicating through the use and presence of the amulet that bears Thamanya Sayadaw's picture. Because it is found in both sacred and private places it serves as a connection between the sacred and private realms at the same time that it signifies commonality of view and a safe context in which to talk. I found that whenever I wore my amulet of Thamanya Sayadaw (I visited the venerated monk) people were willing to talk to me. There was not only political safety implied but also a kind of magical safety.

It does not require much prodding for a discussion of Thamanya Sayadaw to turn to political issues. Thamanya Sayadaw's longtime refusal to come to the capital and be honored by the State Law and Order Restoration Council/State Peace and Development Committee (SLORC/SPDC) has remained a deep source of irritation to the military. In response to inquiries about why the Sayadaw refuses to come to Rangoon, I was told by a variety of people there that it was a sign the monk did not view the government as legitimate. Thamanya Sayadaw, they said, refused to become a "government monk," decorated with the titles of an illegitimate regime. (The regime has taken to securing its own hierarchy of monks by awarding prizes to feats of scholarship by learned monks. It apparently hopes this will mirror the populace's own values and criteria for good monks.) Elaborate rumors contrasting the circumstances and events surrounding the Sayadaw's aloof reception of the military ruler, Khin Nyunt, with that of National League for Democracy (NLD) leader, Aung San Suu Kyi, circulate. These accounts often include miraculous and magical details evidencing Thamanya Sayadaw's sainthood. Discussion of his remarkable qualities is transposed into a discourse critical of the ruling junta and lionizing Aung San Suu Kyi. In the context of severely restricted freedom of speech and assembly in contemporary Burma, such active and visible support for an exemplary monk allows a speaker to communicate political views while leaving open the possibility of shifting ground to the safety of orthodox Buddhist rhetoric.

One might add that this is where slippage between conversation levels takes place. For example, in my presence a person said, "No, he [Thamanya Sayadaw] is a very good monk, he only supports the good people, he knows this government is insincere so he won't support them." In this comment we discern that *sasana* language subsumes the political realm. However, the line about the government could as easily be left off, so what remains is a language purely about *sasana* and which only by extension and in some contexts also incorporates a political commentary. Even where the intention is to focus explicitly on the unfairness of the regime, one can immediately code switch and say, "Oh, I'm just talking about *sasana*." And in that zone there is no fear.

That Thamanya Sayadaw's overt rejection of the junta reinforces perceptions of his saintliness,[5] while his saintliness demonstrates the illegitimacy of the regime, has its roots both in political rhetorical practices of Burmese Buddhists and in understandings of what the transcendent sources of power are. Contemporary Burmese ideas about political rule still draw heavily on the rhetoric of kingship and associated notions of the role of the Sangha in conferring legitimacy to the political order. Answering to this populist and indeed social structural demand, the regime supports the Sangha in the role of king and chief donor. However, it would be insufficient to think of these processes of legitimation and the military clique's engagement with the Sangha as mere performative spectacles in pursuit of the appearance of legitimate political rule. Moral performative acts such as donation or pagoda building and repair, in which the government conspicuously participates,[6] are believed to create the actual transcendent causal circumstances that result in political power. Min Zin explains:

> The Burmese concept of *hpoun,* . . . originally meant the cumulative result of past meritorious deeds, but later came to be synonymous with power. . . . The discourse of *hpoun* is so deeply embedded in Burmese culture that few even think to question it. Since *hpoun* is theoretically a "prize" earned through past good deeds, it is self-legitimating: Simply by virtue of possessing power, one has demonstrated that one has acquired considerable merit in past lives. Thus the question of moral legitimacy does not arise. As long as one remains in the ascendancy (whether socially, politically, or economically), one is presumed to possess merit. . . . In the political realm, this reliance upon the notion of *hpoun* is even more pronounced. No matter how morally unfit a ruler may appear to be, as long as he is able to cling to power, he can claim that his *hpoun* is still flourishing. (Min Zin 2001: 1)

Appreciating how potency translates into power and political legitimacy in Burmese Buddhist terms is integral to understanding government actions.[7]

Thamanya Sayadaw's refusal to place his considerable field for merit making at the disposal of the ruling junta was understood to be a practical determination to prevent the military from accruing merits that might sustain their hold on power. This last interpretation is supported by a remarkable event recounted to me by the director of Religious Affairs in 2002. It helps draw into focus the dimensions of a shared set of representations held by the state and Buddhist populace over what the sources of political legitimacy are.

In May 2002 Thamanya Sayadaw, who was suffering from diabetes, slipped into a coma. In desperation his guardian committee *(kopaka apwe)* rushed him to a Rangoon hospital where he remained comatose for several days. While Thamanya Sayadaw lay unconscious, the military leaders and key high-ranking members of the government came to "pay their respects" and to make offerings in his hospital room. A high official from Religious Affairs took pride over the fact that he had the good *paramis* (moral perfections cultivated over incalculable lifetimes) to be in the proximity of the great monk and also that he was able to offer him *dana* (donations).

The official's boast reveals a double claim. First, his high status is justified as the consequence of prior meritorious actions for which his present incarnation is the result. Privilege and status is not conceived as subtracting from another person's natural rights. Relationships of exploitation and privilege say things about prior *kammic* (Sanskrit, karmic) relationships. The present is always justly warranted because each individual reaps the consequences of his own prior intentions and actions. Second, the director's smug relating of how he had offered *dana* to Thamanya Sayadaw in such intimate circumstances was meant to communicate to me his privileged access to the great monk. It was understood that leveraged merit-making opportunities would ultimately translate into auspicious conditions in the future. The genuine respect that the Sayadaw garners from both government officials and their critics is one evidential moment of the force exertible on the regime through religious or cosmological means.

The government's surreptitious attempt to exploit the moral causal assets of Thamanya Sayadaw provides us with an interpretive key for understanding the process by which the regime seeks to control monks, the Buddhist populace, and the many merit fields that are the leveraged locations for the production of *hpoun,* or merit-based power. A survey of its activities demonstrates that the SLORC/SPDC has made greater efforts than any other post-independence government to demonstrate that the military clique is foremost among all the laity in their support of the Sangha and Buddha *sasana.* Acting as primary donors among the laity in support of *sasana* and the Sangha is not a mere metaphorical effort directed at associating the symbols of classical kingship with military rule, thereby presuming political legitimacy from the populace. State efforts to "capture potency" are as much a concern about controlling monks' merit fields as about controlling the moral communities surrounding monks. Inasmuch as the government did not maintain a relationship of official patronage with Thamanya Sayadaw, its legitimacy (at best) remained in doubt among the monk's many devotees.[8]

Mass Meditation and the Double Order of Law

On one level what emerges thus far is a model only slightly emending that of the public/private sphere theory of Habermas and Fink. That is, there is a deflection or perhaps sublimation of public political discourse to an alternate sphere and in an alternate mode. Monks are both the symbolic and tangible fields for merit production of rulers. As the legitimate living continuity of the Buddha's *sasana,* they represent ultimate truth (the *dhamma*) and may also legitimately evaluate the moral actions of political authority. The Sangha both asserts and justifies public metavalues and is the empirical grounds for its warrant. They are therefore the legitimate critics of political authority. However, as world renouncers they are also constrained by their moral code *(viniya)* not to be involved in the politics of worldly life. For this reason, it is primarily through forms of public justification rather than criticism that monks are best able to redress unjust rulers. This sort of assertion of the moral terms of public life needs to be evaluated as a form of context framing that is not explicitly political but that has political implications. The terms of moral reality are made by way of reference to intention *(cettana).* It is to this that I turn next in consideration of the mass lay meditation movement and the prominent place women have taken in it.

Where public space is repressed and controlled by an oppressive regime, Buddhist Burmese (especially among the urban middle class) claim control *over the private space of their intention* in pursuit of creating better future life circumstances. This is accomplished through the widespread practices of meditation, which I discuss presently. From this place, I claim, the populace can challenge the sincerity of the government's *sasana*-supporting actions while simultaneously exerting a sort of pressure on them. The overall effect is that a seemingly very private and individualistic practice, meditation, conceived as acting on one's own psychophysical processes, becomes a fulcrum of action in the social and political world. The emergence of a mass lay meditation movement (Jordt 2007) is the vehicle for this action on the world in both the logic of its encounter and the sheer force of numbers of adherents—millions.

The mass lay meditation movement is a relatively recent historical phenomenon that began as a rural millenarian movement in reaction to British colonialism in the mid- to late 1800s. One of the implicit goals of the early movement was to protect the Buddha *sasana* from degeneration and decay in the absence of a Buddhist king, whose first responsibility as head of society was to guard and preserve the Buddha's teachings and dispensation. The goals of the state and the goals of *sasana* perpetuation were so fundamentally intertwined that when the British deposed the Burmese king (including removing his throne from the country so that no usurpers might lay claim to it), monks began in earnest to teach the laity how to practice meditation for enlightenment, believing that the end of the world was approaching.

The mass lay meditation movement is characterized by the breadth of socioeconomic differences of its participants—from educated elite to farmers, who come from the countryside by the busload during the agricultural slow season to undertake brief courses—and by the wide range in ages. It is common, for instance, for children and university students to spend a portion of their summer vacation together practicing silent meditation. The most distinguishing feature of this "new laity" is that women are by far the main participants.[9] They outnumber men five to one in, for example, Burma's largest and most renowned center, Mahasi Thathana Yeiktha. Yet despite the massive entry of women into the lay meditation movement over the past fifty years, it is not perceived as a women's project.

The mass lay meditation movement is more than a revitalization movement but stops somewhere short of a civil society movement. Civil society movements tend to be considered in terms of their goals of power and resource sharing by authoritarian rule. The mass lay meditation movement, by contrast, is not in search of a particular political solution, for example, democracy.[10] It also does not challenge the state in the sense Scott (1985) describes in his "weapons of the weak" argument. And yet the movement has definite implications for the political environment that need to be explored.

The mass lay meditation movement, I argue, has shaped new dimensions in Buddhist practice and has asserted a sacred public sphere critical of the coercive power of the regime. It has been influential in defining the politics of sincerity and ultimately the terms for unforced political legitimacy.

Also characteristic of the new laity is its emphasis on temporary world renunciation to engage in *satipatthana vipassana* (insight) meditation and enlightenment here and now, followed by reintegration into worldly life. Reintegration is a key feature especially for women since men can become long-term monks and thereby embody the category of world renouncers. Women who practice for a long time may at most become "ten precept" lay nuns. Usually they practice and then go back to the life of a householder. They reincorporate their experiences in meditation into daily life. And there are millions of women doing this. What happens for these millions of women who practice meditation and then return to their normal lives is a reformulation of their attitude toward everyday suffering.

I asked one woman, a yogi at the Mahasi Yeiktha, how she has been able to endure all the suffering under military rule. She responded, "With *kanti* [patience] we can endure" (Thee kan kwin lwet dey). It would be theoretically facile to explain (or reduce) the mass practice of meditation as (to) a psychological impulse for survival. However, explanations of how mental states are cultivated to withstand poverty and violent repression only distantly approximate the sense in which these experiences are meaningfully felt. "Thee kan kwin lwet dey" includes the idea that having *kanti* necessarily implies that one has also "dropped," or let go of, the reasons you hold against a person for their wrongful actions. In the act of forbearance is included the act of forgiveness. Forms of consciousness are interrelated on a separate level, the level people experience when they meditate. *Kanti* thus becomes not just a psychological defense but also a social space that conforms to certain collective values and dispositions and that incorporates distinct means of communication. People inhabiting that "space" respond to the keywords associated with meditation.

Thus, to reiterate the idea in a slightly different way, it is not merely the psychological value of patience or equanimity cultivated by practitioners through *vipassana* meditation that I mean to use as an explanation for how vital experiences encountered in meditation become the empirical reference for the assertion of metavalues in the public domain. The appeal to a transcendent truth through the experiences of *vipassana* insights (*nyanzin*) becomes in the public sphere a form of public justification asserting the terms of a politics of sincerity. It is precisely because these assertions are not criticisms but verifications that they are capable of positively differentiating a separate moral arena from that of the state.

To discern this it is best to start with a certain notion of interiority, or privacy, which becomes the space in which one copes with the contradictions of the contemporary historical moment, its violations against the *sasana*. The only place one can take refuge is in one's own intentions toward oneself. Once this becomes a mass movement, regulated by the systematic technique of *satipatthana vipassana* meditation, and with institutional apparatuses to support its practice, the experience of shared insight (there are twelve stages of insight) itself becomes a reality—a verification procedure. It becomes a warrant about the truth of a lived reality.

It is important to differentiate the "lived reality" that emerges from the mass lay meditation movement, with all its latent criticism of the regime included, from an explicit "antilaw" reality. The state versus civil society model in which students (for example) oppose the regime would conform to a law versus antilaw scenario. To antilaw activities the regime responds with force: increased enforcement, suppression, violence. By contrast, here I wish to introduce the notion of a double order of law, in which the moral orders invoked by separate groups accommodate, overlap with, or conflict with one another according to circumstance. Two statements from my field interviews are sufficient to signal the concept in action.

One woman explained to me, "Just to live you have to break your precepts." Once you have reached the insight stage of being unable to break your precepts,[11] this situation presents a contradiction. Yet here is a woman who claims to be enlightened (and therefore incapable of breaking her precept not to lie), and she tells me that just to live you have to break your precepts. "This is no law. Sometimes we have to not tell the truth just so we can live. The government is trying to make criminals out of the whole population. So we think, 'This is not the real law.' Only the *dhamma* is the real law, so we just do like this [i.e., break the first precept not to lie]. In our minds we know." This negation of the lie by imagining a double order of law—the conventional one imposed and the transcendent law of *dhamma*—depends on the understanding that an alternative public space exists within which the conventions of truth-saying remain consistent. Words and intentions become perversely separated in a practical act that interiorizes the public space of moral society.

How does the internal versus external, private versus public distinction as described here apply to politics? It is perceived that there will be a consequence for the regime's insincere actions. The junta's good deeds are regarded by some as sorcery, because there is no sincerity behind the actions. A committee member of the lay women's association of the Mahasi Thathana Yeiktha meditation center offers an interpretation:

> This government is only trying to look like they support the Sangha. They say the monks have so much influence on the public. So they claim that the *dayakas* [lay supporters of monks] were doing politics. First they arrested so many monks in 1988. They searched monasteries and kicked out people and arrested monks saying they were sleeping with women. They showed bodices and suspenders of ladies to show how the monks were bad. They planted all these things. They said the monks were dealing in gems. Then they created rival factions within the *sasana*. They elected all the big names, the old Sayadaws, the monks who wouldn't speak politics. They created a nomination process [by] which the Sangha elects their members, but the government tries to push their own candidates by putting pressure on monks they think are on their side. Formerly, every monk was against them. This government is bluffing. They're not sincere. Why don't these monks do something?

We see here that Sangha purification is not in itself considered a bad thing, but the government's intentions are dubious, that is, politically motivated. They are accused of insincerity, of "bluffing." The dual recognition of the blunt efficacy of sacred acts in reproducing auspicious circumstances for agents and of the fact that sacred acts may be enacted with thoroughgoing duplicity—for example, as manipulation of the *dhamma* through sorcery— is here being hinted at. Intention and action in Burmese Buddhist reckoning are recognized as two kinds of acts that produce future ontological realities. Acts disconnected from an agent's intentions are believed to be causally efficacious, despite the stress on intention as the forerunner of action. Even so, intention inflects speech and bodily acts, with the *kammic* resultant effect to take place in some unspecified future. And it is understood to have causal efficacy independent of actions.

The mass lay meditation movement has brought about the conviction among its members that the technique for the objective foundations of psychic experiences can be attained through the practice of *satipatthana vipassana* meditation. The inner process of systematic insights is outwardly verified according to criteria that cannot directly impute evidence of inner states in other people. However, as is true of language, there is agreement and consent about the systematic structure of experiences and the criteria for their validation. Whether or not there is understanding in the sense of individual primary experience of sense structures, there is nevertheless participation in these assertions about inner states, vis-à-vis the military and beyond. Thus there has emerged a concern over the sincerity of intentions and the interpretation of the true meaning of outer actions as they correspond to inner states. This is the level at which public political discourse takes place. The question asked of military actors is, is their action connected to their inner states?

Discourses about sincerity of intentions are therefore simultaneously about contemporary and ultimate reality. Legitimate claims to power can only be made if one is sufficiently endowed with merits cultivated in this and previous lifetimes. And, as in a Calvinist model, election is evaluated on the basis of what is seen from the outside as sincere efforts by an individual to perform meritorious acts in support of *sasana*. The "withdrawal of trust," to borrow an expression from Veena Das, in words and actions has created a profound skepticism among the population concerning the intentions of the junta that places their legitimacy-seeking performances under scrutiny and question.

I have referred to the existence of three levels at which one can discern action spheres vis-à-vis evaluation of the regime's activities. These action spheres lie socially and analytically on a continuum relative to each other. On the simplest level, a shunting of debate and formation of public opinion to a kind of underground railroad–level discussion, as among students, is found. The second level entails a kind of code switching, often not recognized as strategically enacted, in which political commentary is inserted in the context of religious discourse and institutions. The pilgrimages and amulets and so on concerning Thamanya Sayadaw are an example of this second level of action sphere. Third, the interior-focused practice of meditation can be seen as also encompassing a form of political commentary. The preponderance of women in the mass lay meditation movement shades this category in a particular way, filtered as it is through silence, accommodation in everyday life, and moral adaptation to the strictures of living under corrupt rule. In the case of the students, if they are caught, then the regime will respond quickly to root out and imprison offenders. In the case of religious practitioners, however, among whom many senior members of the military junta (and their wives) can also be found, the response can be described as accommodation. Ironically, it is on the very question of whether the regime is being sincere in its Buddhist practices that public critique rests.

The other point I wish to reinforce in these concluding remarks is that any critique we wish to find of the regime in the two more subtly manifested political action spheres would be situated more immediately in people's experiences of everyday life. By this, I mean experience as opposed to ideology and, again, not just forms of gossip and rumor but efforts directed toward remaking the moral world. The popularly held conception is that through the revitalization of meditation an enlightened society is being produced. Meditation is a place in which you have a shared experience with other meditators, which invokes an idea about a mythical society from the past that serves as an exemplar for a civilized and enlightened society in the future. This is one reason one cannot regard critique that takes place in the context of the religious sphere as merely a sublimated form of public debate, in the Habermasian sense. The moral issues at stake are more broadly conceived (i.e., on the level of cosmology) and are applied to matters other than politics, which at times appears to be only a tertiary application. Devout women may not be looking to act politically even though their actions might have political effects. In 1990, after a regime-conspired massacre of monks took place in Mandalay, military wives refused to cook for their husbands because their merit field was being cut off. They were not trying to bring down the regime or even to meddle in affairs of state, yet their domestic defiance brought about a cessation of the violence.

NOTES

1. "The bourgeois public sphere may be conceived above all as the sphere of private people coming together as a public; they soon claimed the public sphere regulated from above against the public authorities themselves, to engage them in a debate over the general rules governing relations in the basically privatized but publicly relevant sphere of commodity exchange and social labor" (Habermas 1991: 27).

2. Closed since 1963, when Ne Win replaced U Nu's fledgling parliamentary democracy with a military dictatorship and a military-run Burmese Socialist Program Party (BSPP) government, the new military junta sought to draw new resources to a country badly in need of economic rescue. Aung San Suu Kyi's call to the international community to boycott Burma as a tourist destination has largely been successful. The boycott has not, however, resulted in the intended goal of bringing down the military regime. The regime has only tightened its own grip on power and resources. In 2002 many Rangoon residents I spoke with said that democracy issues had been completely eclipsed for them by bread and butter issues.

3. Burma's first military dictator (1962–88) but thought to be the éminence grise to later dictators until his death in 2003.

4. I use the term *sasana* to refer to the sense in which Burmese regard their "religious" practices. Unlike the term "Buddhism" (which has analytic value and meaning in comparative contexts), *sasana* refers to the teachings of a Buddha and to the dispensation in which a Buddha's teachings exist.

5. I am, of course, not making a causal argument reducing popular recognition of Thamanya Sayadaw's saintliness to a political barometer for antiregime sentiment. Thamanya Sayadaw participated in far more embedded contexts of religious practice.

6. For more detailed accounts of how the military regime participates in religious activities, see Jordt 2003, 2003a, 2003b, 2005, 2007; Houtman 1990, 1999; Schober 1997, 2005.

7. "Spectacular performances" of the sort in which the regime routinely participates I define as association at face value, usually in a highly visual medium, through events or displays by an individual or collectivity (e.g., the military junta) with an identity with a symbolic counterpart. This is the metonymic association of charismatically or morally inflected affects or events with persons. I borrow Stanley Tambiah's (1985) use of "performative action" in the sense of an action undertaken in order to produce an effect and assert a metaphorical relation between things. Thus the junta's attempt to effect material demonstrations of their power and authority through traditional symbols of kingship and sponsorship of religion, which is the purview of kings, makes a claim about the relationship between present and transcendent realities.

8. The military regime's efforts to gain the support of the Buddhist population by making claims about their moral actions and standing in Buddhist terms are recognized by the populace to be manipulative in a variety of ways I consider below. However, it should not go unrecognized that from the point of view of the ordinary Burmese Buddhist citizen the fact that duplicity is involved does not necessarily imply that the junta's actions will not have auspicious transcendent efficacy. The military's efforts to *extract* magical efficacy from sacred acts are reviled and feared by the public. The law of *dhamma* is understood to be a universal law, and manipulation of the law for private gain is not outside the realm of possible affective actions. It is recognized by the general populace that such practices are in direct pursuit of power. Moreover, that rulers have attempted to balance their merit stores in order to secure their continued hold on power is an active concept drawn from classical Buddhist kingship. In these instances, interpretations of the military's moral actions are described as acts of sorcery and not sincere *(yu)* actions on behalf of the *sasana*.

9. I thank F. K. Lehman for suggesting this term.

10. Although the possibility for democratic interpretation of the earliest mythical political institutions has been interpreted by Aung San Suu Kyi as an incipient democratic form.

11. The yogi's experience of insights leads in an inevitable progression from one insight to the next, eventually culminating in enlightenment consciousness. The *sotapanna,* "stream winner" (first-stage enlightened being), has uprooted gross mental defilements. As a consequence, the yogi is presumed to be no longer capable of breaking the five precepts (not to kill, not to steal, not to lie, not to commit adultery, not to take intoxicants).

10

To Marry a Man or a Spirit?

Women, the Spirit Possession Cult,
and Domination in Burma

BÉNÉDICTE BRAC DE LA PERRIÈRE

Frank Lehman, a leading American scholar of Burmese studies, told me that according to one of his informants, a lawyer and longtime friend in Mandalay, female spirit mediums of the Burmese spirit possession cult are known to have been "despotic" wives to their human husbands. Their difficult dispositions made their marriages unworkable, even grounds for divorce, and that is why they had to marry spirit husbands.

This statement highlights the feminine dimensions of the ritual specialization in the Burmese spirit possession cult and raises questions such as whether spirit mediumship gives to Burmese women a kind of agency by offering them an alternative to marriage. In this chapter I want to extend the analysis by looking at how the feminine dimensions of spirit mediumship involve not only Burmese gender construction but also, more generally, Burmese construction of difference and its encoding in the hierarchical system. Following current trends in gender studies, I consider that "gender meanings are not autonomous but intersect with other hierarchies of power" (Werner 2005: 27). Thus the feminine dimensions of spirit mediumship enter into general structures of domination in Burmese culture and may be untangled as a particular instantiation of the Burmese way to delineate others and to establish authority.

Spirit Possession as a Feminine Vocation

Let us first look closer at the feminine dimensions of spirit mediumship in Burma. Spirit mediums, whether men or women, are called Natkadaw in Burmese, which means "spirit wives" according to the best-accepted etymology.[1] Furthermore, they are drawn into spirit possession through a spiritual attack understood by the Burmese as the seduction by a spirit of the Burmese cult pantheon, who then becomes their main spirit, or *khaung swe*, "the head-dragging one." The initiation ritual for becoming a recognized spirit medium, at least for women, is to marry the male spirit. Those who have recently been drawn into the vocation speak readily about the sexual relationship their main spirit has with them, how they make themselves ready for his visit, bathing and perfuming themselves, on the night of the spirit's birthday, when he is expected to appear. These references to the main spirit's nocturnal visits tend to disappear from the accounts of spirit mediums as their experience as mediums progresses (Brac de la Perrière 1989).

Men may also become spirit mediums. About half of my sample of Burmese mediums, established in the 1980s, are men, most of them called Natkadaw.[2] Although they may be linked to female spirits, as sons to mothers, or to male spirits, as younger brothers to elder brothers, many of them are actually married to Ma Ngwe Taung, a female spirit well known for seducing men in order to transform them into transvestites. Many male spirit mediums are transvestites (*meinma sha*) and, although there are no statistics on this development, it seems that their number has increased during the past twenty years. However, male spirit mediums are suspected of homosexuality, which underlines the feminine character of this vocation. And that the mediums are called "spirit wives" whatever their sex further underlines that their relationship is conceived of, on the level of gender representation, as a marital one.[3]

That spirit mediums occupy a feminine position when considered as part of the whole symbolic system makes it all the more interesting to look at the issue from the perspective of gender. How does the cultural construction of the mediums' role in society reflect the construction of gender in Burma? The temperamental character of the women engaged in spirit mediumship, highlighted by Lehman's informant, is indeed a widely recognized explanation of their vocation among the Burmese themselves. This is in sharp contrast to the normative modest behavior imposed on Burmese wives in the presence of their husbands, especially in public.

In analyzing the life stories of female spirit mediums, one encounters various situations leading to spirit possession (Brac de la Perrière 1989). I would more readily characterize these as life crises, often stemming from problematic marital situations such as celibacy, divorce, widowhood, or infertility, whether due to a difficult character or not. On the one hand, the Burmese account of the seduction of these women by the spirits—that their "soul" is "soft" *(leippya nu-)*[4]—contradicts their alleged insubordinate character and supports the common explanation given for women's greater ability to excel at meditation (an alternative path offered to them), namely, the capacity of their bodies to endure pain (Jordt 2005). Both explanations ground the gendered difference in the sexed body of the women. On the other hand, that the Burmese explain the failure of female spirit mediums to have successful marital lives by their willful character raises the question of whether spirit mediumship allows them to reach an acceptable social status without being married and to exercise a certain kind of power or whether encountering the spirit is a way to transform their personality disorder through a process of pacification.

Thus the feminine dimension of spirit possession and the sexual as well as the marital aspect of the relationship established with the spirits are salient aspects of the Burmese cult: in this tradition, special importance is given to the marital link through the celebration of a marriage ritual. These aspects also characterize the ideology of possession cults in general.[5] More generally, the feminine dimension is often associated with the subversive aspect of the spirits. This has been interpreted primarily as evidence that in highly stratified societies possession cults deal with marginal segments of societies, even, in some cases, with expressing opposition to the established order (Lewis 1971).

This is where gender construction and overall structures of domination intersect with spirit possession cults. It is this intersection that I want to depict by asking whether it gives agency to dominated segments of societies that includes contestation of the established order or whether it is a part of the hierarchical setting. I address these questions in the Burmese case by examining first the construction of gender in the Burmese cultural system and the role of the marital bond in it, then the place of the spirit cult and spirit possession in the structures of domination, and finally the contemporary dynamics of this cult.

Women's Status in Theravada Buddhist Society

First, I identify the parallels that can be made between the positions of spirit mediums and women in the Burmese cultural system and how these positions are built up through a marital bond. The construction of gender in Burmese culture has not been the object of much study.[6] However, one can assume that it rests on bases of gender similar to those of other Southeast Asian societies. The image of gender in these societies is a complex: although its economic or material aspects seem to contradict its spiritual aspects, they are actually complementary.

Among the first studies dealing with women's status in Southeast Asia, those conducted by Penny Van Esterik in 1982 already emphasize that the cliché of the strong woman who is economically active conceals the actual construction of gender status in these societies. Indeed, if economic functions and powers may give women a kind of autonomy, they do not bestow prestige on them according to Southeast Asian value systems, as has been stated by Shelly Errington (1990: 6–7), among others.

If it is characteristic of Southeast Asia in general, it is especially true in societies whose predominant religion is Theravada Buddhism. In these societies materialistically oriented activities are held in lower esteem than spiritual achievements as expressed in Buddhist terms. Buddhism accords the highest value to the religious vocation, that is, to monkhood, which entails withdrawal from worldly pursuits and entering Sangha, the monastic order founded by Gautama Buddha. This condition is theoretically the path to *neibban*, or liberation from the cycle of rebirth governed by one's own acts according to karmic law. It provides the main context for spiritual practice, and only those who have already reached a certain level in the spiritual hierarchy may succeed in renunciation. Therefore, the religious vocation has the highest status in Buddhist society.

It is said that women have been banned from monkhood for historical reasons. Although a female order was founded after due controversy in Buddha's time, this institution long ago disappeared in the Theravada school (Watson Andaya 2002). This is the reason given for the fact that in Burma there is no valid ordination for women in the religious system: they are only allowed to become *thilashin*, or nuns, who are of inferior status compared to that of monks or renunciates.[7] This is still the case in Burma and in other Theravadin countries, although allowing ordination of women is again under discussion in modernist circles of Buddhism.

In this configuration, the main spiritual achievement open to women is to struggle in this world for a better rebirth, that is, rebirth as a man: this is the karmic path available to a lay devotee. Their means is the practice of meritorious deeds, mainly religious donations among which the most important are food given to the monks or sons given to Sangha. Both rest on the traditional maternal and nurturing roles of women, roles that further bind them to worldly activities.

In Burma the radical distinction between monks and laypeople persists, and monkhood is still considered by most Burmese the main way to strive for *neibban*, although some alternative paths do exist.[8] As women are banned from the religious order, they are considered spiritually inferior to men, whatever their eventual economic success. According to Burmese Buddhist doctrine, they are born women because of their lower karmic qualification.

In addition to this karmic inferiority, there is a set of taboos regarding spatial relations between men and women the trespassing of which will endanger masculine *phon:*, the characteristic that makes men and monks superior.[9] Actually, these Burmese taboos have a hierarchical component, as observed by Valerio Valeri (1990: 243) among the Huaulu: they imply that women "are superior to men in terms of destructive power and this is why they are considered inferior to them in terms of positive value," a notion based on the assumption that women's blood is polluting.[10] These taboos remind us that the Buddhist construction of male spiritual superiority rests on a deeper construction of gender.

Barbara Watson Andaya (2002) addressed the issue of the success of Theravada Buddhism in attracting female support in spite of the conservatism of its dogmatic assertion of male spiritual superiority. She argues that beliefs about female spiritual inferiority in early Southeast Asia were actually "countered by the public space Theravada ritual permitted women as lay devotees and by the affirmation of their nurturing and maternal role" (3). In addition, "moving into Southeast Asia at a time when its basic receptivity to lay involvement had been enhanced, Theravada offered continuing opportunities for all women to acquire merit through gift-giving and thereby counter their relegation to an inferior position" (29).

Watson Andaya's hypothesis concerning the role of women is a stimulating one for renewed studies of the reception of Buddhism in Southeast Asia. Concerning the construction of gender, however, one cannot fail to see that this agency paradoxically contributed to keeping women in an inferior position, as beings whose access to a direct path to salvation is restricted. That is, they have an inferior position in the realm in which the gender hierarchy is ultimately defined, despite resistance through trends such as the mass lay meditation movement in contemporary Burma. The gender construction in these societies is layered, Buddhism seeming to have reinforced previous cultural constructions. But it is in Buddhist terms that the ideological framework of gender construction in Burma is formulated.

The Marital Bond in Contemporary Burmese Gender Construction

Let us now examine how this gender construction is expressed in contemporary Burma, insofar as I have been able to observe in my field research, primarily in urban contexts. In the cities the traditional couple partnership of agricultural production has been replaced by the preponderance of wage work or small business. In these contexts, the economic role that women retain of overlooking the domestic budget takes on another dimension: women's responsibility as managers of the household may lead them to view men as irresponsible.[11]

Indeed, women who have marital and economic difficulties may say that they would prefer to be rid of men. However, this proposal seems unrealistic. In practice, relatively young women having no husbands very seldom live alone with their children; they usually depend on parents. The reasons for this are not only pragmatic, such as the difficulty of earning a living and taking care of a family at the same time. Underlying the situation is the cultural prejudice that a woman's sexuality requires male control. Melford Spiro ([1967] 1978) has noted that Burmese confer on women an unquenchable sexuality (the source of their destructive power)[12] and that male authority is assessed through the ability to check this sexuality.

Notwithstanding the pervasiveness of the images of the strength of women and of the irresponsibility of men in the new urban districts, Burmese women may adopt a strategy of running away from the men with whom they have been involved. This behavior seems all the more paradoxical if we consider the supposed autonomy of Burmese women and the accessibility of divorce. A young woman I know well was intensely afraid of a man she had been married to, and whom she still loved, although she had left him and was hiding from him. Leaving aside the psychological aspects and without going into the details of her case (see Brac de la Perrière 2000b), I have tried to understand the cultural aspects of her behavior from the way she explained her feelings. She associated her fear with her "shame of woman" *(meinma ashek)*, a kind of shame that was, according to her, specific to women willing to comply with the more sophisticated values of urban Buddhism, that is, women aspiring to rise in the Buddhist hierarchy of values. In her case it was linked to the attachment she had for the man *(thanyozin)*, a feeling she believed was not consistent with Buddhist unworldliness and contrary to feelings such as compassion *(thana:)*. This shame allowed the man to "show his power" *(ana: pya-)*. The word *ana:* used here implies brutal force and is contrasted with the authority conferred on men because of their spiritual superiority, best expressed through the concept of *phon:*. The only way for this woman to counter male domination was to escape from the marriage, a move that allowed her to reverse the situation and take the dominant position in the relationship *(naïn-)*.

This example reveals that the combination of a marital tie with love, which is felt to be inconsistent with Buddhist values, and the ensuing shame gives the man an ascendancy that seems intolerable. It is the concrete marital tie that upholds the Buddhist gender hierarchy analyzed earlier—authority on the male side and power on the feminine one—and transforms it into domination by the man of the woman: it allows the submerging of the female threat within the Buddhist system of values.

The Spirit Cult in the Burmese Overall System of Difference

We now return to the spirit possession cult to examine its position in the Burmese system of difference. Spirit possession is linked to the existence of a cult in honor of the Nat, known as the cult of the Thirty-seven Lords. The emergence of the Thirty-seven as a national pantheon can be considered a result of the construction of Burmese territory under Burmese Buddhist kings or, in other words, of the unification of Burma. Burmese historiography credits King Anawratha with unifying the Irrawaddy valley under Burmese Buddhist rule and with the recognition of the local cult figures that form the pantheon and their placement under the authority of Sakka, guardian of Theravada Buddhism in Burma. The cult of the Thirty-seven is thus the result of the religious policy of the Buddhist Burmese kings, which, concerning local or autochtonous cults, consisted of their unification into a centralized pantheon, as well as in their Burmanization through the casting of historical characters from Burmese dynasties as cult figures.

These local cult figures, or Nat, are spirits resulting from the violent death of human beings, the kind of death that, according to Burmese Buddhist conceptions, prevents reincarnation and leaves potentially dangerous spirits free to roam about. Their violent death is connected to the fact that they were, typically, former rebels or heroes belonging to a rival community that the Burmese royalty wanted to subdue. In many of these cases, the Burmese king first uses the well-known practice of marriage alliance, marrying the hero's sister. But when the alliance turns out to be inadequate, he finally brings about his brother-in-law's death and resorts to a symbolic procedure, the transformation of the malevolent spirit into a potentially positive spirit by appointing him tutelary spirit of the region and establishing a local cult around him. Buddhism is central here, as is Sakka, who gives the scepter to the king, bestowing on him karmic legitimacy and allowing him to transform the malevolent spirit into a Nat subservient to Buddhist symbols. That the establishing of a Nat involves the use of Buddhism has to be stressed: it reveals that this is a process of conversion, or civilization. In short, the Nat are subversive local powers captured by the central kingdom and enshrined in the Buddhist system of values.

From a symbolic point of view, women and spirits are thus in the same hierarchical position, that of "localities" encompassed in Buddhist society. It is because women are endowed with a power able to endanger the masculine quality of men *(phon:)* that they have to be subdued by integration into the Buddhist system of values. In the same way, it is because spirits are local powers that pose a threat to Burmese order that they must be overpowered by the dominant Buddhist royalty.

Spirit Mediums as Agents of Power in the Possession Cult?

At the local level, the Nat is a sovereign as expressed in the name of the cult, the cult of Thirty-seven Lords, and by local rituals that evoke royal ones. Taken together, they form a pantheon that had been the subject of a royal cult whose specialists were court officers dependent on royal patronage. At the end of the nineteenth century, a new policy of local rituals was implemented that led to more standardization and the creation of an independent profession of ritual specialists. This development explains the continuation and even expansion of the "national" cult after the collapse of Burmese royalty,[13] under a central government that has drawn its legitimacy from Buddhism.[14]

It is probably in this context that spirit possession developed. Spirit mediums who must participate in the main local rituals, or "royal festivals" *(pwe daw)*, in their capacity as ritual specialists, mainly make their living, as professionals, from the celebrations of private ceremonies to the Thirty-seven *(nat kanna: pwe)*. This category of ritual seems to be a relatively recent development: today performances are mainly urban, with economic success being the main incentive for their organization. A medium and his troupe are needed for the celebration because it is necessary for all of the Thirty-seven Nat of the pantheon to be entertained consecutively, being embodied by mediums for three days. These rituals are the main context of spirit possession through which one can have direct access to the spirits and call on their potency.

As discussed above, the relationship of mediums with their main spirit is conceived as a marital one, ideally the marriage of a male spirit with a woman. The Burmese believe that the spirits take the initiative both in seducing the woman and in appearing in rituals, embodied in their mediums. The latter are supposed to forget what has happened during possession rituals, which are under the direction of the musicians, at least in theory. For the Burmese, the people dancing, eating, drinking, smoking, and interacting with them during the ceremonies to the Thirty-seven are the Nat acting through their mediums. The ritual specialists are held to be the passive repositories of the Nat. From their first encounter with their main spirits, when they submit to the spirit seduction, and throughout the process of achieving the status of spirit mediums organizing ceremonies to the Thirty-seven for clients, their relationship with their spirits is transformed such that they are able to both master this main relationship—that is, to embody the spirit when needed for ritual purpose—and incarnate any of the Thirty-seven. They become virtuosi of spirit possession.

However, this does not mean that the mediums are the masters of the spirits. In the Burmese symbolic system, the "king"—the figure of central power whose legitimacy rests on Buddhist values—retains this function. The position of mediums is to submit to the spirits through possession, and this is consistent with its feminine aspect and the symbolic expression of the relationship through marriage. In a sense, if problematic marital relations of women may be seen as a failure of their socialization, of the subduing of their threat to Buddhist values, in the case of the spirit mediums a new socialization process has been accomplished through marriage with the spirit that ultimately has the same effect.

However, spirit mediums achieve a status of a kind in the context of their specialists' practice that is in contrast with their accounts of the life crisis that they had to go through before being called by the Nat. They achieve a certain control over their own lives that was previously beyond them. They also ascend to an active social role within the limits of their followings and which can only be exercised in the rituals. The scale of their influence depends on their competence as mediums. If through their mediation they manage to gather an important clientele, in number or in quality, they are said to "have great powers" *(ta 'go 'gyi-)*. This means that they are credited with a kind of spiritual power that derives from their particular relationship with Nat. The phrase *nat shi-*, "he gets the Nat," expresses the same idea. Thus, at least on an ideological level, spirit mediums are credited not so much with a power of their own as with the ability to draw on the Nat's power.

Nat as a Source of Symbolic Empowerment

The Nat are a link in the symbolic chain of authority in Burma. Their relationship to humans is one of domination—of the communities for which they are the tutelar spirits, as well as of the women they marry. At all the levels of the cult to the Nat, domination is initiated by a marriage alliance, the king marrying the sister of the local hero, or the Nat marrying his medium. The entity subdued in such a way by the superior order retains in both cases a margin of power: the Nat keeps its subversive powers; the spirit medium comes to master possession by the Nat. In both cases the relation is strongly ambivalent, mainly because it allows certain forces to continue to function, despite the fact that they are not consistent with Buddhist values and are believed to be negative if they operate outside the Buddhist context. Another aspect of this ambivalence is that the subordination of these marginal forces through the symbolism of a marital link allows their integration.

Indeed, one has to look more closely at the ambivalence of spirits deriving from the fact that their establishment is based on the integration through subordination of these marginal but potentially dangerous forces (which I have also called marginalities or localities). On a symbolic level, Nat do retain a potential subversive power enacted in the local rituals known as royal festivals.[15] These rituals are addressed annually to the Nat at their main shrines, situated in the domains of which they are the tutelary spirits. They consist of homage ceremonies grounded in the traditions of the local population and

attended by spirit mediums from throughout Burma and of the commemo-
ration of the installation of the Nat in his shrine, that is, the transformation
of the malevolent spirit into a tutelary spirit. The commemorative ritual enacts the subversive dimension of the spirit prior to its transformation into
Nat, the source of its potency. However, this potency is available only after
the spirit has been subdued through the installation of its image inside the
shrine.

The most suggestive example is the festival dedicated to the Taungbyon
brothers, mighty servants of King Anawratha who were condemned by the
king because they had neglected to take part in the building of a pagoda. The
commemorative part of the ritual is made up of the "hunting of the hare"
and the "felling of the trees," during which the most condemned behaviors—
sexual provocation and violence—are staged outside the temple, with the
local population playing the parts of the local heroes and the malevolent
spirits. Meanwhile, the Nat and high-ranking spirit mediums sit inside the
temple, except for the crucial moments when the mediums appear at the
threshold, to accept the offering of the hare that has been caught and prepared
by the locals, and then, just outside the entrance, to consecrate the tree as it
is planted there and to take a branch inside the temple to be saved before the
tree is destroyed by the villagers. In contast to the local population and the
malevolent spirits, the mediums' and the Nats' remaining inside the temple
symbolizes their allegiance to the monarchy and to the pagoda. The moments
when the two parties come together are those when the powers of the spirits are taken from the outside into the temple, where they are then established and converted into tutelary spirits.[16] In other words, if the subversive
dimension of the former local heroes and malevolent spirits is enacted, it is
to commemorate their submission to the Buddhist royal order that formed
the cult.

This is the same process, although reproduced on a broader scale, as the
marriage ritual that allows women or spirit mediums to be controlled. In
this sense, although rituals to the Nat offer the possibility of expressing the
localities' potential threat to Burmese order, they actually participate in their
integration into Buddhist society. This is the point I want to emphasize. Although at a symbolic level the cult of spirit possession may be seen as allowing the expression of marginal values and, as such, an opposition to central
authority, the Burmese cult displays these images of marginalities only in
order to enact their pacification through their integration into the Buddhist
system of values.

State Initiatives in the Spirit Possession Cult

On various sociological levels, the Burmese cult of spirit possession functions more to ensure the integration of marginal forces into the Burmese Buddhist order than to allow any protest of the established order, as royal support for the cult during the monarchy also revealed. Looking at the present situation, it is striking that although the Burmese military dictatorship has been facing a major crisis of legitimacy since 1988, one almost never hears open criticism of the militaries through Nat "voices." What I mean by this is that whatever the political positions of the participants may be, they are not expressed during the ceremonies, although the rituals would appear to offer an ideal opportunity for this. During the ceremonies to the Thirty-seven, the Nat are held responsible for whatever may occur during the possession sequences, which allows for expression not tolerated under everyday circumstances. The Nat are supposed to express themselves through their mediums, during their interactions with the worshipers present, either donors or guests, and also through the singers. The latter perform not only stereotyped hymns corresponding to the different figures represented but also improvised songs inspired by the context and stimulating the interactions between a Nat and his followers (Brac de la Perrière 1994). Although this setting allows for the complaint of a wife against her husband, or of children against their parents, for instance, it does not seem that the permissiveness ever reaches the level of expressing political opposition. During all the ceremonies I attended in the 1990s, I only once heard an oblique reference to the political opponent Aung San Suu Kyi, and this reference was made, I think, because the ritual was performed in the district where she was then under house arrest. On the whole, one can say that political opposition is not at stake in the spirit possession cult.

As for the official government position regarding the cult to the Thirty-seven Nat, the government does not support it. This attitude is based mainly on the grounds that the practices involved are mere superstitions, whose persistence is explained as remnants of pre-Buddhist practices.[17] Even if the government on the whole neither sponsors nor intervenes in the cult, on a private and individual basis Burmese officials do participate in it. This is why the most influential spirit mediums are those who have high-ranking military officers or their wives among their clients.

Moreover, during the 1988 "events,"[18] when Burma was under emergency law, with public meetings forbidden and travel severely limited, the Nat festivals continued to be performed in central Burma, although there were fewer spirit mediums from Yangon and locals in attendance. This meant that officers in charge of the local administrations did not take any action against them, either because they did not feel these celebrations were a threat (a threat that any huge gathering might represent to "public order") or, on the contrary, because they were themselves afraid of punitive action by the spirits. Instead of forbidding the festivals, they took whatever measures were necessary to make the gatherings possible during this troubled period so as to better control them, in particular, by taking charge of organizational aspects not under local hereditary control. This is how, for example, at Taungbyon, the supervision of the part of the festival held at the pagoda was taken over in 1991 by official Mandalay religious authorities, whereas it had been previously organized by an unofficial Mandalay religious association (see Brac de la Perrière 2005).

Military intervention in the cult is not limited to local authorities' supervision of the festivals. A visit to various local ritual institutions in central Burma reveals shrines displaying testimonies of embellishments by officials — or more typically by their wives — who are natives of that place, as thanks to the local tutelary spirit for their social promotion or other favors. In this way Burmese officials have sometimes initiated new ritual developments. This is the case with the local ritual of Hlegyi, west of Sagaing, that had been evolving into a quasi-festival during the 1980s with high-ranking spirit mediums coming to perform at the initiative of the mayor of Yangon, who comes from this village.

However, these donations to some cult institutions by military officers are individual acts for personal motives and are not evidence of an explicit governmental policy, at least as far as I am aware. In contrast, when, during the 1950s, Prime Minister U Nu offered an image of Min Mahagiri, to be installed in the shrine of this Nat domain, at the site of Popa city, this did have the connotation of government sponsorship. It is therefore especially significant that after General Ne Win took power (1962), the ritual focus of the festival celebrated there annually, in December, moved from Min Mahagiri to the Lady of Popa (Popa Medaw). A monk, famous for having developed an important religious complex at the foot of Mount Popa, dedicated the shrine to her there and invited the two highest-ranking spirit mediums to perform, thus "reinventing" the local cult to the Lady. Since this time, the December festival of Popa has no longer been held in homage to Min Mahagiri and his sister but to the Lady of Popa.[19] The temple of Min Mahagiri and its image donated by U Nu are still visited by spirit mediums during the festival of the

Lady of Popa, but they are ignored by the crowds of pilgrims and tourists. In most tourist guidebooks, pictures of the "Nat of Popa" show images in the Lady's temple and not of the original Nat, Min Mahagiri and his sister. What is striking here is that this shift of ritual focus marks both the dramatic political change that occurred in 1962 when U Ne Win took power and the end of recognized governmental initiatives in the sponsorship and expansion of the cult.

The present military government has followed this trend by not taking any open, decisive measures in relation to the cult: it only takes charge, through the local authorities, of the supervision of festivals and of the regulation of their ritual institutions, as interest in the gatherings increases. Indeed, local ritual institutions have been, and are still, undergoing significant transformations involving the main agents of the cult, namely, local populations and institutions, on the one hand, and professional spirit mediums and their clients, on the other. Although these transformations may vary according to the specific context, the general trend is toward further integration of local rituals into the Burmese cult of the Thirty-seven by means of their standardization.

Ritual Institutions and Social Integration within the Burmese Order: The Example of the Amei Kyan Festival

A striking example of the trend toward the standardization of rituals is the Amei Kyan festival, celebrated annually in June at the village of Ethigon, in the Kyaukse district, close to the remnants of the royal city of Ava.[20] It used to be a remote site, only accessible from Kyaukse after two days of travel by bullock cart. Professional spirit mediums came only from Mandalay and a few other places to pay tribute to this female spirit *(nat thami:)*. However, villagers from the surrounding districts came, and continue to come, by the hundreds. At dawn on the first day of the festival, lines of villagers could be seen across the plains converging toward the small shrine, situated on the top of a small hill, where the image of the female spirit had been brought in from Ethigon by its custodian family. The villagers were accompanied by their musicians, whose hereditary duty was to play throughout the celebration to allow the devotees to dance for the spirit, with each group of villagers taking turns, in front of the shrine and around the site.[21] The mediums alone took part in this spectacular performance. Later in the day, when the image was brought back to Ethigon and the ritual shower performed by the custodians, the mediums and the devotees danced in front of her shrine.

Things have changed somewhat since the old Mandalay airport, situated in the town some thirty miles north and across the Myitnge, has been rehabilitated as an international airport and moved to the site of Ethigon village. The site consisted of a group of nine small hills, of which Amei Kyan was considered the Lady. For the construction of the new international airport, Ethigon village was displaced and the ground flattened. But, at least as the story goes, as military officials were surveying the project by helicopter, they saw that the Lady's shrine hill was crawling with serpents. They interpreted this as a sign of the spirit's wrath and decided to spare both that hill and the one on which the pagoda is located. Private contractors encountered further problems during building work that were interpreted in the same way; these problems were resolved by the donation of a new temple to the custodian family of the spirit's image in the displaced village of Ethigon and by holding a ceremony to the Thirty-seven in the temple.

This image had previously been kept in a small shrine that could not accommodate large-scale rituals performed by professional spirit mediums. These are now possible in the new temple, built on the model of those of the main festivals. In addition, roads built for the new airport have made the site much more accessible, allowing for attendance of greater numbers of mediums. Moreover, stories of how the spirit blocked the displacement of her shrine have created a momentum that has attracted more mediums to the festival than ever before. This, in turn, has had an effect on the celebration of the festival: there are more professional mediums and a modernized ritual structure. It has become possible to create a system of rotation of dances, as in the main festivals, which are offered as tribute to the spirit by the spirit mediums and for which the profits (from dance fees and fixed offerings) go primarily to the custodian family. So we now have a situation in which, after taking the spirit to the hill shrine at dawn and after performing the ritual shower in the village temple, spirit mediums take turns dancing there for the spirit. They pay for this and for the musicians, as in the main festivals; devotees or local mediums from surrounding neighborhoods still dance around the temple to the sound of free village music.

This case raises a number of issues. This festival is an old one; it is linked to the Burmese royalty as shown by the proximity of the ruins of Ava, the Burmese royal city until 1782.[22] When the site of the royal city was moved across the river Myitnge to Amarapura and then Mandalay, this royal festival became marginalized and isolated from the main royal festivals. In other words, there has been a phase of localization. The actual transformation is a rehabilitation of the old royal festival—different in this sense from a "reinvention"—according to present-day standards of the main festivals.

The process of standardization has taken place because of the opening of the new international airport nearby. This dramatic change in the local context has created a web of opportunities that merits closer study. The airport construction created economic opportunities, attracting building contractors, developing access facilities unknown before, and bringing in a market for spirit possession. On a pragmatic level, however, the construction of the airport initially posed a threat to the site of the cult. The original village of the Lady has been displaced. However, the villagers managed to get the building contractors, who were afraid of arousing the Lady's anger, to sponsor the new ritual infrastructure, which has in turn added to the attraction for spirit mediums. This gave the villagers, especially those of the custodian family, the ability to retain economic control of the festival, whereas in the case of other festivals usually attended by spirit mediums, the professionals themselves financed the new ritual institutions and kept the profits. Thus, finally, the villagers managed to turn a threat to their cultural heritage to their own financial advantage.[23]

It is clear that the process of standardization in itself directly involves spirit mediums and villagers, whose interests converge on some points. Both parties benefit from the consequent enlargement of ritual institutions—spirit mediums because their growing numbers require ever more ritual spaces and villagers because the participation of spirit mediums is a new source of cash income and local development.

There are other recent or not so recent stories of how the participation of spirit mediums, mainly from Rangoon, in local festivals has enhanced standardization of the rituals and therefore also their integration into the "national" cult. This case is especially illuminating on this point, in that the actual sociological processes involved are those of intense interaction between local populations and the spirit mediums representing the central cult. However, in the spirit mediums' accounts, the ultimate reference is that of a governmental initiative that appears in this way as a symbolic imperative.

Governmental institutions did not intervene directly except through the decision to build a new airport, the kind of decision on the part of central administrations that always seems extremely arbitrary from a local perspective.

The local population was then confronted with huge transformations of the locality imposed by the central authorities. Stories told by the spirit mediums about the resistance of the Lady express this confrontation on a symbolic level. The festival transformations reveal how villagers overcame the difficulties encountered by adapting to the new situation.

One can say that the threat posed to the Lady's domain was transformed into an opportunity on a symbolic level. I have not been able to verify whether the story of the officers alarmed by the vision of serpents on the hill actually occurred or whether the two spared hills had in fact been scheduled for removal. Nevertheless, the story is told by the spirit mediums as the story of how they rediscovered the Lady's potency, hence their arrival in growing numbers at the festival. In this sense the threat to the Lady's domain has been transformed by both the locals and the spirit mediums into an opportunity to demonstrate her strength. This is expressed through the spirit possession idiom as a result and a mark of the Lady's powers.

However, the accounts of the spirit mediums credit the authorities with this decision. What is more, the case of the Ethigon festival is not an isolated one in this regard. Indeed, the story of the military government being forced to recognize the potency of the Lady just as they were planning to erase her domain sounds very similar to the numerous cases of kings being forced to recognize the potency of the local forces they had wanted to eradicate. This kind of story is significant in that it points to the complexity of the structure of domination in the Burmese spirit possession cult. The subduing of localities by the Burmese central power cannot be properly understood without taking into account the part played by these localities in their integration into the national society.

At the sociological level, the transformations of the festival were made possible by interactions between the villagers and the spirit mediums, but according to the spirit cult idiom, these transformations are credited to the authorities' decision to recognize the potency of the Lady. In this sense one can say that the spirit possession cult allows the locals a kind of agency through their identification with a local spiritual strength such as that of the Lady. However important this agency may be in overcoming the threats to the local societies and cultural heritages by the frequently brutal interventions of the central government in implementing integrative policies, it does not put the locals in a position to contest the state but merely to adapt or become involved in the integrative process. It does not enhance their position in the hierarchical setting but, on the contrary, delineates it.

Conclusion

We have seen that women and spirits are in the same hierarchical position of "localities" encompassed in the Burmese central order, that is, the Burmese Buddhist order. Both also retain a similar ambivalence in the hierarchical structure that rests on the threat they seem to pose to the social order. However, this threat contributes more to their delineation as an inferior segment in the hierarchical structure than to contestation of this structure. In other words, their stigmatization as threatening to the order is the very process that motivates both their overcoming and their location as inferior members of society.

This accounts rather well for the articulation of gender and domination in the spirit possession cult, that is, for its feminine dimensions. The analysis of its contemporary dynamics through the transformations of a festival demonstrates that what is really at stake is the endless integration of local or marginal strengths or "localities" into the Buddhist system of values.

The Nat are conceived of as having been subdued by the Buddhist royalty and the king as their master. Now that the monarchy has disappeared, it seems rather that the government does not intervene directly in their control. As part of a national profession, spirit mediums are the main agents of the standardization of local rituals. The power of the Nat they embody gives them this influence on cult institutions. On the whole, however, as under the monarchy, the effect of the cult has been more to subordinate and integrate the potentially subversive local forces than to create a platform for contesting the central power of the state.

NOTES

I would like to thank Monique Skidmore for inviting me to give a presentation at the conference "Women and the Contested State" and Juliane Schober whose comments have been especially useful.

1. Burmese words are given here according to the usual transcription found in English-language publications. In my works in French, I prefer a transcription adapted for French speakers. Here, for example, I use *Nat* instead of *Naq,* which renders the glottal stop. I find it more convenient to keep the better-known terms *Burma* and *Burmese* rather than the official name *Myanmar* that the present government has adopted.

2. A few of them prefer to be called *natshaya,* meaning roughly a "specialist of the Nat," obviously out of discomfort with the feminine denotation of Natkadaw.

3. On these questions, see Brac de la Perrière 1998b.

4. Another expression often used is *leippya hla-,* "their 'soul' is beautiful." The explanation for why some women are more vulnerable to spirit possession is that their *leippya* is more fragile than men's, which implies that it is less firmly attached to their bodies.

5. Marriage with spirits in the possession cults of other Southeast Asian cultures had not been emphasized (see, e.g., the special issue on spirit possession and shamanic cults of ASEMI [1973–74]) until Monique Selim (2000) mentioned it in the Laotian case. It is difficult to determine whether the celebration of marriage of female spirit mediums to spirits is a new development due to territorial delocalization and local idiosyncratic variations of the cult in Laos (Brac de la Perrière 2000b) or if it had simply escaped the attention of previous scholars.

6. One can readily compare the state of Burmese studies to that of Vietnamese studies that demonstrate a focus on gender linked to the fact that Vietnam opened to the field at the time gender studies came of age in the Western academy (Werner 2005: 20). Burma was hardly opened to the field before the 1990s, so Burmese studies still suffer from a lack of development in many fields of research, including gender.

7. The status of *thilashin* is best demonstrated by the fact that they cannot take the vow to observe more than ten rules or precepts, whereas monks have to take the vow to comply with the 227 rules prescribed by the *vinaya* to enter the Sangha. It means that *thilashin* are still considered members of the laity, as explained by Jordt (2005), among others, although she has tried to introduce other criteria to define the ambiguous position of the *thilashin* in the Burmese socioreligious system (see also Kawanami 2001).

8. The mass lay meditation movement in Burma, as it has been qualified by Jordt (2001, 2005), has recently opened a new path to salvation that does not require renunciation. This movement has developed in the context of a religious revival sponsored by the government through a meditation center called the Mahasi Thathana Yeiktha that has promoted a kind of spiritual practice, *wipathana* meditation, open to laymen and laywomen as well as monks (see also Houtman 1990). According to Jordt (2005: 50), the dimensions of the movement have been so far-reaching that monk–lay relations "have undergone substantial transformation" and have "implications for women's spiritual practice and gender conceptions more generally." Without discounting the influence of this movement, principally in urban modernist circles, one has to recognize nevertheless that it has not undermined the radical distinction between monks and lay people, as Jordt duly states.

A way to strive for salvation without entering the Sangha, besides the spiritual practice of meditation by laypeople, is the *weikza* path, which has been the object of much debate but which is supposedly not open to women (Rozenberg 2005).

9. This is how *phon:* is presented in the normative Burmese discourse and in most Western academic discourse (see, for an outstanding instance, Spiro 1993: 317). However, this is the masculine vision of *phon:*. As for Burmese women, some of them claim that they also have *phon:* but locate it precisely in their hair, while that of men is supposed to be in their right shoulders.

10. The supposed negative power of feminine blood accounts for the fact that Burmese soldiers traditionally carried a piece of their mothers' soiled loincloth as a protection against enemies.

11. Although my data have been collected in an urban context, the fact that men are considered domestically irresponsible is more widely held, as Juliane Schober rightly pointed out to me in a personal communication.

12. This supposed unquenchable sexuality of women is also a threat to monastic celibacy. On the other hand, women cannot retreat to the forest, a step considered necessary to strive for the highest spiritual achievements, because, according to Jordt's (2005) informants, they would be vulnerable to sexual attack by men. In both cases women's sexuality needs to be controlled or protected by men.

13. The present-day cult is here qualified as "national," to distinguish it from the cult as it existed under the monarchy and to reflect the fact that it is the cult of Burmese Buddhists. However, this qualification, far from being "official," would probably be contested both by government authorities and by "orthodox" Buddhists.

14. For more information on hypotheses on the historical development of spirit mediums and possession, see Brac de la Perrière 1998a. This hypothesis of the impact of kingship collapse on the formation of contemporary ritual institutions of the cult of the Thirty-seven has to be paralleled with those reached separately by scholars of Buddhist studies concerning a similar impact on the development of contemporary Buddhist institutions such as the Shwegyin branch of the Sangha and practices such as lay meditation. This sheds light on the dramatic change that colonial rule effected on Burmese society and culture by not taking over the traditional role of the Burmese kings as keeper of the cosmos and patron of religions.

15. For analysis of festival rituals, see Brac de la Perrière 1993, 1998b, 1998c, 2005.

16. For a more detailed description of this festival, see Brac de la Perrière 1993, 2005.

17. A good example of official reluctance to admit the prevalence of the cult practices today is the reactions that my research topic immediately provokes. I am systematically told that it is not a proper subject, or in more relaxed contexts, jokes are made in defense. Officials are sometimes puzzled by the interest shown by foreigners even as they are beginning to understand the tourist potential of the rituals.

18. "Events" is my translation of the Burmese expression used to refer to this period, *A yé A khin*. Major demonstrations occurred during summer 1988 to protest the previous military government, that of General Ne Win. This resulted in bloody repression and a coup d'état. Elections organized later were won decisively by the democratic opposition. The new military government, then known as the SLORC, refused to recognize the result and to hand over power.

19. Eventually another temple to the Lady of Popa was built by a rival monastery. Both temples dedicated to the Lady actually contain a collection of images representing the whole pantheon of the Thirty-seven, which sets them apart from the usual context of festival and ritual institutions.

20. I conducted field research concerning this ritual in June 2002.

21. The spirit's image is brought again the next day, also at dawn. This time hundreds of monks gather on one side, around the pagoda facing the spirit shrine, at the top of a second hillock, to be fed by the population after they have paid homage to the spirit.

All this *dana* is said to be done in the name of the spirit, and the benefits are considered to be distributed by her.

22. The obligations of the villagers regarding the festival are mentioned in official reports of the end of the eighteenth century, which attests to the long history of this tradition.

23. The opportunities created by these developments can create conflicting interests, both within the village, since the custodian family is the main benefactor, and between the villages participating in the festival. Some incidents occurred during the 2002 festival that bear witness to this: a group from a nearby village came to the hillock with its own image of the Lady, attempting to enter the shrine to dance in front of it and trying to attract part of the audience. The medium of Ethigon in charge of the image expelled them on the grounds that this was not part of the "traditional" ritual *(yoya)*.

Bibliography

Abedi, Mehdi, and Marcus M. J. Fischer. 1993. "Etymologies: Thinking a Public Sphere in Arabic and Persian." *Public Culture* 6: 219–30.

Abraham, Itty. 1999. *The Making of the Indian Atomic Bomb: Science, Secrecy and the Postcolonial State.* New Delhi: Orient Longman.

ADHUNA. 1998. *Grass-Roots Democracy.* (In Bengali.) Dhaka: ADAB Publications.

African Rights. 1995. *Not So Innocent: When Women Become Killers.* London: African Rights.

Afshar, Haleh. 2004. "War and Peace: What Do Women Contribute?" In *Development, Women, and War: Feminist Perspectives,* edited by Haleh Afshar and Deborah Eade, 1–7. Oxford: Oxfam.

Afshar, Haleh, and Deborah Eade, eds. 2004. *Development, Women, and War: Feminist Perspectives.* Oxford: Oxfam.

Agamben, Giorgio. 1998. *Homo Sacer: Sovereign Power and Bare Life.* Translated by D. Heller-Roazen. Stanford: Stanford University Press.

———. 1999. *Remnant of Auschwitz: The Witness and the Archive.* Translated by D. Heller-Roazen. New York: Zone Books.

Ahamad, Emajuddin, and Jinnat Ara Nasrin Dil Roushan. 2003. "Islam in Bangladesh." http://www.powerxs.de/delta/islam.html (accessed April 9, 2003).

Akhtar, S., S. Begum, H. Hussain, S. Kamal, and M. Guha Thakurata. 2001. *Narir Ekatur O Judho Poroborti Katho Kahini.* (In Bengali.) Dhaka: Ain-O-Salish Kendra.

Ali, Daud. 1999. *Invoking the Past.* New Delhi: Oxford University Press.

Alvarez, Sonia E. 1993. "Deepening Democracy: Social Movement Networks, Constitutional Reform and Radical Urban Regimes in Contemporary Brazil." In *Mobilizing the Community: Local Politics in the Era of the Global City,* edited by Robert Fischer and Joseph Kling, 191–222. Newbury Park, CA: Sage.

Amarasinghe, Oscar. 1989. "Technical Change, Transformation of Risks and Patronage Relations in a Fishing Community of South Sri Lanka." *Development and Change* 20: 701–33.

Amin, Shahid. 1988. "Gandhi as Mahatma." In *Selected Subaltern Studies,* edited by Ranajit Guha and Gayatri Spivak, 288–351. New York: Oxford University Press.

Amnesty International. 1993. "Sri-Lanka: 'Disappearance' and Murder as Techniques of Counter-Insurgency." In *Disappearances and Political Killings: Human Rights Crisis of the 1990's: A Manual for Action.* London: Amnesty International.

Anderson, Benedict. 1991. *Imagined Communities: Reflections on the Origin and Spread of Nationalism.* London: Verso.

Anderson, Mary. 1999. *Do No Harm: How Can Aid Support Peace—or War.* Boulder, CO: Lynne Rienner.

Appadurai, Arjun. 2002. "Deep Democracy: Urban Governmentality and the Horizon of Politics." *Public Culture* 14, no. 1: 21–47.

Arendt, Hannah. [1953] 1994. "On the Nature of Totalitarianism: An Essay in Understanding." In *Essays in Understanding,* 328–60. Edited by J. Kohn. New York: Harcourt Brace.

Argenti-Pillen, Alex. 2003. *Masking Terror: How Women Contain Violence in Southern Sri Lanka.* Philadelphia: University of Pennsylvania Press.

Asad, Talal. 1986. *The Idea of an Anthropology of Islam.* Washington, DC: Georgetown University Press.

———. 2003. *Formations of the Secular: Christianity, Islam, Modernity.* Stanford: Stanford University Press.

ASEMI. 1973. "Chamanisme et possession en Asie du Sud-Est et dans le monde insulindien." *Bulletin of Asie du Sud-Est et Monde Insulindien* 4, nos. 1–2, 3–4. Special issues.

Asia-Pacific Media Service. 2003. "Is Religious Extremism on the Rise in Bangladesh?" http://www.asiapacificms.com/articles/bangladesh-extremism (accessed June 14, 2003).

Aung San Suu Kyi. 1991. *Freedom from Fear: and Other Writings.* New York: Penguin Books.

Azza, Karam. 2001. "Women in War and Peace-Building: Roads Traversed, the Challenges Ahead." *International Feminist Journal of Politics* 3, no. 1: 2–25.

Bachofen, Johann Jakob. [1897] 1967. *Religion and Mother Right: Selected Writings of J. J. Bachofen.* Translated by Ralph Manheim. Princeton: Princeton University Press.

Baker, Keith M. 1990. "Public Opinion as Political Invention." In *Inventing the French Revolution: Essays on French Political Culture in the Eighteenth Century,* edited by Keith M. Baker, 167–99. Cambridge: Cambridge University Press.

Banerjee, Sikata. 2000. *Warriors in Politics: Hindu Nationalism, Violence, and the Shiv Sena in India.* Boulder, CO: Westview Press.

Bangladesh Bureau of Education and Information Statistics (BANBEIS). 2003. http://www.banbeis.org/db (accessed February 28, 2003).

Bar-On, Bat-Ami. 2002. *The Subject of Violence: Arendtean Exercises in Understanding.* New York: Rowman & Littlefield.

Basham, A. L. 1976. "The Practice of Medicine in Ancient and Medieval India." In *Asian Medical Systems: A Comparative Study,* edited by Charles Leslie, 18–43. Berkeley: University of California Press.

Basu, Amrita, and Patricia Jeffrey, eds. 1997. *Appropriating Gender: Women's Activism and the Politicization of Religion in South Asia.* New York: Routledge.

Basu, Amrita, and Atul Kohli, eds. 1998. *Community Conflicts and the State in India.* New York: Oxford University Press.

Bayly, Chris A. 1985. "The Pre-History of Communalism? Religious Conflict in India, 1700–1860." *Modern Asian Studies* 19, no. 2: 177–203.

Beck, Linda J. 2003. "Democratization and the Hidden Public: The Impact of Patronage Networks on Senegalese Women." *Comparative Politics* 35, no. 2: 147–69.

Bekker, Sarah M. 1994. "Talent for Trance: Dancing for the Spirits in Burma." In *Tradition and Modernity in Myanmar: Proceedings from an International Conference Held in Berlin from May 7 to May 9, 1993*, vol. 2, edited by Uta Gärtner and Jens Lorenz, 287–98. Berlin: Berliner Asien-Afrika-Studien.

Belak, Brenda. 2002. *Gathering Strength: Women from Burma on Their Rights*. Chiang Mai: Images Asia.

Bellah, Robert. 1970. "Civil Religion in America." In *Beyond Belief: Essays on Religion in a Post-Traditional World*, 168–89. New York: Harper & Row.

Benhabib, Seyla. 1992. *Situating the Self: Gender, Community and Postmodernism in Contemporary Ethics*. Cambridge: Polity Press.

Bennet, Olivia, Jo Bexley, and Kitty Warnock, eds. 1995. *Arms to Fight, Arms to Protect: Women Speak about Conflict*. London: PANOS Oral Testimony Series.

Bhabha, Homi, and John Comaroff. 2002. "Speaking of Postcoloniality, in the Continuous Present: A Conversation between Homi Bhabha and John Comaroff." In *Relocating Postcolonialism*, edited by D. T. Goldberg and L. A. Quayson, 15–46. Oxford: Basil Blackwell.

Bhasin, Kamla, and Ritu Menon. 1998. *Borders and Boundaries: Women in India's Partition*. New Brunswick, NJ: Rutgers University Press.

Bleifuss, Joel. 1997. "Land of Pagodas . . . and Pimps; Trouble Brewing." *These Times*, 21 (March 31–April 13): 9.

Bloch, Maurice. 1977. "The Past and the Present in the Present." *Man*, n.s., 12: 278–93.

Bordo, Susan. 1991. "Docile Bodies, Rebellious Bodies: Foucauldian Perspectives on Female Psychopathology." In *Writing the Politics of Difference*, edited by H. Silverman, 202–341. Albany: State University of New York Press.

Brac de la Perrière, Bénédicte. 1989. *Les rituels de possession en Birmanie: Du culte d'Etat aux cérémonies privées*. Paris: ADPF, Recherches sur les civilisations.

———. 1993. "La fête de Taunbyon: Le grand rituel du culte des naq de Birmanie (Myanmar)." *Bulletin de l'Ecole Française d'Extrême-Orient* 79, no. 2: 201–232.

———. 1994. "Musique et possession dans le culte des 37 naq birmans." *Cahiers de Littérature Orale* 35: 177–88.

———. 1998a. "Le cycle des fêtes en Birmanie centrale: une circumambulation de l'espace birman." In *Etudes birmanes en hommage à Denise Bernot*, edited by Pierre Pichard and François Robinne, 289–331. Etudes thématiques 9. Paris: Ecole Française d'Extrême-Orient.

———. 1998b. "'Etre épousée par un naq': Les implications du mariage avec l'esprit dans le culte de possession birman (Myanmar)." *Anthropologie et Sociétés* 22: 169–82.

———. 1998c. "'Le roulis de la Dame aux Flancs d'Or': Une fête de naq atypique en Birmanie centrale." *L'Homme* 146 (April–June): 47–85.

———. 2000a. "Bouddhismes et chamanisme en Asie." In *La politique des esprits: Chamanismes et religions universalistes*, edited by Denise Aigle, Bénédicte Brac de la Perrière, and Jean-Pierre Chaumeil, 17–24. Nanterre: Société d'Ethnologie.

———. 2000b. "Petite en Myanmar: Destin et choix de vie d'une femme birmane." In *L'Enigme conjugale: Femmes et mariage en Asie,* edited by Josiane Cauquelin, 33–50. Clermont-Ferrand: Presses Universitaires Blaise Pascal, collection Anthropologie.

———. 2005. "The Taungbyon Festival: Locality and Nation Confronting in the Cult of the 37 Nat." In *Burma at the Turn of the Twenty-first Century,* edited by Monique Skidmore, 65–89. Honolulu: University of Hawai'i Press.

Braidotti, Rosi. 1994. *Nomadic Subjects: Embodiment and Sexual Difference in Contemporary Feminist Theory.* New York: Columbia University Press.

Brass, Paul. 1996. *Riots and Pogroms.* London: Macmillan.

Brison, Susan. 2002. *Aftermath: Violence and the Remaking of a Self.* Princeton: Princeton University Press.

Brow, James. 1988. "In Pursuit of Hegemony: Representations of Authority and Justice in a Sri Lankan Village." *American Ethnologist* 15, no. 2: 311–27.

———.1996. *Demons and Development: The Struggle for Community in a Sri Lankan Village.* Tucson: University of Arizona Press.

Burton, Frank, and Pat Carlen. 1979. *Official Discourse: On Discourse Analysis, Government Publications, Ideology and the State.* London: Routledge & Kegan Paul.

Butalia, Urvashi. 2000. *Other Side of Silence: Voices from the Partition of India.* Durham, NC: Duke University Press.

———, ed. 2002. *Speaking Peace: Women's Voices from Kashmir.* New Delhi: Kali Press for Women.

Butler, Judith. 1993. *Bodies That Matter: On the Discursive Limits of "Sex."* New York: Routledge.

———. 1997. *Excitable Speech: A Politics of the Performative.* New York: Routledge.

Cahill, Ann J. 2001. *Rethinking Rape.* Ithaca, NY: Cornell University Press.

Calhoun, Craig. 2002. "Imagining Solidarity: Cosmopolitanism, Constitutional Patriotism, and the Public Sphere." *Public Culture* 14, no. 1: 147–71.

Carter, April. 1998. "Should Women Be Soldiers or Pacifists?" In *The Women and War Reader,* edited by Lois A. Lorentzen and Jennifer Turpin, 33–37. New York: New York University Press.

Chakrabarty, Dipesh. 1993. "The Difference-Deferral of (a) Colonial Modernity: Public Debates on Domesticity in British Bengal." *History Workshop* 36: 1–34.

Chatterjee, Partha. 1993. *The Nation and Its Fragments: Colonial and Postcolonial Discourses.* Princeton: Princeton University Press.

Clark, Fiona, and Caroline Moser. 2001. *Victims, Perpetrators or Actors? Gender, Armed Conflict and Political Violence.* London: Zed Books.

Cockburn, Cynthia. 1998. *The Space between Us: Negotiating Gender and National Identities in Conflict.* London: Zed Books.

Condominas, Georges. 1985. "Quelques aspects du chamanisme et des cultes de possession en Asie du Sud-Est et dans le monde insulindien." In *L'autre et l'ailleurs, hommages à Roger Bastide,* edited by Jean Poirier, 215–32. Paris: Berger-Levrault.

Coomaraswamy, Radhika. 1997. "Women of the LTTE." *Frontline,* January 10.

———. 2001. "Peace and Suffering." *Tamil Times* 20, no. 4: 21–24.

———. 2003. "Forms, Life, and Killable Bodies." Keynote address presented at the conference "Women and the Contested State: Religion, Violence and Agency in South

Asia," Joan B. Kroc Institute for International Peace Studies, University of Notre Dame, April 11–12.

Daniel, E. Valentine. 1994. *Charred Lullabies: Chapters in an Anthropography of Violence.* Princeton: Princeton University Press.

Das, Veena. 1995. *Critical Events: An Anthropological Perspective on Contemporary India.* Delhi: Oxford University Press.

———. 1996. "Sexual Violence, Discursive Formations and the State." Paper presented at the conference "Violence against Women: Victims and Ideologies," March 28–31, Sri Lanka Foundation, Colombo, Sri Lanka.

———. 2001. "Crisis and Representation: Rumor and the Circulation of Hate." In *Disturbing Remains: Memory, History and Crisis in the Twentieth Century,* edited by Michael S. Roth and Charles G. Salas, 37–62. Los Angeles: Getty Research Institute.

———. 2006. *Life and Words: Violence and the Descent into the Ordinary.* Berkeley: University of California Press.

———, ed. 1990. *Mirrors of Violence: Communities, Riots, and Survivors in South Asia.* New Delhi: Oxford University Press.

Das, Veena, Arthur Kleinman, Mamphela Ramphele, and Pamela Reynolds, eds. 2000. *Violence and Subjectivity.* Berkeley: University of California Press.

De Lauretis, Teresa. 1989. "The Violence of Rhetoric: Considerations on Representations and Gender." In *Violence of Representation: Literature and the History of Violence,* edited by Nancy Armstrong and Leonard Tennenhouse, 239–57. London: Routledge.

De Mel, Neloufer. 2002. "Fractured Narratives: Notes on Women in Conflict in Sri Lanka and Pakistan." *Development* 45, no.1: 99–104.

Derrida, Jacques. 2001. *On Cosmopolitanism and Forgiveness.* London: Routledge.

Dixon, Ruth B. 1982. "Mobilizing Women for Rural Employment in South Asia: Issues of Class, Caste, and Patronage." *Economic Development and Cultural Change* 30, no. 2: 373–90.

Dollimore, Jonathan. 1991. *Sexual Dissidence: Augustine to Wilde, Freud to Foucault.* New York: Oxford University Press.

Dunn, John. 1969. *The Political Thought of John Locke.* Cambridge: Cambridge University Press.

Eade, Deborah. 2004. "Preface." In *Development, Women, and War: Feminist Perspectives,* edited by Haleh Afshar and Deborah Eade, 1–3. Oxford: Oxfam.

Elias, Norbert. 1994. *The Civilizing Process.* Oxford: Basil Blackwell.

Engels, Friedrich. 1942. *The Origin of the Family, Private Property and the State: In the Light of the Researches of Lewis H Morgan.* London: International Publishers.

Enloe, Cynthia. 1990. *Bananas, Beaches, and Bases: Making Feminist Sense of International Politics.* Berkeley: University of California Press.

Errington, Shelly. 1990. "Recasting Sex, Gender and Power: A Thematic and Regional Overview." In *Power and Difference: Gender in Island Southeast Asia,* edited by Jane Monnig Atkinson and Shelly Errington, 1–15. Stanford: Stanford University Press.

Escobar, Arturo. 1992. "Culture, Economics, and Politics in Latin American Social Movements Theory and Research." In *The Making of Social Movements in Latin America: Identity, Strategy and Democracy,* edited by Arturo Escobar and Sonia E. Alvarez, 62–85. Boulder, CO: Westview Press.

Escobar, Arturo, and Sonia E. Alvarez. 1992. "Introduction: Theory and Protest in Latin America Today." In *The Making of Social Movements in Latin America: Identity, Strategy, and Democracy,* edited by Arturo Escobar and Sonia E. Alvarez, 1–18. Boulder, CO: Westview Press.

Farquhar, Judith. 2001. "For Your Reading Pleasure: Self-Health (Ziwo Baojian) Information in 1990s Beijing." *Positions* 9, no. 9: 105–30.

Feit, Mario. 2003. "Mortality, Sexuality and Citizenship: Reading Rousseau, Arendt and Nietzche." Ph.D. dissertation, Johns Hopkins University.

Feldman, Allen. 1991. *Formations of Violence: Narrative of the Body and Political Terror in Northern Ireland.* Chicago: University of Chicago Press.

———. 1995. "On the Actuarial Gaze: From 9/11 to Abu Ghraib." *Cultural Studies* 19, no. 2: 203–26.

Feldman, Shelley. 2001. "Gender and Islam in Bangladesh: Myth and Metaphor." In *Understanding Bengali Muslims,* edited by Rafiuddin Ahmed, 209–35. New Delhi: Oxford University Press.

Fell McDermott, Rachel, and Jeffrey J. Kripal, eds. 2003. *Encountering Kali: In the Margins, at the Center, in the West.* Berkeley: University of California Press.

Felman, Shoshana, and Dori Laub. 1992. *Testimony: Crises of Witnessing in Literature, Psychoanalysis, and History.* New York: Routledge.

Ferguson, Frances. 1984. "The Nuclear Sublime." *Diacritics* 14, no. 2 (Summer): 4–10.

Ferguson, James, and Gupta Akhil. 2002. "Spatializing States: Toward an Ethnography of Neoliberal Governmentality." *American Ethnologist* 29, no. 4: 981–1002.

Filmer, Sir Robert. [1652] 1991. *Patriarcha and Other Writings.* Edited by Johann P. Sommerville. Cambridge: Cambridge University Press.

Fink, Christina. 2001. *Living Silence: Burma under Military Rule.* London: Zed Books.

Foucault, Michel. 1977. *Discipline and Punish.* Harmondsworth: Penguin Books.

Gamage, Siri, and Siri Hettige. 1997. "Democracy, Ethno-Nationalist Politics and Patronage Sri Lankan Style." *Asian Studies Review* 21, nos. 2–3: 134–49.

Gamburd, Michelle. 1995. "Women's Work, Women's Wages: Sri Lankan Labor Migration and the Microprocesses of Gender Transformations." Paper presented at the 5th Sri Lanka Conference, August 10–13, University of New Hampshire.

Gärtner, Uta, and Jens Lorenz, eds. 1994. *Tradition and Modernity in Myanmar: Proceedings from an International Conference Held in Berlin from May 7 to May 9, 1993.* Vol. 2. Berlin: Berliner Asien-Afrika-Studien.

Gautam, Shobha, Amrita Banskota, and Rita Manchanda. 2001. "Where There Are No Men: Women in the Maoist Insurgency in Nepal." In *Women, War and Peace in South Asia: Beyond Victimhood to Agency,* edited by Rita Manchanda, 214–51. New Delhi: Sage.

Geertz, Clifford. 1973. *The Interpretation of Culture.* New York: Basic Books.

Gibson, Thomas. 1986. *Sacrifice and Sharing in the Philippine Highlands: Religion and Society among the Buid of Mindoro.* London: Athlone Press.

Giddens, Anthony. 1991. *Modernity and Self-Identity: Self and Society in the Late Modern Age.* Cambridge: Polity Press.

Godse, Gopal. 1978. *May It Please Your Honour: Statement of Nathuram Godse.* Pune: Gopal Godse for Vitasta Prakashan.

Goldstein, Joshua S. 2001. *War and Gender: How Gender Shapes the War System and Vice Versa.* Cambridge: Cambridge University Press.

Gombrich, Richard F. 1971. *Precept and Practice: Traditional Buddhism in the Rural Highlands of Ceylon.* Oxford: Clarendon Press.

Gombrich, Richard, and Gananath Obeyesekere. 1988. *Buddhism Transformed.* Princeton: Princeton University Press.

Gottschang Turner, Karen. 1999. *Even the Women Must Fight: Memories of War from North Vietnam.* Hoboken, NJ: John Wiley.

Government Publications Bureau. 1997. *Final Report of the Commission of Inquiry into the Involuntary Removal or Disappearance of Persons in the Northern and Eastern Provinces,* Colombo, Sri Lanka. (Released 1998.)

Graham, Laura. 1993. "A Public Sphere in Amazonia? The Depersonalized Collaborative Construction of Discourse in Xavante." *American Ethnologist* 20, no. 4: 717–41.

Grimsley, Ronald. 1982. "Rousseau and His Reader: The Technique of Persuasion." In *Rousseau after Two Hundred Years: Proceedings of the Cambridge Bicentennial Colloquium,* edited by R. A. Leigh, 225–38. Cambridge: Cambridge University Press.

Gunaratna, Rohan. 1987. *War and Peace in Sri Lanka.* Colombo, Sri Lanka: Institute of Fundamental Studies.

Gunasalingam, V. S. 2004. "Human Rights Commission Indifferent to Atrocities Committed under PTA." *Beyond the Wall,* Home for Human Rights Quarterly Journal on Human Rights News and Views (January).

Gupta, Akhil. 1995. "Blurred Boundaries: The Discourse of Corruption, the Culture of Politics and the Imagined State." *American Ethnologist* 22, no. 2: 375–402.

Gupta, Charu. 2001. *Sexuality, Obscenity and Community: Women, Muslims and the Hindu Public in Colonial India.* New Delhi: Permanent Black.

Gupta, Mehandra Nath. 1957. *The Gospel of Sri Ramakrishna.* Madras: Sri Ramakrishna Math.

Habermas, Jürgen. 1991. *The Structural Transformation of the Public Sphere.* Cambridge, MA: MIT Press.

Hansen, Thomas Blom. 2001. *Wages of Violence.* Princeton: Princeton University Press.

Harcourt, Wendy, and Arturo Escobar. 2002. "Women and the Politics of Place." *Development* 45, no. 1: 7–14.

Hashmi, Taj. 2000. *Women and Islam in Bangladesh: Beyond Subjection and Tyranny.* New York: St. Martin's Press.

———. 2002. "Islamist Resurgence in Bangladesh." http://www.islaminterfaith.org/sep2002/article.html (accessed June 23, 2003).

Hayner, Priscilla B. 2002. *Unspeakable Truths: Facing the Challenge of Truth Commissions.* New York: Routledge.

Held, Virginia. 1993. *Feminist Morality: Transforming Culture, Society, and Politics.* Chicago: University of Chicago Press.

Hirschmann, David. 1998. "Civil Society in South Africa: Learning from Gender Themes." *World Development* 26, no. 2: 227–38.

Hobbes, Thomas. [1651] 1991. *Man and Citizen: De Homine and De Cive.* Edited by Bernhard Gert. Indianapolis: Hackett.

Hobsbawm, Eric, and Terence Ranger, eds. 1983. *The Invention of Tradition.* Cambridge: Cambridge University Press.

Houtman, Gustaff. 1990. "Traditions of Buddhist Practice in Burma." Ph.D. dissertation, London University.

———. 1999. *Mental Culture in Burmese Crisis Politics: Aung San Suu Kyi and the National League for Democracy.* Tokyo: Institute for the Study of Languages and Cultures of Asia and Africa, Tokyo University of Foreign Studies.

———. 2005. "Sacralizing or Demonizing Democracy? Aung San Suu Kyi's 'Personality Cult.'" In *Burma at the Turn of the Twenty-first Century,* edited by Monique Skidmore, 133–53. Honolulu: University of Hawai'i Press.

Houtzager, Peter P., and Marcus J Kurtz. 2000. "The Institutional Roots of Popular Mobilization: State Transformation in Brazil and Chile 1960–1995." *Comparative Studies in Society and History* 42: 394–424.

Hui, Wang, Leo Ou-fan Lee, and Michael M. J. Fischer. 1994. "Etymologies: Is the Public Sphere Unspeakable in Chinese? Can Public Spaces (Gonggong Kongjian) Lead to Public Spheres?" *Public Culture* 6: 597–605.

Humphrey, Caroline. 1994. "Shamanic Practices and the State in Northern Asia: Views from the Centre and the Periphery." In *Shamanism, History and the State,* edited by Nicholas Thomas and Caroline Humphrey, 191–228. Ann Arbor: University of Michigan Press.

Humphrey, Michael. 2002. *The Politics of Atrocity and Reconciliation: From Terror to Trauma.* London: Routledge.

Jaranson, James M., and Michael K. Poplin. 1998. *Caring for Victims of Torture.* London: American Psychiatric Press.

Jayawardena, Kumari, and Malathi de Alwis, eds. 1996. *Embodied Violence: Communalising Female Sexuality in South Asia.* New Delhi: Kali Press for Women.

Jean-Klein, Iris. 2000. "Mothercraft, Statecraft, and Subjectivity in the Palestinian Intifada." *American Ethnologist* 27, no. 1: 100–127.

———. 2003. "Into Committees, out of the House? Familiar Forms in the Organization of Palestinian Committee Activism during the First Intifada." *American Ethnologist* 30, no. 4: 556–77.

Jeganathan, Pradeep. 1998. "In the Shadow of Violence: 'Tamilness' and the Anthropology of Identity in Southern Sri Lanka." In *Buddhist Fundamentalism and Minority Identities in Sri Lanka,* edited by Tessa J. Bartholomeusz and Chandra R. de Silva, 89–109. Albany: State University of New York Press.

———. 2000. "A Space for Violence: Anthropology, Politics and the Location of a Sinhala Practice of Masculinity." In *Community, Gender and Violence: Subaltern Studies XI,* edited by Partha Chatterjee and Pradeep Jeganathan, 37–66. London: Permanent Black.

Jordt, Ingrid. 1988. "Bhikkhuni, Thilashin, Mae-Chii: Women Who Renounce the World in Thailand, Burma and the Classical Pali Texts." *Crossroads* 4, no. 1: 31–39.

———. 2001. "The Mass Lay Meditation Movement and State-Society Relations in Post-Independence Burma." Ph.D. dissertation, Harvard University.

———. 2003a. "The Social Organization of Intention: Sacred Giving and Its Implications for Burma's Political Economy." In *Anthropological Perspectives on Economic Development and Integration,* edited by Norbert Dannhaeuser and Cynthia Werner, 325–44. Research in Economic Anthropology, vol. 22. Oxford: Elsevier.

———. 2003b. "From Relations of Power to Relations of Authority: Epistemic Claims, Practices, and Ideology in the Production of Burma's Political Order." *Social Analysis* 47, no. 1: 65–76.

———. 2005. "Women's Practices of Renunciation in the Age of *Sāsana* Revival." In *Burma at the Turn of the Twenty-first Century,* edited by Monique Skidmore, 63–98. Honolulu: University of Hawai'i Press.

———. 2007. *Burma's Mass Lay Movement: Buddhism and the Cultural Construction of Power.* Athens: Ohio University Press.

Joseph, Ammu, and Kalpana Sharma, eds. 2003. *Terror, Counter-Terror: Women Speak Out.* London: Zed Books.

Joseph, Betty. 2002. "Gendering Time in Globalization: The Belatedness of the Other Woman and Jamaica Kincaid's *Lucy.*" *Tulsa Studies in Women's Literature* 21, no. 1: 67–83.

Joseph, Suad. 1991. "Elite Strategies for State-Building: Women, Family, Religion and State in Iraq and Lebanon." In *Women, Islam, and the State,* edited by Deniz Kandiyoti, 176–200. London: Macmillan.

———. 1997. "The Public/Private—The Imagined Boundary in the Imagined Nation/State/Community. The Lebanese Case." *Feminist Review* 57: 73–92.

Joseph, Suad, and Susan Slymovics, eds. 2001. *Women and Power in the Middle East.* Philadelphia: University of Pennsylvania Press.

Kabeer, Naila. 1991. "The Quest for National Identity." In *Women, Islam and the State,* edited by Deniz Kandiyoti, 115–43. London: Macmillan.

Kakar, Sudhir. 1996. *The Colors of Violence: Cultural Identities, Religion, and Conflict.* Chicago: University of Chicago Press.

Kalam, A. P. J. Abdul. 1999. *Wings of Fire.* Hyderabad: Universities Press.

Kaldor, Mary. 2003. *Global Civil Society: An Answer to War.* Cambridge: Polity Press.

Kapferer, Bruce. 1983. *A Celebration of Demons: Exorcism and Aesthetics of Healing in Sri Lanka.* Bloomington: Indiana University Press. Reprint, Washington, DC: Smithsonian Institution Press, 1991.

———. 1988. *Legends of People, Myths of State: Violence, Intolerance and Political Culture in Sri Lanka and Australia.* Washington, DC: Smithsonian Institution Press.

———. 1997. *The Feast of the Sorcerer: Practices of Consciousness and Power in Sri Lanka.* Chicago: University of Chicago Press.

Kapur, Rajiv. 1984. *Sikh Separatism: The Politics of Faith.* London: Allyn and Unwin.

Karim, Lamia. 2001. "Politics of the Poor? NGOs and Grass-Roots Political Mobilization in Bangladesh." *Political and Legal Anthropology Review (POLAR)* 24, no. 1: 92–107.

Kaul, Suvir. 2002. *The Partitions of Memory: The Afterlife of the Division of India.* New Delhi: Permanent Black.

Kawanami, Hiroko. 2000. "Theravadin Religious Women." In *The Life of Buddhism,* edited by Frank E. Reynolds and Jason A. Carbine, 86–95. Berkeley: University of California Press.

———. 2001. "Can Women Be Celibate?" In *Celibacy, Society, and Culture: The Anthropology of Sexual Abstinence,* edited by Elisa J. Sobo and Sandra Bell, 137–56. Madison: University of Wisconsin Press.

Keeler, Ward. 2005. "But Princes Jump: Performing Masculinity in Mandalay." *In Burma at the Turn of the Twenty-first Century,* edited by Monique Skidmore, 308–41. Honolulu: University of Hawai'i Press.

Kelly, Michael, and Lynn M. Messina, eds. 2002. *Religion in Politics and Society.* The Reference Shelf, vol. 74, no. 3. New York: H.W. Wilson.

Kendall, Laurel. 1985. *Shamans, Housewives, and Other Restless Spirits: Women in Korean Ritual Life.* Honolulu: University of Hawai'i Press.

Khandro, Karma Sangye. 2002. "The Dakini's Dance: Meaning and Myth in [Tibetan] Buddhism." Unpublished manuscript.

Kordon, Diana R., Lucila I. Edelman, et al. 1988. *Psychological Effects of Political Repression (Efectos psicológicos de la represión political).* Buenos Aires: Sudamericana/ Planeta.

Koselleck, Reinhart. [1959] 1988. *Critique and Crisis: Enlightenment and the Pathogenesis of Modern Society.* Oxford: Berg.

Kumar, Krishna, ed. 2001. *Women and Civil War: Impact, Organizations, and Action.* Boulder, CO: Lynne Rienner.

Kumar, Pramod, ed. 1992. *Towards Understanding Communalism.* Chandigarh: Centre for Research in Rural and Industrial Development.

Landes. Joan B. 1988. *Women and the Public Sphere in the Age of the French Revolution.* Ithaca, NY: Cornell University Press.

Lawrence, Patricia. 1995. Report on the Summary Execution of 184 Tamil Civilians at Sathurukondan on September 9, 1990, to the Presidential Commission of Inquiry into Involuntary Removal or Disappearances of Persons in the Northern and Eastern Province, Ministry of Justice, Hulftsdorp, Colombo, Sri Lanka, through the International Legal Studies Program, University of Denver Law School.

———. 1997. "The Changing Amman: Notes on the Injury of War in Eastern Sri Lanka." *Journal of South Asian Studies* 20: 215–38.

———. 2000. "Violence, Suffering, Amman: The Work of Oracles in Sri Lanka's Eastern War Zone." In *Violence and Subjectivity,* edited by Veena Das, Arthur Kleinman, Mamphela Ramphele, and Pamela Reynolds, 171–204. Berkeley: University of California Press.

———. 2003a. "Kali in a Context of Terror: Tasks of a Goddess in Sri Lanka's Civil War." In *Encountering Kali: In the Margins, at the Center, in the West,* edited by Jeffrey J. Kripal and Rachel Fell McDermott, 100–123. Berkeley: University of California Press.

———. 2003b. *The Ocean of Stories: Children's Imagination, Creativity, and Reconciliation in Eastern Sri Lanka.* Colombo, Sri Lanka: International Centre for Ethnic Studies.

Lentin, Ronit, ed. 1997. *Gender and Catastrophe.* London: Zed Books.

Lerner, Gerda. 2002. *Fireweed: A Political Autobiography.* Philadelphia: Temple University Press.

Levine, Philippa. 2002. "The Cordon Sanitaire: Mobility and Space in the Regulation of Colonial Prostitution." In *Trans-Status Subjects: Gender in the Globalization of South and Southeast Asia,* edited by Sonita Sarker and Esha Niyogi De, 51–55. Durham, NC: Duke University Press.

Lewis, I. M. 1971. *Ecstatic Religion: An Anthropological Study of Spirit Possession and Shamanism*. New York: Penguin Books.

Lorentzen, Lois Ann, and Jennifer Turpin, eds. 1998. *The Women and War Reader*. New York: New York University Press.

Ludden, David. 1996a. *Contesting the Nation: Religion, Community, and the Politics of Democracy in India*. South Asia Studies Seminar Series. Philadelphia: University of Pennsylvania Press.

———. 1996b. *Making India Hindu: Religion, Community, and Politics of Democracy in India*. New Delhi: Oxford University Press.

McClintock, Anne. 1995. *Imperial Leather: Race, Gender and Sexuality in the Colonial Contest*. London: Routledge & Kegan Paul.

McDonald, Sharon. 1987. "Drawing the Lines — Gender, Peace and War: An Introduction." In *Images of Women in Peace and War: Cross-Cultural and Historical Perspectives*, edited by Sharon McDonald, Shirley Ardener, and Pat Holden, 1–26. London: Macmillan Education.

McDonald, Sharon, Shirley Ardener, and Pat Holden, eds. 1987. *Images of Women in Peace and War: Cross-Cultural and Historical Perspectives*. London: Macmillan Education.

McGilvray, Dennis. 1989. "Households in Akkaraipattu: Dowry and Domestic Organization among the Matrilineal Tamils and Moors of Sri Lanka." In *Society from the Inside Out*, edited by John N. Gray and David Mearns, 192–235. New Delhi: Sage.

———. 1998. "Arabs, Moors, and Muslims: Sri Lankan Muslim Ethnicity in Regional Perspective." *Contributions to Indian Sociology*, n.s., 32, no. 2: 433–83.

———. 2008. *Crucible of Conflict: Tamil and Muslim Society on the East Coast of Sri Lanka*. Durham: Duke University Press.

———, ed. 1982. *Caste Ideology and Interaction*. Cambridge: Cambridge University Press.

McKay, Susan R. 1998. "The Psychology of Societal Reconstruction and Peace: A Gendered Perspective." In *The Women and War Reader*, edited by Lois Ann Lorentzen and Jennifer Turpin, 348–62. New York: New York University Press.

McKenna, Thomas M. 1999. "Murder or Martyrdom? Popular Evaluations of Violent Death in the Muslim Separatist Movement in the Philippines." In *Death Squad: The Anthropology of State Terror*, edited by Jeffrey A. Sluka, 189–203. Philadelphia: University of Pennsylvania Press.

McLennan, John Ferguson. 1970. *Primitive Marriage: An Enquiry into the Origin of the Form of Capture in Marriage*. Edited by Peter Riviére. Chicago: University of Chicago Press.

Mahmood, Cynthia Keppley. 1999. "Trials by Fire: Dynamics of Terror in Punjab and Kashmir." In *Death Squad: The Anthropology of State Terror*, edited by Jeffrey A. Sluka, 70–90. Philadelphia: University of Pennsylvania Press.

Mahmood, Cynthia Keppley, and Stacy Brady. 1999. *The Guru's Gift: An Ethnography of Exploring Gender Equality with North American Sikh Women*. New York: McGraw-Hill.

Manchanda, Rita. 2001a. "Where Are the Women in South Asian Conflicts?" In *Women, War and Peace in South Asia: Beyond Victimhood to Agency*, edited by Rita Manchanda, 9–41. New Delhi: Sage.

———, ed. 2001b. *Women, War and Peace in South Asia: Beyond Victimhood to Agency*. New Delhi: Sage.

Manderson, Lenore, and Linda Rae Bennett, eds. 2003. *Violence against Women in Asian Societies.* London: Routledge Curzon.

Mannan, Maznurul, et al. 1994. *Fatwabazz against BRAC: Are They Alone?* Dhaka: BRAC Research and Development.

Marshall, John. 1994. *John Locke: Resistance, Religion, and Responsibility.* Cambridge: Cambridge University Press.

Mascarenes, Anthony. 1971. *The Rape of Bangladesh.* New Delhi: Vikas.

———. 1986. *Bangladesh: A Legacy of Blood.* London: Hodder & Stoughton.

Maunaguru, Sitralega. 1995. "Gendering Tamil Nationalism: The Construction of 'Woman' in Projects of Protest and Control." In *Unmaking the Nation: The Politics of Identity and History in Modern Sri Lanka,* edited by Pradeep Jeganathan and Qadri Ismail, 158–75. Colombo, Sri Lanka: Social Scientists' Association.

Mayaram, Shail. 1997. *Resisting Regimes.* New Delhi: Oxford University Press.

Mbembe, Achille. 2001. *On the Postcolony.* Berkeley: University of California Press.

Mehta, Deepak. Forthcoming. "Words That Wound: Archiving Hate in the Constitution of Hindu and Muslim Publics in Bombay." In *Beyond Crisis: A Critical Second Look at Pakistan,* edited by Naveeda Khan. New Delhi: Routledge.

Mehta, Ved. 1993. *Mahatma Gandhi and His Apostles.* New Haven, CT: Yale University Press.

Meintjes, Sheila, Anu Pillay, and Meredeth Turshen, eds. 2001. *The Aftermath: Women in Post-Conflict Transformation.* London: Zed Books.

Mercier, Jacques. 1993. "Corps pour Corps, corps a corps: De la regulation sacrificialle de la possession a la "Mise en Corps" du sacrifice par la possession." *L'Homme* 32, no. 1: 67–87.

Min Zin. 2001. "The Power of Hpoun." *Irrawaddy* 9, no. 9: 1–3. http://www.irrawaddy.org/aviewer.asp?a=2471&z=107.

———. 2003. "Engaging Buddhism for Social Change." *Irrawaddy* 11, no. 2: 1–4. http://www.irrawaddy.org/aviewer.asp?a=2854&z=107.

Mitchell, Joshua. 1993. "Hobbes and the Equality of All under the One." *Political Theory* 21, no. 1: 78–100.

Moore, Erin P. 1998. *Gender, Law, and Resistance in India.* Tucson: University of Arizona Press.

Morgan, Lewis Henry. 1877. *Ancient Society: or, Researches in the Lines of Human Progress from Savagery through Barbarism to Civilization.* London: Macmillan.

Morrison, Toni. 1993. Nobel Lecture. December 7. http://nobelprize.org/nobel_prizes/literature/laureates/1993/morrison-lecture.html.

Mosse, David. 2003. *The Rule of Water: Statecraft, Ecology, and Collective Action in South India.* Oxford: Oxford University Press.

Muhith, A. M. A. 1978. *Bangladesh: Emergence of a Nation.* Dhaka: Bangladesh Books International.

Mukta, Prita. 2000. "Gender, Community and Nation: The Myth of Innocence." In *States of Conflict: Gender, Violence and Resistance,* edited by Susie Jacobs, Ruth Jacobsen, and Jennifer Marchbank, 163–78. London: Zed Books.

Mulder, Niels. 2001. *Inside Thai Society: Religion, Everyday Life, Change.* Chiang Mai: Silkworm Books.

Muller, Friedrich Max. 1876. *Chips from a German Workshop.* New York: Scribner.

————. [1898] 2002. *Ramakrishna: His Life and Sayings.* New Delhi: Rupa & Co.

Murshid, Tazeen. 2003. "Women, Islam and the State: Subordination and Resistance." http://www.lib.uchicago.edu/e/su/southasia/Tazeen.html, 119–34 (accessed March 22, 2003).

Musengezi, Chiedza, and Irene McCartney, eds. 2000. *Women of Resilience: The Voices of Women Ex-Combatants.* Harare: Zimbabwe Women Writers.

Myrdal, Gunnar. 1968. *Asian Drama.* London: Penguin.

————. 1970. *The Challenge of World Poverty.* London: Penguin.

Nandy, Ashis. 1990. "The Politics of Secularism and the Recovery of Religious Tolerance." In *Mirrors of Violence,* edited by Veena Das, 69–93. New Delhi: Oxford University Press.

————. 1998. *Exiled at Home.* New Delhi: Oxford University Press.

————. 2002. *Time Warps: Silent and Evasive Pasts in Indian Politics and Religion.* New Brunswick, NJ: Rutgers University Press.

Nemoto, Kei. 1996. "Aung San Suu Kyi—What Does She Aim At?" *Genbunken,* no. 73: 21–32.

Nissan, Elizabeth. 1996. *Sri Lanka: A Bitter Harvest.* London: Minority Rights Group International Report.

Nissan, Elizabeth, and R. L. Stirrat. 1990. "The Generation of Communal Identities." In *Sri Lanka: History and the Roots of Conflict,* edited by Jonathan Spencer, 19–44. London: Routledge.

Nordstom, Carolyn. 2004. *Shadows of War: Violence, Power and International Profiteering in the Twenty-first Century.* California Series in Public Anthropology. Berkeley: University of California Press.

Obeyesekere, Gananath. 1969. "The Ritual Drama of the Sanni Demons: Collective Representations of Disease in Ceylon." *Comparative Studies in Society and History* 11, no. 2: 174–216.

————. 1976. "The Impact of Āyurvedic Ideas on the Culture and the Individual in Sri Lanka." In *Asian Medical Systems: A Comparative Study,* edited by Charles Leslie, 201–26. Berkeley: University of California Press.

————. 1984. *The Cult of the Goddess Pattini.* Chicago: University of Chicago Press.

Obeyesekere, Gananath, and Richard Gombrich. 1988. *Buddhism Transformed: Religious Changes in Sri Lanka.* Princeton: Princeton University Press.

Orjuela, Camilla. 2003. "Building Peace in Sri Lanka: A Role for Civil Society?" *Journal for Peace Research* 40, no. 2: 195–212.

Ortner, Sherry. 1995. "Resistance and the Problem of Ethnographic Refusal." *Comparative Studies in Society and History* 37, no. 1: 173–93.

Pandey, Gyanendra. 1990. *The Construction of Communalism in Colonial North India.* New Delhi: Oxford University Press.

————. 1994. "The Prose of Otherness." In *Subaltern Studies VIII: Essays in Honour of Ranajit Guha,* edited by David Arnold and David Hardiman, 188–221. New Delhi: Oxford University Press.

————. 2001. *Remembering Partition: Violence, Nationalism and History in India.* Contemporary South Asia. Cambridge: Cambridge University Press.

————. 2006. *Construction of Communalism in Colonial India.* New Delhi: Oxford University Press.

Parkel, Anthony J. 1997. *Gandhi: Hind Swaraj and Other Writings.* Cambridge: Cambridge University Press.

Parker, Andrew, Mary Russo, Doris Sommer, and Patricia Yaeger, eds. 1992. *Nationalisms and Sexualities.* New York: Routledge.

Pateman, Carole. 1988. *The Sexual Contract.* Stanford: Stanford University Press.

Pearlman, Wendy. 2003. *Occupied Voices: Stories of Everyday Life from the Second Intifada.* New York: Nation Books.

Perera, Sasanka. 2001. "Spirit Possessions and Avenging Ghosts: Stories of Supernatural Activity as Narratives of Terror and Mechanisms of Coping and Remembering." In *Remaking a World: Violence, Social Suffering, and Recovery,* edited by Veena Das, Arthur Kleinman, Margaret Lock, Mamphela Ramphele, and Pamela Reynolds, 157–200. Berkeley: University of California Press.

Perry, Sir Eskine. 1853. *Cases Illustrative of Oriental Life and the Application of English Law to India Decided in H.M. Supreme Court of Bombay.* London: S. Sweet.

Peteet, Julie. 2001. "Women and the Palestinian Movement: No Going Back?" In *Women and Power in the Middle East,* edited by Suad Joseph and Susan Slymovics, 135–49. Philadelphia: University of Pennsylvania Press.

Pettigrew, Joyce. 1999. "Parents and Their Children in Situations of Terror: Disappearances and Special Police Activity in Punjab." In *Death Squad: The Anthropology of State Terror,* edited by Jeffrey A. Sluka, 204–25. Philadelphia: University of Pennsylvania Press.

Platteau, Jean Philippe, and Anita Abraham. 2002. "Participatory Development in the Presence of Endogenous Community Imperfections." *Journal of Development Studies* 39, no. 2: 104–36.

Pocock, J.G.A. 1971. *Politics, Language, and Time.* New York: Atheneum.

Pollock, Sheldon. 1993. "Ramayana and Political Imagination in India." *Journal of Asian Studies* 52, no 2: 261–97.

Poovey, Mary. 2002. "The Liberal Civil Subject and the Social in Eighteenth-Century British Moral Philosophy." *Public Culture* 14, no. 1: 125–45.

Prakash, Gyan. 1997. "The Modern Nation's Return in the Archaic." *Critical Inquiry* 23: 536–56.

Rajagopal, Arvind. 2000. *Politics after Television.* Cambridge: Cambridge University Press.

Rajasingham-Senanayake, Darini. 1999. "Democracy and the Problem of Representation: The Making of Bi-polar Ethnic Identity in Post/Colonial Sri Lanka." In *Ethnic Futures,* edited by Joanna Pfaff-Czarnecka and Darini Rajasingham-Senanayake, 99–134. New Delhi: Sage.

————. 2001. "Ambivalent Empowerment: The Tragedy of Tamil Women in Conflict." In *Women, War and Peace in South Asia: Beyond Victimhood to Agency,* edited by Rita Manchanda, 102–30. New Delhi: Sage.

Ram, Kalpana. 1992. *Mukkuvar Women: Gender, Hegemony and Capitalist Transformation in a South Indian Fishing Community.* New Delhi: Kali Press for Women.

Ramachandran, R. 1999. *Frontline Online* 16, no. 2, January 16–29. http://www.flonnet.com/fl1602/16020730.html.

Rancière, Jacques. 1992. "Politics, Identification, and Subjectivization." *October* 61: 58–64.

Reilly, Niamh, ed. 1996. *Without Reservation: The Beijing Tribunal on Accountability for Women's Human Rights*. New Brunswick, NJ: Rutgers University Press.

Renan, Ernest. [1882] 1999. "What Is a Nation?" In *The Nationalism Reader*, edited by Omar Dahbour and Micheline Ishay, 143–55. New York: Humanity Books.

Renou, Louis. 1941–42. "Les connexions entre le rituel et la grammaire en Sanskrit." *Journal Asiatique* 233, no. 1: 105–65.

Reynolds, Frank E., and Jason A. Carbine, eds. 2000. *The Life of Buddhism*. Berkeley: University of California Press.

Reynolds, Holly Baker. 1980. "The Auspicious Married Woman." In *The Powers of Tamil Women*, edited by Susan S. Wadley, 35–60. South Asian Series 6. Syracuse: Syracuse University Foreign and Comparative Studies.

Robben, Antonius C.G.M., Marcelo M. Suarez-Orozco, and Naomi Quinn, eds. 2000. *Cultures under Siege: Collective Violence and Trauma*. Publications of the Society for Psychological Anthropology. Cambridge: Cambridge University Press.

Rogers, John. 1995. "Racial Identities and Politics in Early Modern Sri Lanka." In *The Concept of Race in South Asia*, edited by Peter Robb, 146–64. New Delhi: Oxford University Press.

Rostami Povey, Elaheh. 2004. "Women in Afghanistan: Passive Victims of the *Borga* or Active Social Participants?" In *Development, Women, and War: Feminist Perspectives*, edited by Haleh Afshar and Deborah Eade, 172–87. Oxford: Oxfam.

Rousseau, Jean-Jacques. 1911. *Emile*. New York: Everyman's Library.

Roy, Arundhati. 1999. *The Cost of Living*. New York: Modern Library.

Rozenberg, Guillaume. 2005. "The Cheaters: Journey to the Land of the Lottery." In *Burma at the Turn of the Twenty-first Century*, edited by Monique Skidmore, 19–40. Honolulu: University of Hawai'i Press.

Sadan, Mandy. 2005. "Respected Grandfather, Please Bless This Nissan." In *Burma at the Turn of the Twenty-first Century*, edited by Monique Skidmore, 90–111. Honolulu: University of Hawai'i Press.

Sarker, Sonita, and Esha Niyogi De, eds. 2002. *Trans-Status Subjects: Gender in the Globalization of South and Southeast Asia*. Durham, NC: Duke University Press.

Scarpaci, Joseph L. 1991. "Primary-Care Decentralization in the Southern Cone: Shantytown Health Care as Urban Social Movement." *Annals of the Association of American Geographers* 81, no. 1: 103–26.

Scheper-Hughes, Nancy. 1992. *Death without Weeping: The Violence of Everyday Life in Brazil*. Berkeley: University of California Press.

Schirmer, Jennifer. 1994. "The Claiming of Space and the Body Politic within National-Security States: The Plaza de Mayo Madres and the Greenham Common Women." In *Remapping Memory: The Politics of Timespace*, edited by Jonathan Boyarin, 185–220. Minneapolis: University of Minnesota Press.

Schober, Juliane. 1989. "Paths to Enlightenment: Theravada Buddhism in Upper Burma." Ph.D. dissertation, University of Illinois.

———. 1995. "The Politics of Contested Meanings: State Patronage of the Chinese Tooth Relic and the Construction of Burmese National Culture." Paper prepared for AAR Seminar on Relics, Philadelphia, November 19.

————. 1997. "Buddhist Just Rule and Burmese National Culture: State Patronage of the Chinese Tooth Relic in Myanmar." *History of Religions* 36, no. 3: 218–43.

————. 2005. "Buddhist Visions of Moral Authority and Modernity in Burma." In *Burma at the Turn of the Twenty-first Century,* edited by Monique Skidmore, 113–33. Honolulu: University of Hawai'i Press.

Schreiter, Robert J. 1992. *Reconciliation.* Newton, MA: Boston Theological Institute.

————. 1997. "Buddhist Just Rule and Burmese National Culture: State Patronage of the Chinese Tooth Relic in Myanmar." *History of Religions* 36, no. 3: 218–43.

Scott, David. 1994. *Formations of Ritual: Colonial and Anthropological Discourses on the Sinhala Yaktovil.* Minneapolis: University of Minnesota Press.

Scott, James. 1976. *The Moral Economy of the Peasant: Subsistence and Rebellion in Southeast Asia.* New Haven: Yale University Press.

————. 1985. *Weapons of the Weak: Everyday Forms of Peasant Resistance.* New Haven: Yale University Press.

————. 1988. *Gender and the Politics of History.* New York: Columbia University Press.

Selim, Monique. 2000. "Génies, comunisme et marché dans le Laos contemporain." In *La politique des esprits: Chamanismes et religions universalistes,* edited by Denise Aigle, Bénédicte Brac de la Perrière, and Jean-Pierre Chaumeil, 105–24. Nanterre: Société d'Ethnologie.

Severance, Mary Laura. 2000. "Sex and the Social Contract." *English Literary History* 67, no. 2: 453–513.

Shehabuddin, Elora. 1999. "Beware the Bed of Fire: Gender, Democracy and Jamaat-i-Islami in Bangladesh." *Journal of Women's History* 10, no. 4: 148–71.

Shehadeh, Raja. 2003. *When the Birds Stopped Singing: Life in Ramallah under Siege.* Hanover, NH: Steerforth.

Shrimali, K. M. 2003. "The History and Politics of 'Trishul' and 'Diksha.'" *Frontline Online* 20, no. 11. May 24–June 6. http://www.flonnet.com/fl2101l/stories/20030606001308 400.html.

Siddiq, Salik. 1977. *Witness to Surrender.* Karachi: Oxford University Press.

Simpson, Robert. 1997. "Possession, Dispossession and the Social Distribution of Knowledge among Sri Lankan Ritual Specialists." *Journal of the Royal Anthropological Institute* 3, no. 1: 43–60.

Sinha, Mrinalini, 1995. *Colonial Masculinity: The "Manly Englishman" and the "Effeminate Bengali" in the Late Nineteenth Century.* Manchester: Manchester University Press.

Sisson, Richard, and Leo E. Rose. 1990. *War and Secession: Pakistan, India and the Creation of Bangladesh.* Berkeley: University of California Press.

Sivaramakrishnan, Kalayanakrishnan. 2000. "Crafting the Public Sphere in the Forests of West Bengal: Democracy, Development, and Political Action." *American Ethnologist* 27, no. 2: 431–61.

Skidmore, Monique. 2003. "Darker than Midnight: Fear, Vulnerability, and Terror-Making in Urban Burma (Myanmar)." *American Ethnologist* 30, no. 1: 5–21.

————. 2004. *Karaoke Fascism: Burma and the Politics of Fear.* Philadelphia: University of Pennsylvania Press.

————, ed. 2005. *Burma at the Turn of the Twenty-first Century.* Honolulu: University of Hawai'i Press.

Skielsboek, Inger, and Dan Smith, eds. 2003. *Gender, Peace and Conflict.* Oslo: International Peace Research Institute.

Sluka, Jeffrey A. 2000. "Introduction: State Terror and Anthropology." In *Death Squad: The Anthropology of State Terror,* edited by Jeffrey A. Sluka, 1–45. Philadelphia: University of Pennsylvania Press.

Sobhan, Rehman. 1997. "The Political Economy of Micro-Credit." In *Who Needs Credit? Poverty and Finance in Bangladesh,* edited by Geoffrey Wood and Iffath Sharif, 131–41. Dhaka: University Press Ltd.

Somasundaram, Daya. 1998. *Scarred Minds: The Psychological Impact of War on Sri Lankan Tamils.* New Delhi: Sage.

———. 2003. "Collective Trauma in Sri Lanka." *International Journal of Mental Health, Psychosocial Work and Counselling in Areas of Armed Conflict* 1: 11.

Spencer, Jonathan.1990. *A Sinhala Village in a Time of Trouble: Politics and Change in Rural Sri Lanka.* New Delhi: Oxford University Press.

Spiro, Melford. [1967] 1978. *Burmese Supernaturalism: A Study in the Explanation and Reduction of Suffering.* Philadelphia: Institute for the Study of Human Issues. 1967.

———. 1993. "Gender Hierarchy in Burma: Cultural, Social, and Psychological Dimensions." In *Sex and Gender Hierarchies,* edited by Barbara Diane Miller, 316–33. Cambridge: Cambridge University Press.

Starn, Orin.1992. "I Dreamed of Foxes and Hawks: Reflections on Peasant Protest, New Social Movements, and the *Rondas Campesinas* of Northern Peru." In *The Making of Social Movements in Latin America: Identity, Strategy, and Democracy,* edited by Arturo Escobar and Sonia E. Alvarez, 89–111. Boulder, CO: Westview Press.

Stephen, Lynn. 1995. "Women's Rights Are Human Rights: The Merging of Feminine and Feminist Interests among El Salvador's Mothers of the Disappeared (CO-MADRES)." *American Ethnologist* 22, no. 4: 807–27.

Suarez-Orozco, Marcelo. 1992. "A Grammar of Terror: Psychocultural Responses to State Terrorism in Dirty War and Post-Dirty War Argentina." In *The Paths to Domination, Resistance, and Terror,* edited by Carolyn Nordstrom and JoAnn Martin, 219–59. Berkeley: University of California Press.

Tambiah, Stanley Jeyaraja. 1976. *World Conqueror, World Renouncer: A Study of Buddhism and Polity in Thailand against a Historical Background.* Cambridge: Cambridge University Press.

———. 1985. *Culture, Thought, and Social Action.* Chicago: University of Chicago Press.

———. [1986] 1991. *Sri Lanka: Ethnic Fratricide and the Dismantling of Democracy.* Chicago: University of Chicago Press.

———. 1992. *Buddhism Betrayed? Religion, Politics, and Violence in Sri Lanka.* Chicago: University of Chicago Press.

———. 1997. *Leveling Crowds: Ethno-Nationalist Conflicts and Collective Violence in South Asia.* Comparative Studies in Religion and Society 10. Berkeley: University of California Press.

Tamilnet. 2004. "Women's 'Coming Together' Event." http://www.Tamilnet.com. October 3.

Taraki, Sivaram. 1992. *The Eluding Peace.* Sarcelles: Arts Social Sciences of Eelam Academy.

Taussig, Michael T. 1992. *The Nervous System.* New York: Routledge.

Taylor, Charles. 1998. "Modes of Secularism." In *Secularism and Its Critics*, edited by Rajeev Bhargava, 31–53. New Delhi: Oxford University Press.

———. 2002. "Modern Social Imaginaries." *Public Culture* 14, no. 1: 91–124.

Taylor, Philip. 2004. *Goddess on the Rise: Pilgrimage and Popular Religion in Vietnam*. Honolulu: University of Hawai'i Press.

Taylor, Robert. 1987. *The State in Burma*. London: C. Hurst & Co.

Thiruchandran, Selvy. 1999. *The Other Victims of War: Emergence of Female Headed Households in Eastern Sri Lanka*. Vol 2. Women's Education and Research Centre. Colombo, Sri Lanka: Vikas.

Thomas, Philip. 2002. "The River, the Road, and the Rural-Urban Divide: A Postcolonial Moral Geography from Southeast Madagascar." *American Ethnologist* 29, no. 2: 366–91.

Trawick, Margaret. 1997. "Reasons for Violence: A Preliminary Ethnographic Account of the LTTE." *Journal of South Asian Studies* 20: 153–80.

———. 2007. *Enemy Lines, Warfare, Childhood, and Play in Batticaloa*. Berkeley: University of California Press.

Tripp, Ali M. 1998. "Expanding 'Civil Society': Women and Political Space in Contemporary Uganda." *Journal of Commonwealth and Comparative Politics* 36, no. 8: 84–107.

———. 2001. "Women's Movements and Challenges to Patrimonial Rule: Preliminary Observations from Africa." *Development and Change* 32: 33–54.

Trouillot, Michel-Rolph. 1995. *Silencing the Past: Power and the Production of History*. New York: Beacon Press.

Turshen, Meredith, and Clotilde Twagiramaiya. 1998. *What Women Do in Wartime: Gender and Conflict in Africa*. London: Zed Books.

Uribe-Uran, Victor M. 2000. "The Birth of the Public Sphere in Latin America during the Age of Revolution." *Comparative Studies in Society and History* 42, no. 2: 425–57.

Valeri, Valerio. 1990. "Both Nature and Culture: Reflections on Menstrual and Parturitional Taboos in Huaulu (Seram)." In *Power and Difference: Gender in Island Southeast Asia*, edited by Jane Monnig Atkinson and Shelly Errington, 235–72. Stanford: Stanford University Press.

van der Veer, Peter. 1994. *Religious Nationalism: Hindus and Muslims in India*. Berkeley: University of California Press.

———. 1997. "The Victim's Tale: Memory and Forgetting in the Story of Violence." In *Violence, Identity and Self-Determination*, edited by Samuel Weber and Hent De Vries, 186–200. Stanford: Stanford University Press.

———. 2001. *Imperial Encounters*. Princeton: Princeton University Press.

———. 2002. "Religion in South Asia." *Annual Reviews in Anthropology* 3, no. 1: 173–87.

———, ed. 1996. *Conversion to Modernities: The Globalization of Christianity*. New York: Routledge.

Van Esterik, Penny. [1982] 1996. *Women of Southeast Asia*. Occasional Paper no. 17. DeKalb: Northern Illinois University Press.

Villa, Dana R. 1992. "Postmodernism and the Public Sphere." *American Political Science Review* 86, no. 3: 712–21.

Viswanathan, Gauri. 1998. *Outside the Fold*. Princeton: Princeton University Press.

————. 2002. "Literacy in the Eye of the Conversion Storm." In *The Invention of Religion*, edited by Derek Peterson and Darren Walhof, 190–208. New Brunswick, NJ: Rutgers University Press.

Wadley, Susan S., ed. 1980. *The Powers of Tamil Women*. South Asia Series 6. Syracuse: Syracuse University of Foreign and Comparative Study.

Waller, Marguerite, and Jennider Rycenga, eds. 2000. *Frontline Feminisms: Women, War and Resistance*. New York: Garland.

Warner, Michael. 2002. "Publics and Counterpublics." *Public Culture* 14, no. 1: 49–90.

Watson Andaya, Barbara. 2002. "Localising the Universal: Women, Motherhood and the Appeal of Early Theravada Buddhism." *Journal of Southeast Asian Studies* 33, no. 1: 1–30.

Weber, Max. 1978. "Political Communities." In *Economy and Society: An Outline of Interpretive Sociology*, edited by Guenther Roth and Claus Wittich, 901–40. Berkeley: University of California Press.

Werbner, Pnina. 1999. "Political Motherhood and the Feminization of Citizenship: Women's Activisms and the Transformation of the Public Sphere." In *Women, Citizenship and Difference*, edited by Nira Yuval-Davis and Pnina Werbner, 221–45. London: Zed Books.

Werbner, Pnina, and Helene Basu, eds. 1999. *Embodying Charisma*. London: Routledge.

Werner, Jayne. 2005. "Gender Matters: Gender Studies and Vietnam Studies." In *Le Vietnam au féminin*, edited by Gisele Bousquet and Nora Taylor, 19–35. Paris: Les Indes Savantes.

West, Lois A., ed. 1997. *Feminist Nationalism*. New York: Routledge.

Wickramasinghe, Nira. 2001. *Civil Society in Sri Lanka: New Circles of Power*. New Delhi: Sage.

Wirz, Paul. 1954. *Exorcism and the Art of Healing in Ceylon*. Leiden: E. J. Brill.

Woolf, Virginia. 1938. *Three Guineas*. New York: Harbinger Books.

Zaman, Muhammad Qasim. 2002. *The Ulama in Contemporary Islam*. Princeton: Princeton University Press.

Zarkov, Dubravka. 1997. "War Rapes in Bosnia: On Masculinity, Feminity and Power of the Rape Victim Identity." *Tijdschrift voor Criminologie* 39, no. 2: 140–51.

————. 2001. "The Body of the Other Man: Sexual Violence and the Construction of Masculinity, Sexuality and Ethnicity in Croatian Media." In *Victims, Perpetrators or Actors? Gender, Armed Conflict and Political Violence*, edited by Cynthia Moser and Fiona Clark, 69–82. London: Zed Books.

Contributors

Alexandra Argenti-Pillen is a lecturer in the Department of Anthropology at University College London. She trained initially in medicine at the University of Louvain, Belgium, and then in medical anthropology at University College London. She is the recipient of numerous awards, including a Harry Frank Guggenheim Foundation Post-Doctoral Research Fellowship. She is the author of *Masking Terror: How Women Contain Violence in Southern Sri Lanka* (2003).

Bénédicte Brac de la Perrière is a professor of anthropology at Laboratoire Asie du Sud-Est et Monde Austronésien, Centre National de la Recherche Scientifique, Paris, France. She trained in anthropology at the Ecole des Hautes Etudes en Sciences Sociales, Paris. She has been working in Burma since 1981 and has published more than forty articles on issues of urbanization and the *nat* spirit cult in Burma. She is the author of *Les rituels de possession en Birmanie: Du culte d'Etat aux cérémonies privées* (1989).

Veena Das is Krieger-Eisenhower Professor and chair of the Department of Anthropology at Johns Hopkins University. Her publications include *Critical Events: An Anthropological Perspective on Contemporary India* (1995) and *Structure and Cognition: Aspects of Hindu Caste and Ritual* (1977) and the edited volumes *The Word and the World: Fantasy Symbol and Record* (1986) and *Mirrors of Violence: Communities, Riots and Survivors in South Asia* (1990).

Mangalika de Silva is a doctoral candidate in anthropology at the Amsterdam School for Social Science Research, University of Amsterdam. She is a scholar-practitioner and has worked on research projects in Sri Lanka concerned with women's rights as human rights, women in parliament, women in the labor movement, and women in armed conflict.

Ingrid Jordt is an assistant professor in anthropology at the University of Wisconsin–Milwaukee. She received a Ph.D. from Harvard University in 2001, for which she wrote the dissertation "The Mass Lay Meditation Movement and State-Society Relations in Post-Independence Burma." She has spent many years in Burma as a Buddhist nun and has published articles and book chapters about the processes of political legitimation, lay-monastic relations, and Buddhist meditation movements. She is currently working on a book titled *Political Legitimacy in Post-Independence Burma*.

Betty Joseph is associate professor of English at Rice University. She received a Ph.D. in English at the University of Minnesota. She is the author of several chapters and articles on gender, colonialism, and eighteenth-century British culture. She is the author of *Reading the East India Company, 1720–1840: Colonial Currencies of Gender* (2004) and is currently writing *Timing the New World Order: Postcolonial Fractures and the Cosmopolitics of Everyday Life*.

Patricia Lawrence is a senior lecturer in the Department of Anthropology at the University of Colorado. She was a Rockefeller Visiting Scholar in 2002–3 at the Joan B. Kroc Institute for International Peace Studies. Her war zone research in Sri Lanka has produced several films and publications. She is currently completing a book titled *Work of Oracles: Violence, Suffering, and Healing in Sri Lanka* and is an ongoing workshop convenor at the Children's Peace Garden in Batticaloa and a consultant to NGOs in Sri Lanka.

Yasmin Saikia is an assistant professor of South Asian history at the University of North Carolina–Chapel Hill. She is the author of *Meadows of Gold: Telling Tales of the Swargadeos at the Crossroads of Assam* (1997). Her forthcoming book is on memory, history, and identity in contemporary Assam. She is currently conducting research on trauma, history, and gendered silence concerning the 1971 war of liberation in Bangladesh.

Monique Skidmore is a fellow at the Australian National University. She is a medical anthropologist with a Ph.D. from McGill University and has been conducting research in Burma since 1994. She was a 2002–3 Rockefeller Visiting Fellow at the Joan B. Kroc Institute for International Peace Studies at the University of Notre Dame. She is the author of *Karaoke Fascism: Burma and the Politics of Fear* (2004), the editor of *Burma at the Turn of the Twenty-first*

Century (2005), and has published numerous articles and book chapters on violence and psychological well-being in Burma.

Peter van der Veer is a professor of comparative religion at the University of Utrecht and former professor of comparative religion and director of the Center of Religion and Society at the University of Amsterdam. He has been a visiting professor in France, England, and the United States. He is the author of *Imperial Encounters: Religion and Modernity in India and Britain* (2001), *Nation and Religion* (1999), *Modern Orientalisme* (1995), and *Conversion to Modernities: The Globalization of Christianity* (1996).

Index